14.99

A scandal of racism still divides the American church. How fitting to have a black and white share words about reconciliation that are timely and loving and constructive.

David and Karen Mains
The Chapel of the Air

Their stories are powerful and from the heart, and display a vulnerability that is rare. This book very well serves as a catharsis as it reflects back to the ethnic people of America a reality that is so familiar to us. But best of all is the remedy for racial reconciliation; the eight principles are well grounded in the Word of God and in the daily realities of life.

Eliezer D. Gonzalez
National Director, The Evangelical Free Church
Leadership Resources Hispanic Ministries

Breaking Down Walls is thrilling, popular, and prophetic—all at the same time. I am convinced that there is little hope for our desperate inner cities without the kind of wholistic ministry that God has enabled Raleigh Washington and Glen Kehrein to develop together. Their story is a dramatic contemporary reenactment of the reconciling work of the early church.

Ronald J. Sider, Professor of Theology and Culture
Eastern Baptist Theological Seminary

One of the greatest needs of our day is racial reconciliation. This delightful book will not only "tell" us how to do it; it will show us how it is being done in a most exciting and unusual way. Raleigh Washington and Glen Kehrein are the living personification of Christian racial reconciliation at its best!

Dr. Paul A. Cedar, President
The Evangelical Free Church of America

This is a brutally honest book concerning the problem of racism—a national disgrace in our society, and worse yet, in the church of the Lord Jesus Christ. The two authors engage the issue head on.

Clayton Brown, Chairman and Chief Executive Officer
Clayton Brown and Associates, Inc.

This book will make a difference . . . convincing evidence of what can be done when people take God seriously.

Ted W. Ward, Professor
Trinity Evangelical Divinity School

BREAKING DOWN WALLS

A Model for Reconciliation in an Age of Racial Strife

RALEIGH WASHINGTON and GLEN KEHREIN

MOODY PRESS

CHICAGO

To our families:

To Paulette Washington, without whose support I could not be who I am; to Coffee, Kimberly, Matthew, Rachel, and Petra, because they are faithfully following Christ and are willing to be racial bridge builders; and especially to Mama, who did not have the cross-cultural opportunities but provided me a splendid model

To Lonni Kehrein, who has embraced our calling with energy and commitment; and to Tara Dawn, Nathan David, and Chelsey Angela, who already show that they will carry the torch of reconciliation to the next generation, the hope of the future

---

© 1993 by
RALEIGH WASHINGTON
and GLEN KEHREIN

All Scripture quotations, unless noted otherwise, are from the *New American Standard Bible*, © 1960, 1962, 1963, 1968, 1971, 1972, 1973, 1975, and 1977 by The Lockman Foundation, and are used by permission.

Photo Credits
©1993 by Jon Warren: Pages 1, 3 bottom, 4 bottom, 5, 7
Bob Mead: 4 top, 6 top and left, 8 top
Raleigh Washington: 2
All other photos courtesy of Circle Urban Ministries

ISBN: 0-8024-2642-5

1 3 5 7 9 10 8 6 4 2

Printed in the United States of America

CONTENTS

FOREWORD

Few issues trouble our world so persistently as the conflict between different races and backgrounds.

From the tensions in our cities that threaten to explode into violence at any moment (as they did recently in Los Angeles), to the tragic ethnic strife in places like the Balkans and the former Soviet Union, this issue is surely the most fundamental social problem of our time. Is there any hope?

Of all people, Christians should be concerned about racial strife. They recall Jesus' summary of the law, commanding us not only to love God with our whole being but to "love your neighbor as yourself" (Matthew 22:39). They remember as well the example of Jesus, who repeatedly went out of His way to show concern for those of the despised Samaritan race.

And yet all too often, we must confess, we have been content to stand on the sidelines and let others take the lead in racial reconciliation. At times we have even been satisfied with the status quo.

Breaking Down Walls is a highly readable but thoughtful book. It points the way out of the paralysis that grips so much of our society and the evangelical church. Writing from a wealth of personal experience, the authors recount how God worked in their own lives and the life of one struggling church to bring about a new and vital multiethnic community of faith.

But it is more than the story of one ministry or one group of individuals. Through careful study of the Bible, Raleigh Washington and Glen Kehrein have drawn together a series of practical principles—principles that can transferred to a wide variety of church situations.

I commend the authors for their vision of reaching their own community for Christ and their burden to see other churches become centers of evangelism and discipleship to all persons, regardless of ethnic background. May this book challenge every reader to a similar vision.

BILLY GRAHAM
Evangelist

■   □   ■   □   ■

As I have traveled this country for the past twenty-five years encouraging Christians to take up the challenge of reconciliation, skeptics have asked me to give examples of where racial reconciliation is being lived out.

"Dr. Perkins, are you just speaking theoretically or can you point us to someone or some place where racial reconciliation is taking place?" I must admit that the models of living racial reconciliation are few, yet for the past ten years I have been able to point them with confidence to two men in the Midwest.

"If you are ever in Chicago," I tell the questioners, "go look at what Glen Kehrein and Raleigh Washington are doing at Circle Urban Ministries and Rock Church."

These two men have been an inspiration to me. Not only has their ministry on Chicago's West Side encouraged me, I am more inspired by their deep personal relationship. They care deeply for one another; they help one another. This book tells their story, a powerful story of a black man and a white man teaming up as equals in order to advance the kingdom of God.

The story of reconciliation is not always glorious. I remember how devastated Glen was at the racial breakup of Circle Church back in the mid '70s (chapter 5). Glen believed in something with all his heart, knew what he was doing would be a witness for the kingdom of God, and yet his hopes for racial reconciliation fell apart. Sometimes, when such hopes are crushed, you can never recover. At that point, Glen struggled with whether racial unity was even possible.

I've gone through that same kind of quandary in my own life, trying to bring together what I know the Word of God is saying—seek racial reconciliation—with the reality of our separate lives as followers of Christ. But I have watched as God brought these two men together, brothers who embrace one another. He has removed from their minds, and mine, the doubt that blacks and whites can be reconciled.

Christians are slowly awakening to the issue of race. We are beginning to understand that unless we can witness to the rest of the world that Jesus is the answer even for racial strife, our credibility as the people who have the answer will diminish.

In *Breaking Down Walls* you will find specific instructions in approaching this crucial issue. The stories of Glen and Raleigh, separate and together, will move you. Clearly God has been preparing this team for this particular work.

With this book the authors have done the body of Christ a great service. As they share their joys and struggles in their personal journeys and their ministries, you will find inspiration and direction for bringing reconciliation among the races.

JOHN PERKINS
Publisher, *Urban Family* magazine

PREFACE

Evangelist Billy Graham, whose integrity has remained un-
questioned during four decades of ministry, recently appeared on "Prime Time Live," interviewed by the host of the
newsmagazine show. Diane Sawyer, the veteran broadcaster,
asked the man of God, "If you could wave your hand and make
one problem in this world go away, what would that be?" Without
pausing for breath, Dr. Graham quickly replied, "Racial division
and strife."

As we sit down to write this preface, the *Chicago Sun-Times* is
running a five-part series entitled "The Great Divide." As the *Sun-
Times* presents what it calls the most comprehensive survey ever on
race relations in Chicago, the newspaper's series title says it all.

This book is about the "great divide" as well, but with very
significant differences.

The *Sun-Times* series is only the latest in a parade of works
that articulate the serious racial divisions in this country. In the
'60s, Charles Silberman warned us about the *Crisis in Black and*

White, while William Grier and Price Cobbs expressed their *Black Rage*. In the '70s Thomas Kochman was teaching about *Black and White, Styles in Conflict*, and in the '80s Charles Murray declared that we were still *Losing Ground*. Finally, in the '90s, Andrew Hacker declares that we are *Two Nations—Black and White, Separate, Hostile, Unequal*. Several hundred—possibly a thousand—books are part of this evolving bibliography. These scholarly works are all eloquent at articulating the problem, but they are nearly void of any solutions.

This book is about a solution. The reality of racial strife in our society is obvious. If the recent Los Angeles riots taught us anything, it is that we have been traveling in circles. Riots, fermenting in the hotbed of racial inequity and poverty, lie dormant only to rise again; each time more vile and destructive. Each time a new generation will write increasingly articulate works about the causes and little about the remedy.

This book talks about the remedy. A remedy coming from the timeless book of irrefutable truth—the Bible. Neither Congress nor the president can apply a remedy to cure our country's ills. However, you, individually, can apply the principles described in this book, regardless of your place in life. Our remedy is distinctly Christian, calling upon those of faith in Christ to be "salt and light" and to "break down walls of hostility." This remedy is at the very foundation of the Christian faith. It is *the remedy of reconciliation;* specifically, the power of the cross of Christ to bring racial reconciliation. The authenticity of the gospel is demonstrated when the dividing walls of racial hostility are broken down.

Many Christians believe the familiar words sung by André Crouch, "Jesus is the answer for the world today." But when it comes to the enormity of racial conflict and the associated problems of America's inner cities, Christians are left perplexed in a kind of "spiritual dissonance." We know Jesus is the answer—yes, even to these problems—but we don't how to apply a specific solution in our lives or at our work or school, let alone in the broader community. We simply do not know how to go about, "breaking down the walls."

As a result, most Christians have allowed society at large to engage the problem, even though we know it is without the spiritual power. We might even join the resulting endless debate over the virtues of the liberal or conservative political causes.

We (Raleigh and Glen) say that Christ is the answer. Let us be about applying His unique and specific answer: racial reconciliation.

The specifics in this book have been learned in the grit and the grind of life's journey. Therefore, the first half of the book begins with the specific journeys of two men—one black (Raleigh Washington) and one white (Glen Kehrein)—from racially stereotypic origins. Our lives began in ghetto projects of the Jim Crow South and a lily-white, "Norman Rockwell" small farming town of the North. We have been on opposite sides of the dividing wall, yet God has brought us together to be brothers, bound more strongly than as by physical blood.

Our journeys will remind you of common racial realities. Our experiences are unique, of course, yet every racial group has a similar reality. Our stories contain specific examples of racial strife, failure, pain, enlightenment, growth, and success. We have been honest and even, at times, transparent in our self-revelation. But we felt no other approach would authentically touch our subject.

Our lives, originally and typically separate, have now been joined, for these past ten years, in inner city ministry. Our personal stories lay the foundation and, we trust, underline the credibility of the book's second half: eight principles of racial reconciliation. Born out of our personal life experiences, these principles have been refined in the crucible of inner city living and ministry. (Other illustrations in this book represent actual people, though in most cases names have been changed in order to preserve confidentiality.) Hardly scholarly, the eight principles are practical and biblically based. At the conclusion of each chapter are practical applications that should help you be a reconciler in your personal life, work, church, and community. We hope it will encourage action—action to cross barriers of race and class in the name of Christ.

Before you begin reading, here are three cautions about *Breaking Down Walls*:

1. *We use the "R" word! Racism* is one of those terms that is used differently by different people. Without clear definitions misunderstanding is a certainty.

   When African-Americans use the term *racism*, the word covers a broad spectrum. Any action on the part of whites that is different because it is directed at a black person can be racist. And any attitude that lessens a black person's ability is racist. For instance, to assume that a black man wearing surgical scrubs and walking through a hospital corridor is an orderly and not a doctor—that's racist.

But white people use the word *racism* for only extreme actions. They agree that when the Ku Klux Klan burns a cross on a person's lawn or threatens a lynching, that's racist. Such actions are also rare. Actions short of that, however, typically are labeled in graduated terms from *bigotry* down to *misinterpretation*.

Dismissing emotional responses to racism by African-Americans, white people often believe their definition of racism is "objective." But like the Jews who recall relatives lost in death camps, blacks have a sensitivity defined by their experience (as do Hispanics and Asian-Americans living in the United States). For African-Americans, racism is racism; degree differentiation is only a trick to avoid facing the reality.

2. *We know about stereotypes.* We will, no doubt, receive criticism that this book is fraught with stereotyping. We live in an age of individuality and may be insulted when our behavior is described as being part of a group; that is "Black folks believe . . ." or, "White people generally do . . ." We know that we risk being out of step with our ever growing, politically-correct society as we step upon some toes by drawing such generalities.

   Please understand, we know that "*All* black people don't do . . ." and "*All* white people don't feel . . ." But surely our distinctive subcultures have given shape to our thinking and actions. It is those culturally affected thoughts and actions of us Christians-—whether black, white, Hispanic, Asian (or other)—that often need to be brought to the cross of reconciliation.

3. *It's not just a black and white thing.* Our principles have been developed within the black/white inner city and suburban context. Most examples that we share come from within that context. This book is a pragmatic articulation of what we know, and we punctuate it by our personal experiences. We realize, however, that conflicts exist among all the races: red, brown, yellow, black, and white. Invariably we hear, "What about Hispanics (Asians, etc.)? We go through this too. Don't leave us out!"

Our answer is that these principles have universal cultural application. Although most of our examples are in "black and white," we have presented our principles to audiences in Chinatown and the barrio in Mexico City; to Japanese and Filipino middle class church members; in the homes and churches of wealthy suburbanites; even in the jungles of Zaire. Each time we have been amazed by the effective application our audience makes when hearing them.

That has convinced us that these principles are certainly not "ours" but have been blessed by God. If you are looking for practical help in cross-cultural ministry, no matter the setting, you should find it here.

Finally, a disclaimer. Our publishers generously subtitled this book "A Model for Reconciliation in an Age of Racial Strife." We are reminded that one of Webster's definitions of a model is "a small imitation of a real thing."

The "real thing" is Christ. Jesus Christ reconciled us to God and gave us the ministry of reconciliation (2 Corinthians 5:17–21). We are attempting to imitate that. But neither we nor our ministries are the standard. A close examination of Raleigh Washington and Glen Kehrein and of Rock Church and Circle Urban Ministries will certainly expose all of our frailties and flaws. We don't have all the answers, and we are not the experts. We are merely, in the words of that old black hymn, "soldiers in the army of the Lord."

The racial situation in our nation today cries out for Christians to "pick up our cross," step out of our comfort zones, and build relationships across cultural barriers—beginning with at least one person, one family, one church—whether it is African-American, Asian, Hispanic, or white. No, we cannot be everything to everybody, but we will be surprised how even one relationship that stretches us beyond our natural tendencies will help give us the groundwork for relating to others in the body of Christ who are different from ourselves.

Our prayer is simple: that each person who reads this book will learn from the authors' mistakes and some successes and commit him- or herself toward "breaking down the walls" that divide us.

ACKNOWLEDGMENTS

Dave and Neta Jackson brought their considerable writing expertise to this project, taking what was on our hearts and in our heads and helping us put those words on paper. They have succeeded in the laborious task of taking our thoughts, life experiences, and principles and translating them to the written page. Cowriters of more than thirty-five books, they display their skills clearly on these pages. (This talented couple has also written twenty-four children's books, including the Trailblazer series of historical fiction.)

This was not just another project for Dave and Neta—it was a mission. From the first day we sat to discuss this task we sensed that the Jacksons' hearts beat with a personal hunger and commitment toward racial reconciliation that resonates with our own. With similar life experiences as ours, they have been living out their calling as members of Reba Place Church, a racially mixed church in racially mixed Evanston, Illinois.

This project began with many hours together with Dave and Neta, graciously hosted and facilitated by our good friends John and Vicky Wauterlek. During our times together, the Jacksons often told us personal stories of how the principles of reconciliation were relevant to their own life experiences. At one point during the writing they saw the principles at work as God brought about a magnificent, personal act of racial reconciliation within a relationship that had long been estranged. Even as the book was taking shape the Jacksons were experiencing God's reconciling power!

We express our deepest thanks to the Jacksons who, through this process, have been patient with us (not an easy task) as the daily crises of ministry often carried us past deadlines. They remained steadfast, without voicing frustration for "all the changes" we put them through. And once in a while the phone mail system we set up did work. Didn't it?

Thanks for your dedication and commitment to make this book the best it could be. We'll always be grateful.

PART ONE

APART

CHAPTER 1
"LET'S KILL 'EM ALL!"

The night was surprisingly clear for smoggy Los Angeles. A man named George Holliday stepped out on the balcony of his apartment, mildly curious to see what the wailing sirens and screeching tires were all about. What he saw made him grab his video camera . . . and within days, TV viewers all over America were watching, again and again and again, as four LAPD cops savagely beat and kicked a man named Rodney King while other officers looked on like Saul standing by at the stoning of Stephen. The cops were white; King was black.

A year and one month later, on April 29, 1992, the jury trial of the four white policemen, charged with using excessive force, came to an end. The six o'clock network newscasters blurted out the verdict: *not guilty*. Most Americans were stunned. Because of the video witness, it had seemed an open and shut case. But the jury in Simi Valley, an all-white suburb where the proceedings had been moved so that the policemen could get a "fair trial," ruled otherwise.

By the time the ten o'clock news rolled around, however, shock had turned to alarm. Helicopter camera long-shots showed a virtual firestorm rolling across southcentral L.A.

Arsonists were torching building after building, and rioters were smashing windows, blocking streets, and looting stores. A few even attacked autos and their drivers. All that night, and into the next day and night, TV viewers watched with growing horror the visual images appearing "live" in their living rooms: angry residents pouring into the streets chanting, "No justice! No peace!" . . . a long-haired, blond truck driver being pulled from his tractor-trailer at the intersection of Florence and Normandie, then repeatedly kicked and hit on the head by young black men . . . unruly crowds heaving bricks and stones at passing autos, causing several to swerve and crash . . . a Korean shopowner and his armed employees firing at would-be looters . . . mixed mobs of whites, blacks, and Hispanics smashing store windows, then gleefully reappearing on the street with everything from television sets to groceries, disposable diapers to pet food . . . soon, many of those same stores crumbling to ashes beneath an inferno of flames . . . the curious absence of squad cars and fire trucks. Finally, the man who had become the spark for the conflagration spoke, his words a sad commentary on racial relations in Los Angeles and perhaps America. With his voice quivering, Rodney King pled into the network video cameras, "Can we all get along?"

At the end of thirty-six furious hours, the rage was spent. But the toll in human lives and property damage was staggering: 54 dead, more than 2,380 wounded, and 5,200 buildings destroyed or seriously damaged to the tune of one billion dollars and 40,000 lost jobs.[1]

Powder Keg or a Slow Fuse?

The only real surprise in the aftermath of the Los Angeles riots is that people were surprised. Police Sergeant Mike Schott of North Richmond, California, told a *Newsweek* reporter, "Our cities are not a powder keg waiting to explode, but they're like a slow fuse burning all the time. Daily there are race crimes: shootings, beatings, and violence. L.A.'s flame just got higher. People noticed. But believe me, it's ongoing everywhere. Day and night."[2]

A local minister told *Christianity Today* he didn't think the Rodney King verdict caused the riots; it was simply the spark that ignited existing anger and frustration over "deeper issues, like the loss of jobs, the breakdown of the family, the weakened school system, and a fear that leads to hopelessness."[3]

In cities across America, racism remains an underlying force affecting relationships and attitudes. For a variety of reasons, almost all of us struggle with prejudice and fears toward people of different races. Our feelings rarely explode into racial confrontation; usually our attitudes and actions are more subtle. The consequences, though, are still harmful. As the minister told *Christianity Today*, job opportunities, family life, and education are all affected by the strained relationships among the races. Racial reconciliation is desperately needed. But the question is, how?

The L.A. riots are a reminder of how integration efforts have not brought an end to the prejudice of people's hearts. Racial tensions continue to demoralize, enrage, and explode. Those tensions clearly played a role in the L.A. riots, and they were not just white versus African-American. Businesses owned and operated by Korean-Americans were especially targeted by blacks for looting and torching. Hispanics and white youth also rioted against police officers and businesses. Sam Hines, former chairman of the General Assembly of the Church of God, fingered the sore spot: "The unfortunate thing in America is that we settle for integration, a legal accommodation . . . but [in south central L.A.] it did nothing to establish relationships between estranged and alienated people."[4]

A year after the riot, southcentral L.A. still looks like the aftermath of a World War II bombing raid. The promises of politicians and good intentions of local leaders have not yet materialized into rebuilding the neighborhood. Even when—or if—the buildings go up again, is there any hope for racial reconciliation? Will anything have changed? Will it happen again, here . . . or somewhere else?

Ominous graffiti on the wall of a burned out building says it all: "It's not over yet."

■   □   ■   □   ■

Another city, another inner-city neighborhood. It's summer, and four hundred African-Americans have gathered in the hundred degree heat for a dinner in a gymnasium. They have come to the annual "Harvest Banquet" at Rock of Our Salvation Church and Circle Urban Ministries on Chicago's West Side. Most of the women are single parents and come from nearby apartments, such as the notorious "Murder Building" where, in one week, three people had died in drug-related killings. The young men, many unemployed, are angry and hold little hope for a better life. Most are convinced that their desperate struggle to survive is still resisted by the oppressive "white man."

In planning for the banquet, Pastor Raleigh Washington of Rock Church and Glen Kehrein, executive director of Circle Urban Ministries, decide to speak on the subject of bitterness and the need for black/white reconciliation, a reconciliation they have experienced in their own relationship. It is a message they have often given to predominately white audiences, but the two men know that bitterness and alienation are feelings African-Americans have to resolve within themselves before their hearts can become receptive to the gospel and lasting reconciliation to others.

As a child in Jacksonville, Florida, Pastor Washington, an African-American, had only known white people as the insurance man who came to collect the bill and the policeman who arrested a friend's father. Meanwhile, Glen, of German descent, grew up in Ripon, a town of 6,000 in central Wisconsin. His first conversation with a black person waited until he came to Chicago to attend college. But now the two men work together in a most remarkable interracial relationship.

Their approach on this day will be team speaking, recounting chapters of their lives by handing the mike back and forth. After the sumptuous feast, Pastor Washington stands up and taps on the mike. Chairs still scrape, some people keep talking. Several people look uncertain, not sure what they are in for.

After describing his childhood in the public housing projects in Jacksonville, Pastor Washington begins to open up his life to these Harvest guests. "I escaped the ghetto by getting a baseball scholarship in college," the former army officer booms in his strong voice. "The ROTC program commissioned me as a second lieutenant in the U.S. Army when I graduated from college. Then the army assigned me to the Adjutant General's Corps, a predominantly white, elite, administrative branch.

"In the military I did exceedingly well. The army promoted me to captain, then major, and finally to lieutenant colonel—all ahead of my contemporaries. I was on the fast track to becoming the first black general in that branch of the army."

The shuffling and small talk stops. The people are listening. A black man who has succeeded in a white arena always captures attention in the 'hood (neighborhood).

"I supervised white personnel and even fired some of them. Oh, yeah, I fired a whole lot of white folks!" Washington grins broadly. Then his tone becomes serious. "But a black man does not climb the ladder of success so fast without making enemies. The white officers I climbed past—and sometimes over—and those I fired, they were not about to forget. Eventually, a conspiracy of jealous officers began telling lies about me. Two white colonels—one from Mississippi and the other from Alabama—investigated those lies, and you know what they were thinking."

Heads nod. "Uh-huh." "You got that right."

"They conducted eleven different investigations," Washington continues, stabbing his finger in the air. "I was never informed about any of them. It took a year, and they spent over a million dollars going anywhere—Korea, Germany, Hawaii—and talking to anybody who had any contact with me since I'd become a major. All the charges ended without basis; they couldn't find a thing to pin on me. But, during the course of the investigation, they had talked to many of the people whom I had fired and had an axe to grind. They couldn't use a phony allegation of 'sexual assault' by a white female officer because it had been proven false by military police investigations. But, you know, those colonels from Mississippi and Alabama wanted to believe her lies."

"Finally, the army found some minor technicalities to stick me with, like using the government telephone for a personal call—even though my post commander had given me permission—or having my driver pick up my boots on his way back from some other official errand. That was considered 'misappropriating a government vehicle.'

"Such minor matters would not have done me any damage if the army had specifically charged me. Instead, they said I was guilty of 'conduct unbecoming an officer'—without explanation. Then I was given a choice: sign a paper admitting guilt and taking mandatory retirement or be discharged after nineteen years, eleven months, and twenty-nine days of service—one day before I was eligible for full retirement benefits."

An angry murmur travels around the room. Heads are really shaking now.

"If I would have signed, the government would have given me full retirement pay as a lieutenant colonel. But I would not sign that lie. So they kicked me out of the army—no fond farewells, no medical benefits, no nothin'—one day short of full retirement eligibility!"

Leave It Bitter

The dinner guests are really with him now, punctuating every sentence with their own retorts. A layer of anger fills the air, as the crowd listens to the story of racial injustice.

Pastor Washington is about to wind up the first part of his story. Wanting the poignancy of the moment to be suspended, Glen Kehrein whispers in Washington's ear, "Leave it bitter."

Without skipping a beat, Raleigh Washington continues. "But I didn't want to retire. Soon I would have been making full colonel; I was on my way to becoming a general. But because of a conspiracy of white people, because of their lies, because of racism and prejudice, they kicked me out of the army. It was white folks who kicked me out of the army. It was white folks who took away my retirement—"

As Pastor Washington is about to hand Glen Kehrein the microphone, a black man at a table near the front of the gymnasium suddenly jumps to his feet. With a face contorted by rage, he raises his fist in a black power salute and roars, "Then let's kill 'em all!"

A cheer goes up from hundreds of African-American guests.

The sixty white volunteers in that hot gymnasium, standing around the perimeter, freeze with terror. They have come from various churches in the suburbs to help cook and serve a meal, not to become the targets of an angry mob.

Pastor Washington steps back and leans over to his white friend. "Is that bitter enough for you?"

Fighting Stereotypes

Glen Kehrein grimaces. "I said leave it bitter; not start a riot," he whispers back. His heart is pounding as he begins to speak over the tension that permeates the room. Hundreds of pairs of hostile eyes turn on him. He describes growing up in a small, white Midwestern town that never bothered to question its stereotypes of blacks and other minorities.

"I was a student at Moody Bible Institute when Dr. Martin Luther King, Jr., was assassinated and riots broke out throughout Chicago and in other cities of this country. The president of the United States didn't have the answer. The mayor of Chicago didn't have the answer. Even Moody Bible Institute didn't seem to have the answer.

"But I knew that many of the angry blacks out on those streets were the moms and dads and uncles and cousins of kids in the youth club I worked in. Their grief, frustration, and rage tore at me. That moment shook me to the soul of my being, and I knew I faced a decision: would I be part of the problem or part of the solution?"

Kehrein lets the question hang in the air a moment.

"I decided I wanted to be part of the solution. Still, I was ignorant; I had no experience; I was unaware of my own racism. But I wanted to learn. From Dr. Martin Luther King and others I caught the dream that blacks and whites could join hands in brotherhood. So, nearly twenty years ago my family and I moved into the Austin neighborhood to become part of this community when other whites were moving out. God used us and others to start Circle Urban Ministries as a way to give back some of what white people have taken away. Sometimes I reached out and got slapped down; sometimes I even felt stabbed in the back. But after all these years, we are still here.

"This community is my community. Its people are my people. Its problems are my problems, and I'm not going to run away. The dream is not only alive here at Circle—it thrives!"

Then he sits down. After the angry response to Pastor Washington's story, what will happen now? To his surprise, first one, then another person begins to clap. The applause spreads. The tension in the room eases—for some, but not all. The angry man in the front and others like him still glower with rage.

"You're Bitter, and You Know It"

Pastor Washington stands up again. "Earlier, you only heard half of my story," he tells the Harvest guests. "Several years later a white Jewish lawyer named Jeff Strange found out about my experience and offered to take on my case without charging a penny. For nine years he battled the army, and finally got them to say "uncle" and reverse their decision. I was called to active duty to serve one more day so that I could retire."

The crowd yells and claps.

"Fort Sheridan—the same base that had drummed me out of the army—had to roll out the band to give me a retirement parade. I put on my lieutenant colonel's uniform—after fasting for two weeks—and Glen's dad, Pa Kehrein, picked me up in a limousine he borrowed from his work. I returned to active duty in style."

The crowd roars louder. These people understand Washington's pain and struggle with racism and prejudice; they love the victory story. But in a way it is as alien as a Superman tale. This man's triumph came not by "any means necessary" but through the intercession of white people who cared about him.

In the middle of their cheers, Pastor Washington says, "Wait! Don't shout now about my victory, because I heard the same kind of shouting a few minutes ago when the brother down front here yelled, 'Let's kill 'em all!'

"The truth is, you are bitter and you focus your bitterness on white people. You have just faced that bitterness in yourselves. It's there, brother; it's there, sister. Now let me tell you what Jesus Christ did for my bitterness."

As the volunteers quietly clear away the remains of the Harvest feast, Pastor Washington begins to declare the gospel.

"I had to forget what was behind—like the Bible says—and reach for what lies ahead. Only Jesus Christ, who died on the cross to reconcile us to God and to break down the walls of hate and bitterness between us, can help a person do that. That's the only way I can be a partner with my brother, Glen Kehrein, here today." The former army officer then points out that it was a white church that had given Rock Church a sound system and hymnals; it was white people who, because of the love of Christ, had been providing food for the Harvest events all that week. "White people cooked it and are here serving you right now. All this is only possible because of the gospel of Jesus Christ."

When Pastor Washington gives an invitation, people start coming forward to give their lives to Christ. The eighth person to come forward is the man who wanted to "kill 'em all." With the crowd bursting into spontaneous applause, Pastor Washington embraces Timmy. Tears flow from the eyes of the volunteers ringing the perimeter over this visible display of the power of the gospel. Later, when Timmy emerges from counseling, he walks up to Glen and says, "Hey, man, I'm sorry."

"I understand," Kehrein says. "You don't have to apologize for how you felt."

The new believer looks at the white brother and says, "Well, I want you to know . . . you're one of the good ones."

■   □   ■   □   ■

Two cities, two inner-city neighborhoods walking the edge of death. One exploded in a nightmare of rage and destruction. The other tottered on the brink in a stifling hot gymnasium, then blacks and whites shook hands in reconciliation.

What made the difference?

Exploring that question is the purpose of this book. We, Raleigh Washington and Glen Kehrein, invite you to walk with us along two different, difficult journeys that brought us to where we are today: two men—one black, one white—who have become not only partners in ministry, but spiritual brothers and committed friends.

Along the way we have become convicted and convinced that racial reconciliation is not only possible, it is critical. Reconciliation must first take place among Christians, black and white, Hispanic and Asian. The evangelical church, so dedicated to foreign missions, has neglected the desperate needs of the inner cities of our own country for too long. Not only have we neglected the cities, but we have even abandoned our brothers and sisters in Christ to gang violence, poverty, prejudice, racism, hopelessness, and fear. Even when the church wants to respond, it is at a loss to know how to help or what to do.

Paraphrasing the words of Dr. Martin Luther King, we too have a dream—a dream when Sunday morning, which for centuries has been the most segregated hour of the week, will see black and white together, worshiping our Creator as brothers and sisters in Christ. Not just "chocolate"; not just "vanilla," but honest-to-goodness Fudge Ripple Sundays. The fudge ripple process (see chapter 9), more than just a cute analogy, has pointed us toward realizing this dream.

In the second part of the book, we will discuss biblical principles essential for racial reconciliation; they have been hammered out on the anvil of fifty-five years of combined cross-cultural experience. These principles apply to all relationships, but now, when racial tensions are again at an explosive point, Christians who are willing to pursue reconciliation through cross-cultural relationships may be the only hope for this country and for the effectiveness of our churches to demonstrate God's love in America today.

Charges of racism, riots in L.A., marches in Brighton Park, New York, and racial tension on college campuses have exposed

—□■—

the cancer under this nation's skin. What is the Christian response? Where are Christians living out the answer?

To remain silent is to deny the fundamental truth of the gospel —the power of God's love to break down the walls of separation between us. That is why this story is important. It is important that a black man from the housing projects and a white man from America's heartland can live and work together and love each other as brothers. The story unfolds not where life is easy but in the most difficult setting, in a ghetto on Chicago's West Side.

The first half of this book takes you into our personal world, the crucible in which we experienced racial prejudice and responded with ignorance (Glen) and anger (Raleigh). Alone, and later together, we learned the emptiness of isolation and the lasting peace of reconciliation through Jesus Christ. Ours has been an odyssey from ignorance and alienation to love and hope.

But for us, racial reconciliation has not been easy.

We both brought with us histories of cross-cultural failure and disappointment. Yet by returning again and again to God's Word, we have not only become best friends, we have experienced the truth of Ephesians 2:14-16:

> [Jesus Christ] is our peace, who has made the two one and has destroyed the barrier, the dividing wall of hostility . . . His purpose was to create in himself one new man out of the two, thus making peace, and in this one body to reconcile both of them to God through the cross, by which he put to death their hostility." (NIV*)

NOTES

* *New International Version.*
1. Eloise Salholz, "A New Challenge for Ueberroth," *Newsweek*, May 18, 1992, 45.
2. David H. Hackworth, "This Was No Riot, It Was a Revolt," *Newsweek*, May 25, 1992, 33.
3. Ken Waters, "Searching the Ashes for Hope," *Christianity Today*, June 22, 1992, 50.
4. Kim A. Lawton, "A Wake-Up Call for the Church," *Christianity Today*, June 22, 1992, 4.

CHAPTER 2
"BLACK POWER" IS NOT A WITCH'S BREW
(Glen Kehrein's story—1)

As I climbed to the roof of the dorm, I could hear sniper fire echoing from every direction. The sound of gunfire bounced eerily back and forth off the large buildings, and soon my rooftop perch provided a near panoramic, yet horrific view.

Smoke from a dozen fires hung in the air; below me armored personnel carriers, jeeps, and trucks carrying National Guardsmen with rifles rumbled past the school and off to war—just around the corner.

It was 1968. I was a second year student at Moody Bible Institute (MBI) in Chicago, and we had just heard the shocking news along with the rest of the nation. Dr. Martin Luther King, Jr., the most prominent voice for nonviolent protest in the cause of civil rights for black Americans, had been silenced by an assassin's bullet. In a matter of hours, the whole world as I had known it seemed to spin out of control.

What should have been on a television screen reporting a distant, foreign civil war was happening right before my eyes. Standing across the street, I watched, stunned, as the windows of a neighborhood food store were smashed, the contents looted, and the building burned to the ground. I felt myself being pushed to a crossroads, as the safe world in which I grew up and the "other" world I'd been introduced to on my first foray away from home were colliding.

How in the world did I get from a Wisconsin cornfield to a war zone in the inner city of Chicago in less than two years?

Heartland America

Ripon, Wisconsin, a Norman Rockwell sort of town, is the home of Speed Queen Washers, Rippin-Good Cookies, and me. But its real claim to fame is as the birthplace of the Republican Party. Except for the small college population, most people in town knew each other and most things about each other. This is "heartland America," and it shaped my values and outlook on life.

Both sides of my family come from sturdy, hard-working, German stock. My maternal grandfather immigrated to this country with a dream of a better life. In the "old country" he used to hear stories about American streets paved with gold. When he arrived, of course, he soon found that raising eleven children through the Depression wasn't easy, even in America. But like many other European ethnics, most obstacles could be overcome by hard work. Grandpa easily blended into the "melting pot" of mainstream society by pouring his life into Klein's Bakery and Food Store in Kenosha, Wisconsin, which gained a wide reputation for quality German baked goods.

By today's standards, my family was relatively poor, and my dad left for work (for the fabulous wage of $1.90 an hour!) before the sun rose and also worked a second job each summer. Seasonal work at the "Jolly Green Giant" factory meant long summer hours —fourteen or fifteen hours a days—which left little time for play with my older brother, younger sister, and me.

Still, church was never crowded out of our schedule. We attended several while I was growing up, and each embraced traditional evangelical doctrines. After a campfire message one summer at Bible camp, I remember going forward and throwing a small stick into the fire. As I watched that little stick burn, it represented my desire—as genuine as I knew how as a young boy—to let my life burn brightly for Jesus Christ.

—□■—

Our home was a very accepting and loving place, and I understood God's love because my parents showed consistent, selfless love each day. Always a soft touch, my parents often reached out generously to anyone down and out. It was a secure and loving environment, but sheltered from the world too. Everyone we knew looked and thought about life pretty much like we did. But we had absolutely no personal contact with black folks. And subtle "innocuous," acceptable racism existed, like in the children's rhyme we used without thought: "Eenie, meenie, miny, moe, catch a nigger by the toe; if he hollers let him go. Eenie, meenie, miny, moe." We readily accepted, without question, J. Edgar Hoover's accusation that Martin Luther King, Jr., was a Communist and Malcom X a violent revolutionary. Quite simply, it didn't make any difference to me.

I didn't understand that the gospel had any social implications other than personally living an upright life. As far as the plight of other people, we subscribed to the "pull-yourself-up-by-your-bootstraps" mentality common to much of white America: anyone could get ahead if he or she tried; nothing could stop a person's progress, except perhaps one's own lack of desire.

At sixteen, my first real summer job was in the Green Giant cannery where my dad worked as a mechanic. The factory operated on a clear racial hierarchy: Whites—even the young summer employees—got the best jobs, then came the Mexican migrant workers, and finally the two black employees, who got the dirtiest jobs. I didn't think much about it; that was just the way it was. Each summer through college I returned to the cannery and was given more and more responsibility until in my last year I became the assistant personnel supervisor overseeing all three hundred plant workers.

Working with Raoul Lopez, the migrant recruiter and leader, was my first cross-cultural experience. Seeing the migrants put in twelve-hour days, sometimes for two or three weeks without a break, demolished the stereotype of the "lazy Mexican" I'd acquired.

I didn't take my studies very seriously in high school and dreaded graduating with no plans for my future. One day as I complained about the impending responsibility of adulthood, my mother answered, "You know, Glen, you would be a good social worker. You have a tender heart." At the time, I had no idea what she meant.

———□ ■———

On the other hand, my brother, fourteen months older, knew that he wanted to be a missionary pilot in New Guinea, so he applied to the MBI missionary aviation program. Not knowing what else to do, I decided that I'd follow suit a year later. Everyone thought that was a good idea, except MBI. They rejected my application because my grades were so bad. That was a wake-up call for me! MBI finally allowed me to come, provided I attended summer school on probation first. Adulthood loomed near, but I was still seventeen when I went to Chicago in the summer of '66, totally unprepared for what I was about to experience.

Culture Shock

As far as Moody was concerned, I came as a typical student: white, fundamentalist, conservative. But outside the walls of the Institute, culture shock awaited.

A few blocks in one direction was skid row, with homeless derelicts shuffling aimlessly or "sleeping it off" in a doorway. In another direction, the YMCA and "Bug House Square" Park were well-known homosexual enclaves. (For five consecutive days an older man in a big Cadillac repeatedly, while driving alongside me as I walked to work, solicited me. I, of course, never told my mother; things like that just didn't happen in Ripon.) To the north of the MBI campus was Old Town, Chicago's popular "hippie haven." And to the west began the black ghetto and the Cabrini Green public housing projects, notorious for overcrowding and violence. Its seventy buildings stretched block after block. The sight of Cabrini was almost terrifying, because, as far as I can remember, I had never before even spoken to a black person.

Inside the school, we were in a different world. However, MBI emphasized the importance of practical Christian service assignments, sending students out among the people of the city. Founder Dwight L. Moody's idea was that the school should be a practical "institute," training lay people for mission and ministry. From the very beginning, students attended classes in the morning and went out to practice their faith in the afternoon. Every day the student body flowed into surrounding areas, visiting prisons or hospitals, helping out in skid row missions, teaching Bible studies, or leading kids' clubs.

For my Christian service, I was assigned to a small club program connected to the Sonshine Gospel Mission. With each visit I made a cultural leap from the sheltered halls of the school to the raw streets around the mission. The smells of cheap wine, urine, and rotting buildings bombarded me, a country boy completely out of his element. Still, as soon as I turned eighteen, the mission asked me to drive a twenty-year-old bus through the projects, picking up kids for the club meetings.

And those Chicago kids, with whom I was sure I had nothing in common, were something else! While their innate intelligence amazed me, they spoke a dialect I couldn't understand, and if I asked them to repeat something, they shot back, "Man, what wrong wich you? Don't axe me again. Cain't you hear?" Tough and street-wise, they had experienced more of the shadowy side of life by age ten than I would in my whole life. I groped to find any common ground.

In that grimy, little slum building we called a youth center, I was making a turn that would alter my life's course. Apart from a call from God, I can't articulate why I felt deeply drawn to those kids.

But sometimes they confused me. During the club program they seemed to respond with real interest and understanding as we talked about spiritual things; the moment the meeting was over, however, they might run outside and steal everything they possibly could from the little store next door. Other times we'd be having a great time on the way home, but the moment they'd get off the bus, they'd pick up rocks and bricks—anything they could grab—and throw them at the bus windows. I was perplexed and yet curious and attracted to this different culture.

The stark reality of their life amazed me. For instance, three girls routinely came to club together, but one day only two showed up, their faces sullen. We discovered that on the way home from school the fast friends had been walking arm-in-arm past one of the project buildings when someone threw a brick from an upper story. It struck the middle girl on her head. She collapsed, and her friends dragged her home. By the time they got there, she was dead.

Their story shocked me. I had faced almost no tragedy as I grew up. A kid I knew was killed in an automobile accident, and a good friend almost died when his tractor turned over and broke both of his legs and arms. But the threat to survival these kids faced as young children seemed hostile and intentional. Why was it like this? It was part of the rage and hostility of the black ghetto I groped to understand.

New Black Friends

Soon I began to ask questions about my worldview that seemed about to unravel. What about "truth, justice, and the American way?" In Ripon life seemed so much simpler. Had I just been isolated, protected?

Living in Chicago during the mid-sixties became a crash course in social change. The long, hot summer of '66 was the beginning of urban unrest that would escalate into a series of tragic riots over the next two years. Those were also the days of emerging black militancy. A small group of young black men protesting police brutality armed themselves, put on berets, and called themselves the Black Panther Party. Soon J. Edgar Hoover declared the Black Panther Party to be the number one threat to the security of the United States (even though at its height, the Black Panthers reached only two thousand sworn members).

At three o'clock one Sunday morning police raided the home of Chicago Black Panther leaders; two men died in what was reported as a "gun battle." Later, ballistic evidence showed the police had fired more than one hundred rounds into the apartment while the Panthers managed to return only one. Neither the police nor the state attorney's office that orchestrated the raid were charged with murder or even misconduct, as evidence disappeared and investigations were bungled.

To me, this was a clear injustice, and I now began to acknowledge the reality of racism. Black students at Moody began to open my mind to scrutinize and experience things differently. Mel Warren, an African-American who grew up in the inner city, came to Moody right out of the air force. At first he was very passive, but the longer he remained at Moody the more militant he became, until at graduation he burned his diploma as a protest "against this racist institution." By his actions, Mel was saying the institution gave little thought to the needs of its minorities, assuming that they would merely assimilate into the white culture with ease. As students, we were often totally insensitive to the black experience. The dramatic incident even received coverage in *Time* magazine.

An example of the kind of thing that enraged Mel occurred one day when the president of the Student Missionary Union addressed the whole student body about satanic power. He repeatedly used the term "black power," equating "black" with "evil." Finally, Mel Warren stood up in the middle of the auditorium and yelled, "Do you know what that term means to black people?" It was like cold ice water had been dumped on the auditorium; nobody knew what to do.

Following the assembly, conversation buzzed. "Why does Mel need to be so rude? He knew what Larry meant. It was wrong to stand up and make such a big scene in front of everybody over some words." But I remember thinking, *Mel was right to speak up. The student leader was very insensitive and thoughtless to take a term that embodies black identity and black pride and associate it with something evil.* On behalf of all of us, Larry had demonstrated the total ignorance so many whites have about blacks. But we refused to see it.

In fact, I found myself giving a lot of credence to what Mel and some of the other black students were saying. To me, they were being honest and straightforward, and in the Christian, blue-collar home I had grown up in, we respected those values highly. So when the other side of the story—the poverty and injustice and black rage—confronted me, I began to see a lot of truth that until then had been covered by ignorance and apathy.

I remember having discussions in our dorms, where the few black students were always outnumbered by whites. In one particular discussion about racism, a black student said everyone was racist. "No way!" a white student protested indignantly. "I don't have an ounce of prejudice in me. It doesn't exist, I am color blind!" Black students scoffed at his reply.

That conversation really unsettled me. I didn't want to face that black student's charge, but I also knew the white student wasn't right, either. He was prejudiced in subtle ways he would not admit. I had seen it in him. I knew him. He was just like me, and the black student's claim was more true than I wanted to admit.

The emotional cost of identifying with the black students took its toll on me. At Moody I saw a microcosm of society played out: majority versus minority. In several of our dorm discussions the white students seemingly won arguments about racial issues by sheer numbers and an analytical approach, as though truth depended on majority opinion rather than the reality of what blacks experience. The majority opinion that racial inferiority might play a role in the limited achievements of Afro-Americans held sway. The only alternative was to agree that white racism was the major factor, and most whites, myself included, had a tremendous investment in denying that charge.

But something wasn't right. At some level I had to accept either (1) the theory that black people were inferior and that is why they couldn't rise above their bad conditions, or (2) that widespread systematic injustice kept them from realizing their full potential.

It was, as it remains today, difficult for whites to admit that racism exists and that we participate through overt activity or passive acceptance. Unfortunately, as the scales fell from my eyes and I began to identify with my black friends, my cynicism grew, driving me away from my Christian heritage. The white Christian establishment seemed either oblivious or unsympathetic to the legitimate needs of the black community around us. How could my Christian heritage be right when it participated in or supported the obvious injustice of white society toward blacks?

Two Worlds Collide

The greatest influence upon me at MBI was my friendship with Al Caston, a black student from McComb, Mississippi (where his grandmother lived), and New Orleans (where his mother lived). Al's pastor had graduated from Moody years ago but had neglected to sit down and give him an idea of what to expect, so he came to Moody totally unprepared for what it meant to be immersed in a white institution.

Except for my fledgling social awareness, I felt comfortable at Moody. Why was Al so overwhelmed? We were both Christians in a Christian school, yet little was familiar to Al: different songs, different food, different worship style, different assumptions . . . everything was different. Seeing his experience hit me hard. I became convinced that such a contrast in experiences wasn't right. Institutions (and especially a Christian school) shouldn't feel so normal to one kid and so foreign to another, both of whom grew up in the same country, with the same faith in the same Lord.

—□ ■—

When Al carefully talked about the racial problems at the school he didn't mean everyone was an Archie Bunker-type bigot. He meant there were barriers of being a foreigner in his own country, in a school of his own faith. It was through his eyes that I began to really learn what it was like to be a black person in a white world.

"Everyday I am reminded that I am black," Al told me. "When I walk into a new classroom that is typically all white, every head turns to stare at me. Does that happen when you walk into a classroom? If I walk down the hall with a white girl, having a perfectly innocent conversation, I get icy stares. When we're having a discussion, people want me to give them 'the black perspective.' Do people ask you for 'the white perspective'? It's racist to think that black folks can be reduced to just one perspective on life." Al showed me that being black in a white dominated culture extracted a cost—a cost that white folks cannot understand from personal experience.

But in spite of our friendship and my desire to grow in understanding black people, my own prejudices still slipped out. A "bull" session ("rap" having not yet been invented) in my dorm room turned to news about yet another civil disturbance somewhere. "Those niggers are at it again," I blurted out. As soon as the words slipped out I looked into Al's eyes. He never said anything, but my embarrassment impressed upon me that racism exists within all of us. Yes, even me. As with any sin, we have a hard time admitting prejudice and racism until it spills out and shocks us.

During one semester, Al started to do a survey on racism at Moody Bible Institute. MBI still had a rule that students couldn't date cross-racially, at least not blacks with whites, and Al wanted to document student opinion for a research paper on the topic of racism at Moody. When the deans at the school heard about the survey, they called him in and said, "You are not to do this paper." That's all there was to it.

At that point I couldn't deny it; racism was ingrained in the institution. But this was far more serious than turning up racist attitudes among a few students. The deans knew what the survey would turn up, but rather than face and address it, they preferred to suppress it, wanting unity and the status quo of the majority at the cost of the dignity and concerns of the minority.

Al was deeply hurt by that experience and he would remain at MBI just through the end of the year. I invited him to go home with me for a visit during spring break, his first foray into a white home. Later I visited his home, my first entry into a black home. This relationship, which we maintained for about ten years after I graduated from Moody, was the first close friendship I developed with a black person. But I knew then I was becoming a cross-cultural person, no longer satisfied to remain in cultural homogeneity and isolation.

"You're Nothing but a Bunch of Hypocrites!"

Through my friendship with Melvin and Al, along with my work at the Sonshine Gospel Mission, something was being restructured within me. But in April 1968, when Martin Luther King, Jr., was assassinated, the roof caved in. The rioting that followed erupted right outside the walls of MBI. I felt as though I was being torn in two: part of me intensely opposed the violence; the other part was caught up and angered by the injustice that ignited it.

It wasn't just that a man had been killed. In the context of a centuries-old struggle, Dr. King had represented hope. When that hope was brutally, callously snuffed out, it was a devastating blow to every black person in America.

Thirty of us packed into Mel Warren's dorm room that night. "Why?" someone asked. "Why is this happening?"

"You don't really care why this is happening," Mel shot back. "All you care about is that it is happening. The only reason you are here now is that you're scared. You weren't asking 'why' a week ago when things were just as bad for black people. But now you're scared because these fires are raging right outside your door. You're frightened for yourself, and the school is frightened for itself, afraid someone's going to burn it down. You're nothing but a bunch of hypocrites!"

I wanted to scream, "It's not true! I really am concerned!" But deep down I knew he was absolutely right. None of us were very upset about the way things were for black Americans before the riots and few would be after the fires cooled.

The explosion in the streets following the assassination of Dr. King showed the world the desperation of the black community. But the weak response of white evangelicals exposed the fact that my kind of Christians either did not care or that we had insulated ourselves for so long that we did not know how to care. Either option was intolerable to me. But I couldn't very well point a finger at the church without pointing at myself: I, too, was part of the problem.

As part of the problem, I could no longer dismiss the predicament of the black community as someone else's responsibility. Through the youth club I had learned firsthand that many teens in the projects had lives weighed down with incredible injustices and disadvantages. There I was at MBI, on the path to a good education, even though I did not merit it based on my high school performance. In reality I was not that different from my club kids. The main difference was an accident of birth: I was born white in small-town Wisconsin; they were born black in the Cabrini Green projects. That fact alone accounted for the chief difference in our station in life.

Confronting the shallowness of my church heritage created a crisis of faith for me and other students as well. We began to question everything, and some did not survive the process. One of my cousins, a year behind me at MBI, today professes no real faith at all. He concluded Christianity was only a sham. "People do whatever soothes their fears about the hereafter," he says. "But when it comes to really living out the teachings of Jesus, it's a joke."

I came close to reaching a similar conclusion. Either my faith made sense and would help me live out a faith-driven ethic that dealt with things like injustice and poverty and racism, or it was, as my cousin concluded, just a joke. I cried out, "Oh God, what do I do?" But there was no burning bush to guide me; I didn't know what to do. I began a journey, searching for a way to become part of the solution rather than resigning myself to being part of the problem.

CHAPTER 3

FROM LUKEWARM WATER TO LT. COLONEL

(Raleigh Washington's story—1)

In downtown Jacksonville, Florida, where I grew up, black people knew who they were; the signs all over the city told them they were second-class citizens. Some signs were visible. The chilled water flowing from the city's electric coolers was reserved for "White" folk only. Meanwhile, when I was thirsty, I looked for the little fountain with the lukewarm water and the sign "Colored" above the bowl. When my family and I wanted to eat at the coffee shop, we had to order food at the counter then go around back to pick it up from the colored window. We ate our hot dogs as we walked. The seats at the lunch counter, which could bring rest and relief from the Florida sun, were reserved for whites only.

Some signs were understood. One day Mama and I boarded the bus for home after a sweltering day of shopping for cut-rate school clothes and supplies. Loaded down with bags, we longed for a seat to rest our tired feet as we rode back to the housing projects. We saw the empty seats on the bus, but knew they weren't for us. Those seats were in the "white" section separated by a broad dividing line across the aisle. The front two-thirds of the bus was reserved for whites, even though half the riders were black. So we stood for the long ride home.

Those signs were part of the Jim Crow laws that separated the races. As a child, I really didn't understand the laws nor see these things as injustice. I simply accepted things as the way life was. If anything, I began to think my blackness caused me to be inferior. I had a mark that I couldn't remove and that made me less of a person than whites. Eventually, the laws spurred a competitive spirit within me, and I looked for opportunities to prove, maybe even to myself, that I was just as good as a white person.

"He'll Get Us All Lynched!"

But when I was only five, I learned about the tension between the races, which smoldered just beneath the surface. We lived next door to a confectionery store, owned by Mr. Padgett, where I occasionally stacked bottles to earn spending money.

Sometimes I played with Mr. Padgett's granddaughter, who was about my age. One day we were playing house together out behind the store and near a window of my house. We were "Papa" and "Mama," having a grand time, when my own mother, normally at work during this time, overhead our playing. She was unaware that Mr. Padgett's granddaughter and I ever played together and when she saw us together, she became panic-stricken! The scene was too much: black and white, playing mama and papa in 1943, in Jacksonville, Florida.

Mom dashed outside, snatched me up, and took Mr. Padgett's granddaughter to him. She instructed him, amidst his cries that it was OK, to keep her inside the store. Upon entering our home her first words to my grandmama were, "This boy is about to get us all lynched!" My first job ended over racial conflict.

I was bewildered, but Mama was so concerned that she made arrangements to move us into public housing as soon as possible. Another message at any early age: I was not good enough to play with whites.

Mama had good reason to be scared. Twelve years later, Emmitt Till, age fourteen, came from Chicago to visit relatives in Mississippi when someone accused the black boy of whistling at a white woman. The woman's husband and brother caught the boy and brutally beat him to death, then tied a heavy fan to his leg and threw him in a lake.

The incident received national press coverage. When photos of Emmitt Till's smashed body appeared in newspapers around the country, it made brutally real the prevalence of race hate crimes. During the trial, the murderers laughed and made sport of it all, and in spite of overwhelmingly incriminating evidence, the jury rendered a verdict of not guilty. The incident simply reinforced our belief that, given a chance, whites would beat and lynch blacks, and the police would only watch.

Incredibly, when Emmitt's mother was interviewed regarding the death of her only son, she said, "Vengeance belongs to the Lord. I'm a Christian, and if I had the opportunity to care for the children of those men, I would care for them like they were my very own." (Emmitt's story has been memorialized on the National Civil Rights Memorial and is reviewed every year during Black History Month.)

A Patchwork Heritage

Many black families lived in the Jacksonville "projects," where they could pay rent in proportion to their income. Once people got good jobs, they could move out and buy their families their own homes. That was the dream, and for whole families with a working father who held down two jobs, home ownership became reality. But for single parents like my mama, the "projects" slowly became a dead end with little hope of escape.

My mother, who was only seventeen when I was born, worked the night shift at the King Edward Cigar factory. Mama would see my brother and me off to school, but after school we returned to Grandmama's house four blocks away. In the evening Mama depended on us to go home when it got dark, take a bath, and get to bed on our own. Neighbors would check on us to make sure we were doing what we were supposed to do. This was "traditional black family living"—a strong sense of being an extended family, which drew together people who were not related. People looked out for each other's children, and a neighbor's report of misbehavior was uncontested law.

My family, however, bore the scars typical of many black families today. My brother and I had different fathers, and though Mama married four times, she never married either of our fathers.

From time to time the deacons of the Baptist church where my mother was a member came to visit us to encourage us, but no one ever challenged her about her multiple divorces. As I look back on it, that's not very surprising because the pastor who served that church for forty years fathered at least two children out of wedlock—by women in the church. (One of those children is a cousin of mine.) This sinful behavior was never disciplined or brought into accountability by the governing body of a church of seven hundred members. There was a form of godliness, but the power of the gospel to change lives was absent.

Nonetheless, the church was central to our life. Like many kids my age, I had perfect Sunday school attendance for many years and faithfully went to BYTU (Baptist Youth Training Union). Each year I learned a speech at Christmas and Easter and recited them in the church programs. (I could repeat them word-for-word at family get-togethers at Grandmama's house for two or three years afterward.)

Yet, in spite of all that Sunday school and church attendance, no one ever said anything to me about needing a personal relationship with Jesus Christ. The pastor loved to preach about Jesus and Nicodemus—a passage about being born again—but that's not what came out of it. Instead, the pastor would give an invitation—"opening the doors of the church"—for people to join. We voted for them then and there, and he would always announce, "Everybody voted 'yea.' The only person who says 'nay' is the devil, and he doesn't have a vote!" Then the pastor would ask the new members whether they wanted to be an usher or sing in the choir. Those were the only two choices. Since I didn't like ushering and I couldn't sing, I never went forward to join the church.

I knew all the stories about Jesus; I knew the Ten Commandments; I memorized Scripture and loved Sunday school and BYTU. But I grew up only with a form of godliness. I didn't experience the power of the gospel in my life because I had no concept of Jesus as my personal Lord and Savior.

"You Can Beat That White Guy"

All of my education through college was in segregated schools. When I was in junior high, I walked past a white school to get to the more distant black school. It was the "separate but equal" policy of education, but our schools were not nearly so nice as the white schools and didn't have any of the modern equipment, such as typewriters and duplicating machines. In junior high wood shop, we shared three power tools, while the white school had a dozen or more.

As a way of dealing with my growing sense of inequality, I developed a fiercely competitive spirit in all areas. Baseball was my passion; I made the Little League team two years before I was even eligible by age (yes, I snuck in early). At eleven I began to compete in track, and at first I would always lose to Charlie Williams, a good friend two years older who would outrun me by two steps. Rather than accept his obvious prowess, I challenged Charlie to a race every week for two years until I finally beat him.

I also took this competitive spirit into the classroom. The girls often did better in their lessons, but I couldn't just watch the girls always finish first, so I studied hard and got good grades—not because I wanted to excel in algebra or geometry, but because Raleigh Washington wasn't going to let the girls beat the boys.

Each of those little victories did something for my self-esteem and confidence. Jim Crow said we couldn't officially compete. However, we could find common ground with white youths on the athletic field located in a neutral zone between the black and white sections of town. On occasion we competed in baseball, football, and track, but much more was at stake than simply winning—self-esteem, respect, equality, and the opportunity to be superior to the white dude. The scene was set: common ground with no partial judges (there were no umpires); let the best man win. I was fiercely determined that no white guy would run faster, throw farther, or swing a bat harder than I. When competition was close, adult black spectators would whisper, "You gonna let whitey outrun you?"

It was a strong motivation. I now recognize that I was driven to create my own sense of equality to compensate for the imbalance in a world where white folks always had the upper hand. They were privileged on the bus, at the store, and in their jobs; "they" were the foremen and "we" were the workers. But put us nose to nose and I was going to prove myself equal.

An interesting observation emerges as I look back at my small circle of friends. Today Charles Williams is the principal in St. Petersburg's largest, predominantly white high school, Joe Hines a computer programmer in a large bank, Tom Hines a high school coach, Bill Hines a public school administrator, and Henri Latimer a judge in Miami. Each of us lived in poverty and had single moms who worked hard, long hours, were tough on us, and set good examples.

Mission Impossible

I was the first person in my family to attend college, primarily because another kid in the neighborhood said he was going, which triggered my competitive spirit. So I said, "I'm going to college, too." Even though college was "mission impossible" for most black folks, from then on I felt driven to make that goal come true.

A baseball scholarship was my best hope, but in my last year in high school, my team had played only three or four games when the coach started losing his eyesight. He had to cancel the rest of the season—also canceling any chance I had of being recruited by a college scout.

I worked all summer so I could attend Florida A & M (Agricultural and Mechanical) University in nearby Tallahassee. My freshman year I worked two jobs, but I still couldn't afford books. So each night I'd wait until one of my friends in the men's dormitory finished studying, then I borrowed his books. I'm amazed that I got through that first year. I tried out for baseball as a walk-on and made the team.

For the first ten games of the season I did not start or pinch hit, but I had good speed, so they let me pinch run when someone got on base in the latter innings. I stole twenty bases in ten games by stealing second and then third on the first and second pitches. Then the third baseman got into a slump; I was given his job and a starting position for the rest of the season.

At the end of the year I got good news: I had earned a full baseball scholarship for the next year with everything paid—tuition, board and room (on campus), and books. I played so well the second year that the Chicago Cubs offered me a contract, but I wanted to complete my degree in psychology, since my scholarship continued until graduation.

Two years of Reserve Officers Training Corps (ROTC) were required for all men to graduate, but a guy could get a military commission through advanced ROTC, *if* he passed the tough RQ-4 examination. I hadn't really thought about a military career, but the military thrived on competition—a trainee was always being challenged to aim for the next level of proficiency—and I was the

kind of guy who couldn't pass up a challenge. I took the exam
. . . and passed into advanced ROTC, which led to a commission
as a second lieutenant upon graduation.

A Different Kind of White Guy

My first twenty years I lived almost totally segregated from
white people. My first peer relationship with a white guy developed between my junior and senior year, when I went to ROTC
summer training camp at Fort Benning, Georgia. Summer camp
was very competitive because there were ROTC students—both
black and white—from all over the south.

My cubicle mate was Bill Sweet from the Citadel, a military
college in South Carolina, which meant he understood a whole lot
more about the military than I did. Before breakfast we had to
have our bunks made just right, and I was having trouble getting
mine squared away. "Let me do it, Raleigh," Bill said, and in
three minutes he had it razor sharp. When the sergeant came to
inspect, he dropped a quarter on it, and that bunk was so tight the
quarter bounced back up nearly to his hand. Bill winked at me,
and we went off to breakfast together.

That was a good start to a solid friendship. But the event that
affected me most occurred a few weeks later when we were on bi-
vouac. We'd been doing field maneuvers in ninety degree tem-
perature when we took a mid-morning break. I was standing
under a shade tree drinking from my canteen when Bill ran up
and said, "Raleigh, give me a drink. I forgot my canteen." I
reached back to get my cup out of the canteen cover to pour him
some water. Bill gave me the strangest look, slapped the cup
away, and grabbed the canteen. Then he pulled it straight to his
mouth and took a long drink.

A white man drinking from my canteen! I can hardly express
the feelings that came over me as Bill Sweet drank from my canteen. That was 1959; when we went into town, I had to sit in the
back of the bus while he rode in the front. We couldn't drink from
the same water fountain. But he drank from my canteen. Bill was
from Charleston, South Carolina, and knew exactly what he was
doing. He intentionally used that simple act to break down centuries of alienation between us. Suddenly, I felt the invisible but
ever-present walls between us no longer existed.

After graduation ceremonies from summer training camp, I was going to leave immediately since I had no family visiting. But Bill spent an hour chasing me down so he could introduce me to his mother and father. I remember thinking, "Man, when a white guy wants me to meet his parents, he must be for real." Bill's actions demonstrated two principles of racial reconciliation we will discuss later, intentionality (chapter 9) and sincerity (chapter 10).

Nose to Nose with Whites

When I graduated from Florida A & M on May 30, 1960, with a bachelor's degree in psychology, I was commissioned a second lieutenant in the U.S. Army. My first assignment was to the Adjutant General's Corps (the branch of the army dealing with personnel and administration) to begin active duty at Fort Benjamin Harrison, Indiana, later that summer.

In the Adjutant General's Corps, we had nine weeks of intense training on how to be a professional personnel and administrative officer. Along the way we had to take three major exams; failure to pass not only washed you out of the program, but lost you your commission.

There were sixty second lieutenants in my course at Fort Benjamin Harrison. Fifty-nine where white; then there was me. I looked like a fly in a bowl of milk. On the first major exam I scored 81 percent, but I ranked fifty-sixth out of sixty. The adviser called the five of us who scored lowest into his office and told us that even though we passed, we were on the bottom and needed to do better if we were going to make it. I was devastated.

I decided to work doubly hard to bring myself up to speed, and after class I returned directly to the BOQ (bachelor officers quarters) to study. To my amazement, most of my classmates were at their desks already studying; that's what they'd been doing all along to get better grades.

Three weeks later we had the second major exam. I scored 109 out of a possible 125 points, and finished in the top third of the class. On the third exam, I scored 121. By the end of the nine-week period, I had advanced my ranking from 56th to 13th out of 60.

On the Fast Track

After my training at Fort Benjamin Harrison, I was sent to Fort Ord, California, to complete my required service. But during my three years there, I decided to make the army my career. During my next six years I advanced to captain, volunteered for Vietnam, and was promoted to major there. While in Vietnam I was in charge of assignments for all officers coming into Vietnam from the grade of second lieutenant up through lieutenant colonel.

I wasn't yet thirty years old and had gone from second lieutenant to major in less than nine years. Man, I felt great! Raleigh Washington was on his way.

As I was coming up through the ranks in the military, I knew there was racism in the army, but I also knew that the army operated according to regulations. Early on I decided to know the regulations inside out and comply to the letter—this was my best chance of beating discrimination.

The Adjutant General's Corps was a white world, and I knew I'd succeed only if I played according to the white man's rules. That became my goal. My competitive spirit drove me to understand the political side better than most. I operated according to the rules with a keen ability to understand the personalities and desires of my superiors. I gave them what they wanted, often before they asked, always being careful to remain consistent with the regulations.

At least a half dozen times people would meet me and say, "Hey, I didn't know you were black. You didn't sound black over the phone." I cherished the compliment because it proved I could make it in the white world. I didn't see that as denying my color; I simply understood that speaking "properly" was a requirement to win, a behavior I put on just like my uniform.

A Military Wife

Upon my return from Vietnam, where I earned the bronze star for meritorious service in '68, the army gave me the first of two assignments at Fort Bragg, North Carolina. Here I met Paulette, who later became my wife. We hit it off immediately. She was a unique person with a quick wit. Paulette had a tremendous ability to make other people feel at ease. And besides, she was a knockout, with a million-dollar smile.

Neither Paulette or I were true believers, even though we both attended church regularly. Instead, we lived by worldly standards during the early years of our marriage, accumulating wretched, selfish pasts. That ended in April 1979 when Paulette accepted Christ as her personal Savior. Two weeks later I found peace through Christ. (For our conversion stories, see chapter 4.) A month later we confessed all to each other. For three consecutive days and two nights without sleep, we confessed, prayed, and cried with each other. When we were done, not only did we forgive each other but we saw each other as purified in God's sight. On July 1, 1979, in the chapel at Fort Buchanan, Puerto Rico, we renewed our vows before God. Subsequent to our conversion we've lived a morally pure life, restored by the blood of Christ who has covered all of our sins.

After serving three years in the 82nd Airborne Division, I was selected to go to the Command and General Staff College in Leavenworth, Kansas. (Only half of the field grade officers go to the staff college, and being selected means you are in line for further promotion.) When I completed staff college, I was sent to the Pentagon, where I was responsible for all casualty records of prisoners of war (POWs) and soldiers missing in action (MIAs). An officer stationed in Washington, D.C., is doing well when he or she is asked to brief the Army Chief of Staff once or twice. I felt pretty good, then, when I briefed General Creighton W. Abrams, Army Chief of Staff, daily for six months, describing efforts to bring back our POWs.

Making Enemies

When I left the Pentagon, I was sent back to Fort Bragg to work for Colonel Elmer Pendleton (who later became General Pendleton). My primary job was to inspect all units at Fort Bragg: the 82nd Airborne, 18th Airborne Corps, and Fifth Special Forces Group.

But inspectors are not loved by anyone, and I was tough. In the 82nd Airborne Division, for instance, I discovered that 4,000 soldiers were MOS (Military Occupational Speciality) mismatches —they'd been placed in jobs for which they weren't properly trained. Mismatches aren't good for the army or the soldiers. But the people in the most hot water for improper assignments were the commanders. After all, mismatches could get them fired from command and end their careers.

When I made my report to the three-star general of the 18th Airborne Corps, colonels and battalion commanders along with all other officers involved with assignments filled the room. There I stood, this confident and somewhat cocky black major, threatening the career of the two-star general of the 82nd Airborne Division.

MOS numbers have five digits in them. The first three designate a soldier's basic skill: infantry, armor, artillery, etc. The fourth digit signifies a skill level; the fifth indicates a speciality, such as Airborne Qualified. It's not unusual for the fourth or fifth digit not to match the soldier's specific assignment at various times, but if the first three are off, the mismatch is serious.

The threatened two-star general spoke right up. "Washington doesn't know what he's talking about. Fourth and fifth digit mismatches are no problem. He's new here and just trying to make a big impression."

"General," I said, "I'm not talking about fourth and fifth digits. The 82nd Airborne Division has 4,000 MOS mismatches in the first three digits."

The three-star general looked at the two-star and said, "Did you hear that? Now let him finish." Tension filled the room, and the two-star general grew red as a beet. He had been humiliated. I was respectful, but it was my job to turn MOS mismatches around at Fort Bragg, and that's what I did. People were fired as a result of my inspection.

I became one of the most feared and perhaps hated persons on the post. If a unit passed inspection, it was great. If it flunked—well, some people literally lost their jobs. I did nothing out of malice, but it was devastating for people who didn't have their business together, and I was swinging a mighty big hatchet.

Of course, the better I did my job, the better I looked. Colonel Pendleton was so pleased that he selected me to command the newly forming 18th Personnel and Administration Battalion. However, six lieutenant colonels on the staff were desperately waiting for a battalion command, the stepping stone to full colonel. Only a major, I had jumped right over those other officers to become commander of the new battalion.

The command was a big feather in my cap and a clear indication of an anticipated promotion to lieutenant colonel. But it came with a price: I had made some new enemies who would be glad to make me look bad if they could.

Making My Enemies Squirm

Because I understood my environment, which included a strong element of racism, I used it to my advantage. I was the only black commander in the entire command; with me out of the way, one of the other officers would have my position. I knew they would be coming at me like sharks, so I kept on my toes, fearing an underhanded attack and knowing from experience that "whites know how to talk to whites about blacks."

For instance, one of the lieutenant colonels who desperately wanted my position was in charge of field maneuvers one day, and he positioned my Personnel and Administration Battalion way back in the boonies. "No, no, I can't accept that," I said. "I want to be near General Pendleton."

"You'll be out there where I told you, or I'll have you up for insubordination," he growled.

"I strongly recommend you review your plans and you'll see that it's best for the operation," I insisted. This time I even told him why: Personnel and Administration handles all casualty information, so I needed to be near the general in order to make hourly reports.

Oh, boy, did I have him going! He wasn't about to let some uppity nigger tell him what to do. I went back to my headquarters, and in just a few minutes I got a call from Pendleton: "Washington, get yourself up here right now."

When I walked in, the chubby little lieutenant colonel was sitting there, grinning like a Cheshire cat. Pendleton said, "What's this I hear about you refusing to follow the plans of the man I put in charge of operations?"

I said, "Sir, your operations officer is not aware of the combat necessity plan."

"What do you mean?"

"One of the most important reports you need is the casualty data—on an hourly basis. Apparently this man doesn't realize that regulations stipulate that my headquarters must be within fifty meters of your headquarters. I tried to tell him that, but he wouldn't listen to me."

Pendleton exploded. The poor lieutenant colonel had made a fool of himself because he so desperately wanted to do me in, and I was only too happy to oblige him.

Actually, when I took over the 18th Personnel and Administration Battalion, it was in great disarray, and Pendleton wanted me to clean house. In my first six months of command, I fired eleven officers. Ten of them were white; each were MOS mismatches. I didn't dismiss these people summarily, however. I gave them each sixty to ninety days to demonstrate they could do the job; if not, they were reassigned. But this didn't make me a popular guy.

At a commander's New Year's party I was hosting—a formal function where all the officers were expected to show up for a few minutes—a single, female lieutenant came with an escort dressed in civilian clothes; I didn't realize he was a married, enlisted man. Some days later the man's wife filed a formal complaint with the inspector general about this woman. The complaint was forwarded to my unit, but my executive officer intercepted it, and I never saw the complaint.

At that time it was against regulations for officers to fraternize with enlisted personnel (non-officers). Later, I caught a couple of my other lieutenants fraternizing and decided everyone needed a talking-to. The whole time I was lecturing my staff, consisting of over forty officers, the female lieutenant sat there crying. Back at the office, I asked my executive officer what in the world was wrong.

"Don't you know? She's convinced you called this meeting just to ridicule her," he said. It seems that her relationship with the married enlisted man had been going on for some time and everyone else (except me) knew about it.

I wrote my executive officer a formal letter of reprimand for having covered for her, then reassigned the female lieutenant to a position outside our unit as a protocol officer. She knew she was essentially being fired because being a protocol officer—who organizes receptions for visitors and VIPs—isn't very impressive on your record. She was extremely angry, and I had made another dangerous enemy—this time a white female officer.

By performance standards I did exceedingly well at Fort Bragg. While commanding the 18th Battalion, the army promoted me to lieutenant colonel, and we became the number one battalion on the post. In a formal ceremony I was awarded the NR1 battalion trophy. Then, in my first year of eligibility, the army selected me to attend the War College. Being selected in my first year of eligibility meant that a full colonel promotion would be automatic; if I continued at that pace, I was destined to be considered for promotion to general.

In fact, I seemed destined to become the first black general in the Adjutant General Corps. But I had jealous and angry enemies. They began to plot their revenge.

CHAPTER 4

DRUMMED OUT OF THE ARMY

(Raleigh Washington's story—2)

Thé voice on the other end of the phone said, "Sorry, Washington, we can't send you to Florida. A black district commander would not be acceptable to the government officials in Jacksonville."

I was livid. This was the military; that kind of overt discrimination was not supposed to happen. I wanted a district command because that was clearly my track to a general's star. Besides, I had earned it with my performance.

Usually officers in the Adjutant General Corps do not command and therefore wouldn't have a shot at becoming a general. Being a district commander and then a regional commander as a full colonel was the best position from which to qualify for the rank of general. Selected for War College, promotion to colonel, a regional command—as I looked ahead it seemed like the right track and I was running in the fast lane.

But before going to the War College or assuming a regional command, I needed to be a district commander. Among the openings at that time were district commands in Jacksonville, Florida, and San Juan, Puerto Rico. A recruiting commander has to meet with the mayor and other politicians, as well as make many public presentations. Since I had grown up in Florida, Jacksonville was my first choice. But now the chief of staff of the Recruiting Command was saying I couldn't have it—because of racism.

"Tell you what, Washington," the chief of staff said, seeking a compromise. "Why don't you take the San Juan District Recruiting Command. You'll get credit for an overseas tour, but you'll be so close to the States that you can easily come back for commanders' meetings, to visit family, or whatever. You'll be able to eat your cake and have it, too."

I cooled off somewhat. San Juan sounded like a good option, so I didn't raise a stink about the discrimination in Jacksonville. But a week later, I got a call from the same chief of staff; there was another problem. When the acting commander in Puerto Rico (who would become my executive officer once I arrived) heard who was being sent, he objected. Puerto Ricans don't get along with blacks, he said; therefore a black in command would create a political problem.

"OK. Let me get back to you," I said and hung up. Then I placed a call to Three-Star General Meyer, deputy chief of staff of operations for the whole Army—including the recruiting command. We had been golf buddies when he was at Fort Bragg. "General Meyer, Raleigh Washington here. I have been turned down for two district recruiting commands because I am black." Then I explained.

"Where do you want to go, Raleigh? Jacksonville or Puerto Rico?"

"I kinda like Puerto Rico."

"Pack your bags."

Five minutes later, the chief of staff of the recruiting command called to say that I was going to Puerto Rico. But he had been ripped apart by his superior, and that kind of thing isn't forgotten easily.

While the Cat's Away . . .

In 1977 Paulette and I moved our family from Fort Bragg to Puerto Rico, where I commanded the San Juan District Recruiting Command. There are over fifty district recruiting commands in the army (one or two per state), but I was the first black officer to assume such a command. When I arrived, the San Juan District was ranked about twentieth in the army; one year later it was number one. I'd found another competitive environment, and I loved it.

Unknown to me, however, a conspiracy began among those of the "lighter hue" back at Fort Bragg, including some of the lieutenant colonels I had beaten out for command of the 18th Personnel and Administration Battalion, about half of the eleven officers I had fired when I took over that command, and the white female officer. At their urging, investigations began.

I had no idea what I was in for.

During my army career, I had become both famous and infamous. People either loved me or hated my guts. I was a productive leader, arrogant against my competition, demanding but fair toward everybody else. In this environment I was usually the only black officer, but I always satisfied my superiors, which usually endeared me to them. When I did a first-rate job, that made those generals look good. "Hey, Washington, let's go play golf together," they'd say, and in this way I developed a good relationship with the power brokers.

While in Puerto Rico the conspiracy was fueled when my executive officer (the acting commander) was reassigned from Puerto Rico to Fort Bragg. Learning of the investigations, he volunteered to get involved. Later, his wife was recorded in the official testimony as frequently referring to me as a "super nigger." This major, a close friend of one of the investigators, took every advantage of a fact of life: white people know how to talk convincingly to white people about black people.

In all, this group started nine separate investigations at Fort Bragg, yet I knew nothing about them. Each ended without basis for action. The former executive officer had sworn to get even because he blamed me for a low rating he had received in Puerto Rico from his superior, who had called him disloyal.

Clearly my accusers had their personal motives. One white colonel, embarrassed in an earlier conflict with me, said in a sworn statement, "If you don't stop Raleigh Washington, he'll become the first black general in the Adjutant General Corps." Many others made accusations, but not one allegation was ever confirmed.

One of those who filed a complaint was the female officer I had "fired" back at Fort Bragg for fraternization. To my shock, she charged that I had approached her in a "sexual way." The investigator who contacted her was an inspecting officer I had embarrassed when he sprang an illegal inspection on my newly formed battalion at Fort Bragg. I had pointed out to our superior that regulations permitted a newly formed unit one full year free of inspections. "Why does Washington know the regulations better than you do!" his superior had exploded. Now this man thought he had a chance to get even, but he wasn't taking chances.

"Your claim that Washington approached you in a 'sexual way' sounds pretty lightweight," he told the woman. "I'm afraid General Pendleton will just throw it out. Can you be more specific?"

So she strengthened her statement. "He tried to, you know, force himself on me." When the investigator went back a third time, she finally called it a "sexual assault," which is paramount to rape. Allegations like this created a big stir during this period because of the large influx of female soldiers, and the army wanted to do a better job in helping the female soldier.

Her accusation triggered an investigation by the army CID (Criminal Investigation Department), and I was immediately notified so I could procure a lawyer, but I refused, considering the allegation preposterous. This was my first inkling that I was being investigated. When I found out who my accuser was, I expected a fight because I'd heard this woman had vowed to get even with me.

But when she was asked to give a date when this "assault" supposedly happened, she couldn't have picked a better date: the day of Paulette's birthday. On that day, many people were able to attest that I was with Paulette during the whole time the alleged incident was supposed to have taken place. In a separate statement, one of the people she named to support her story completely contradicted her by saying that he had actually taken her out that evening and was with her the whole time. So her charge was refuted and the CID investigators closed the case without even bothering to interview me.

The Charges

One principle charge had even linked me with General Pendleton, alleging that we had both received high ratings from superiors who were not in the proper channel to rate us. From those ratings Pendleton got his star and I was selected to attend the war college. Investigators were embarrassed to find that their allegations were off base.

The investigators, beginning to look like fools, were more determined than ever to save face. They had to uncover something! They finally assembled three charges: that I had used a government telephone in Puerto Rico to make personal calls, misappropriated a government vehicle for personal use, and violated the regulation that prohibits officers from taking advantage of their rank by asking subordinates for loans—petty charges that would, if valid, have merited a reprimand, at most.

But even these charges were questionable. For instance, whenever I made a call from Fort Buchanan, Puerto Rico, the operator always asked, "Official or personal?" When I inquired why, she said, "I always ask in the evening, because you can make personal calls after five o'clock if you declare that it's personal."

I had my doubts, so I checked with the post commander. "Well, it's OK if you do it," he said, "but be careful how many people you tell. We don't want everyone making personal calls on official post phones, or it might jam up the phone lines." So after that, I made several personal calls in the evening.

The investigators cited an obscure joint services regulation that prohibited personal use of military phone lines; I had violated that regulation. However, I had obtained permission from the post commander and had not done it frequently or secretly. At my hearing, the post commander testified, "If you want to hang somebody for those calls, then you'll have to hang me, because I told him he could make them."

But the investigators still wrote it up as a violation.

As for borrowing money from a subordinate, that did happen. My sergeant major and I traveled frequently all over Puerto Rico, meeting with my recruiters, and I often took them out to lunch. In Puerto Rico we couldn't cash personal checks, and sometimes they ordered more than I could pay for with the cash I had in hand, so I would ask my sergeant major to slip me twenty bucks until we got back to base. That probably happened a half dozen times in two years. But as soon as we got back to Fort Buchanan, I always repaid my sergeant major.

That was technically against the law prohibiting officers from borrowing money from their subordinates, but I certainly didn't think of it as the kind of "loan" the regulation was intended to prohibit. When either one of us was short of cash, my sergeant major borrowed from me, and I borrowed from him.

I was also charged with misappropriating a government vehicle. My driver usually made two or three trips per day in the jeep between my headquarters and post headquarters where he would deliver or pick up some official item. The post cleaners was directly on his route, and sometimes I asked if he would drop off or pick up my fatigues to be cleaned or my boots to be polished. Even though he was not making a special trip, that was technically "using a government vehicle for personal purposes," so they cited me with a violation.

Turning Point

But while these secret investigations were going on, something even more significant was happening in my personal life. And it would affect my military conduct in a new, wholesome way.

As a family, we considered ourselves fairly religious. We sent the kids to chapel each Sunday, even if we had stayed out too late the night before to take them. Involvement in the church was a good thing for my career and part of my heritage, but that was about the extent of my spiritual sensitivity.

In December of 1978, during a Christmas program at our church in San Juan, Paulette realized she hadn't been taking God into account in her life; she resolved to change and "live right." The good feeling from her resolution lasted until April, 1979, when she remarked to a student she was tutoring, a girl named Martha Lopez: "Last Christmas, I decided I was going to live for the Lord and I've been on cloud nine ever since."

"Did you accept Jesus Christ as your personal Savior?" Martha asked.

"Well . . . I don't know."

"If you ask Jesus to live in your heart, He'll give you the gift of the Holy Spirit, and you'll be on cloud twelve."

The only concept Paulette had of the Holy Spirit was what she'd heard about holy rollers, and that was scary. But her heart was ready; as Martha explained the gospel, Paulette confessed that she was a sinner, invited Jesus to be her Savior and Lord, and felt the Holy Spirit giving her inner joy.

—☐ ■—

When Paulette came home, I could tell immediately that something was different. My wife had changed, and it wasn't temporary. I also knew that I wanted what she had, but I was too proud to admit it.

Paulette urged me to give my life to Jesus Christ, too. "I know all about religion," I said proudly. "You can't tell me how to do it; it's my own decision."

About a week later we were sitting in the bedroom when a woman involved with a prison ministry called. Paulette put her hand over the receiver and said to me, "Would you please excuse me? This woman wants to hear how I came to know Jesus."

I was furious. Her conversion wasn't a secret, so why was she kicking me out my bedroom? I stormed out, slamming both the bedroom door and the front door. Then I walked around the house to the bedroom window and eavesdropped while standing in the hedges.

Paulette told her story, and then I heard her tell the caller how she had cut off our physical relationship. For almost a week she had refused to be physically intimate. I remembered her words of condemnation: "You know, Raleigh, ever since I asked Jesus to forgive my sins, I feel really clean. But every time you touch me, I feel soiled. You're still unclean because you haven't accepted Jesus Christ. Will you promise not to touch me anymore till you give your life to Jesus Christ?"

I was a cocky guy—a lieutenant colonel—and I thought, *She'll come to me before I come to her.* So I shrugged. "Do as you please."

A long silence followed as the woman listened to Paulette's story. Finally, Paulette said, "You mean I shouldn't be doing that? That it's a sin?"

More silence.

"Well, OK. I didn't understand. . . . Of course, I love him. . . . Yes, I'll try to win him, not force him to Christ."

A few minutes later when I walked in, Paulette met me in tears. "I'm sorry, Raleigh! I was wrong, so wrong," she said. We embraced and I thought, *Tonight's the night.* Then, right in the middle of that passionate embrace, she said, "Now are you ready to accept Jesus Christ?"

"Paulette!" I said, exasperated. "You can't tell me when."

A few days later—two weeks to the day after Paulette gave her life to Christ—I came home early. Paulette and her Christian friend Martha were in the living room celebrating the completion of a project with three other GED students. I went straight to the bedroom to change clothes, when suddenly I found myself on my knees, tears coming down my cheeks, asking Jesus to forgive my sin, cleanse my heart, and be my Savior and Lord.

We lived on the corner of a very noisy intersection, and there was a party in the living room, but I heard nothing. I was in a world alone with God.

I stayed in the bedroom longer than usual trying to compose myself. I wanted to tell Paulette, but I was embarrassed. However, when I opened the door, she ran at me and leaped into my arms. "You did it! You did it! You did it!"

"Did what?" I challenged.

"I see that tear! You gave your life to Jesus, didn't you?"

I just grabbed her in a big hug. What could I say?

A New Manual

When I became a Christian, I set aside the army regulation manuals that I had memorized to beat my competition and picked up the Bible. It became my new handbook, not on how to compete with others, but to learn what God had to say to me. I had grown up in the church, so I had a lot of head knowledge about the Bible, but that was different from reading it, in the power of the Spirit, as a message from God to me.

Shortly after my conversion, I was transferred from Puerto Rico to recruiting command headquarters in Fort Sheridan, Illinois. Within three months Paulette and I were in a Bible study six nights a week. We'd attend Sunday school and chapel on base and then morning worship at First Baptist Church in Lake Forest, a suburban church of about eighty black folks with a white pastor and organist. We traveled to evening worship with the pastor and choir to churches throughout Chicago. We couldn't get enough of God's Word and fellowship with other believers. God was preparing me for the test I was about to face.

While at Fort Sheridan, I received a summons to appear in May 1980 before a military board of review in Atlanta. Initially, the charges trumped up by those colonels were so ludicrous I had paid no attention; later, when I saw they were not going to quit until they got their revenge, I fell to my knees and asked the Lord to deliver me from fear and bitterness.

The same full colonel who wanted to "stop Raleigh Washington," said, "Washington's the smoothest guy I've ever seen. We'll never trap him on anything specific. But where there's smoke . . . " So they gathered a mountain of material, 4,400 pages that had to be pushed around in a shopping cart. The night before my hearing, my lawyers told me I needed to read the whole thing.

I called Ron Balk, my pastor at First Baptist, to pray for me so I could stay up all night. When he asked why I needed to stay up all night, I told him I had to read 4,400 pages of testimony and reports so I could refute any false charges brought against me the next day.

"Brother Raleigh," he said, "the Word of God says, 'You will know the truth, and the truth will set you free.' You tell the truth, and you'll be free in the sight of our Lord." Then he prayed with me on the phone and promised that the whole church would be praying for me the next day.

His words were powerfully freeing. After we hung up, I watched the news on TV, went to bed, and slept like a baby.

The next day as I stood before the three generals on the review board, I felt as though I was in a bullet-proof bubble where nothing could really hurt me. But they quickly let me know where they were coming from. "Tell me, Washington," began one of the generals, "is it still a feather in the cap of a black man to make it with a white girl?" My stomach churned as I thought, *Where is the justice?* The charge of sexual assault had been resoundingly refuted, so ridiculous the CID did not feel it necessary to even interview me before dropping it. Yet the general from Georgia ignored these facts to strip me of my dignity with his racist question. I felt helpless and angry.

I hoped smoke wasn't curling out of my ears. But after that I answered every question put to me. They came at me six different ways, and I'm sure I came across exactly as the colonel had predicted—too smooth to be trapped. But I simply told the truth, and the truth cannot be trapped.

When the hearing finished, however, the military board of review reported to the Pentagon that I had engaged in "conduct unbecoming an officer"—though they never specified what that conduct had been. They didn't even cite the minor regulation violations against me, none of which would have stood up as just cause for dismissing me from the military. Those charges had only served as the legal tool to bring me before the board.

"Retire, or Be Discharged"

Several weeks went by, and I got closer and closer to completing my twenty years in the army, which would have guaranteed my retirement (through an act of Congress) no matter what happened with my case. Then just three days before July 31 when I would have completed my twenty years, I got a formal offer from the Pentagon: Retire "in lieu" of being discharged. This meant I would receive full retirement benefits and an honorable separation from active duty. But such a retirement was tantamount to admitting guilt to these unsubstantiated allegations. The alternative was to take a other-than-honorable discharge with no benefits whatsoever.

I had three days to respond.

At that time we had four kids and Paulette was pregnant with our fifth child. If I refused to sign, I'd be separated from the army with no income, no job, and no civilian experience. Nevertheless, Paulette said to me, "I think Satan is dangling this carrot in front of us. You're not guilty of 'conduct unbecoming an officer,' and my feeling is that you should not accept it. But you're the head of this family; do what you think best." What freedom to have that support from my wife!

I knew that to accept their offer would be to agree with a lie in order to gain full retirement benefits. But I also felt a tension: I must care for my family (the army was offering a retirement pension), and I must live according to the new regulations for my life—the Word of God. I remembered Pastor Balk's words, "The truth will set you free." And so, with great freedom, I refused the Pentagon's offer for retirement "in lieu of." Thus, with nineteen years, eleven months, and twenty-nine days—one day short of twenty years of service—I was unceremoniously discharged from the Army.

Those attending my case were shocked, not expecting me to refuse the tainted retirement offer. The officers assumed that by dangling my entire pension before me, I would agree to their terms and avoid the embarrassment of an ordinary discharge prior to a full twenty-year career. Still, as I was processed for discharge at Fort Sheridan, empty feelings of defeat filled me.

With the army's decision to kick me out, I experienced a profound sense of loss. I'd given the military twenty years of my life and did not deserve what was happening to me. Racism, jealousy, and envy succeeded in drumming me out of the army, and I was deeply disappointed.

A New Direction

But as I look back on it now, I'm convinced that while they meant it for evil, God meant it for good. I had depended upon the army all of my adult life. God began at this point to teach Paulette and me how to walk by faith. Already God had been giving me hints about new directions even before I faced the crisis. When I gave my life to Christ, I began to lose my appetite for the cocktail parties with generals and politicians and everything else it took to stay in the military fast lane. Instead, I developed an insatiable appetite for talking with other people about the Bible.

On the way home from the post chapel in San Juan, I began to rehearse the chaplain's sermon in my mind, thinking how much more he could have done with that passage. Watching me, Paulette would say, "You're re-preaching that sermon, aren't you?" She knew my heart.

The desire to do something with God's Word kept growing within me until an elderly white woman sparked a vision. First Baptist, our church near Fort Sheridan in Illinois, had a ministry at a nearby nursing home, and Pastor Ron Balk asked me to give several devotionals to the residents. Those were my first opportunities to preach, and they excited me to no end.

One day after I had given the devotional, an elderly white woman named Georgia looked at my uniform and said, "Have you ever been in a war?"

"Yes, ma'am," I said, "Vietnam. But I didn't see combat because I was in Personnel and Administration—behind the lines, you know."

"Don't knock it, sonny," she said. "God brought you back for a reason. Have you ever thought about preaching?"

She must have noticed that the question made me freeze, because she said, "Young man, I perceive God has called you to preach. I also perceive that you're running away. Never run from what God tells you to do." With that she turned her wheelchair around and rolled away.

I just stood there, numb while a cold sweat broke out all over me. But when my military career went up in smoke a short time later, God had already pointed me in a new direction.

All my adult life I had had one professional job: officer in the United States Army. If I was going to preach, God would have to retrain me. After I refused the tainted retirement, the Lord started teaching Paulette and me to walk by faith rather than by sight.

"Where should we go when I'm discharged?" I asked Paulette. "Florida or North Carolina?" There were well-known seminaries in both states, and Florida was my home, while North Carolina was Paulette's. We prayed for direction, but God didn't seem to answer. Then one morning, a major knocked at my door. "Sir, I have your discharge orders here, but it's under 'other than honorable conditions,'" he said apologetically. "I'm really sorry."

Giving this discharge was how the army sought to cover its unsubstantiated actions. They had offered me honorable retirement. When I refused it, because of the "in lieu" issue, they were caught completely off guard. In their haste in the final hours they reversed themselves by issuing a discharge under other-than-honorable conditions.

Without an honorable discharge, I did not qualify for free travel or help in moving our household goods to my home of record, Florida. Now I knew why God hadn't directed us toward Florida or North Carolina. He must have other plans, because without a job, money, or transportation, we were stuck.

I asked the army to let us stay on the base for thirty days while we looked for a job and a place to live. They agreed, and I was in a humbling setting (one I needed). One day I was an airborne lieutenant colonel, and everyone saluted me; the next I was worse than a civilian—a disgraced officer with everyone wondering what I had done.

It would have been easier to get completely away from the military than to be constantly reminded of my humiliation, but the Lord was teaching me new things. At Fort Sheridan, I had been the president of the parish council (similar to a board of elders). When I told Chaplain Gorman that he would have to replace me, he said, "You've got one more year to serve, and I expect you to do so as long as you are in the area." Those were kind words, and I was still a leader; but I was no longer a peer.

The job wasn't easy. On the council, I had to work with a full colonel, a major, a captain, and a sergeant major—but I had no rank at all. On the base I couldn't use my rank to make things happen anymore. The Lord wanted me to learn servant leadership like Jesus—a new experience for me.

—□ ■—

Finding a place for a family of seven was very difficult. We finally moved into the basement of one of the deacons of First Baptist Church, but I could not find a job. In spite of all my experience in administration and personnel, not one employer called back after the interviews, though many promised they would. It was another new experience; dozens of interviews but not one offer.

By this time, Pastor Balk, Paulette, and several others had confirmed that God wanted me to be a pastor. Since I was unable to find a job, Paulette and I began asking God whether I should go to seminary right then. I didn't know very much about Trinity Evangelical Divinity School, but it was only a mile and a half away, so I looked into it.

The more I learned about the school, the more it seemed like the right place for me, but the head of admissions had reservations. The school was already into the second week of the fall quarter; the challenge of starting late, going full time, and not having the money to pay the bill was complicated by my not having a job, having a wife and five kids, and living in the basement of someone else's house. It didn't make sense to him or the other people at Trinity.

My competitive nature clicked in. The more the registrar said how difficult it would be for me to take a full-time load and catch up, the more determined I became to do it. But there was a difference this time. I wasn't out to beat the white man at his game; rather, mine was a dogmatic response to the call of God on my life. I wanted to show the registrar not just what I could do but that God was in the plan.

The registrar permitted my enrollment. Still, school finances weren't easy. At the end of my first quarter I could not pay the $225 owed on my account. Just as I questioned remaining in school, an anonymous donor paid the bill—God was saying don't quit. (Later I was able to personally meet him and give him my thanks.) Toward the end of my first year, I owed over $1,000 and finally decided I couldn't continue. But one day an adjudicator for the Veterans Administration called me. She'd seen my case, and although she had no power to reverse what the army had done, she did have the authority to rule on my eligibility for veteran's benefits.

"The military obviously did you a horrible injustice, but that's not going to happen at the VA," Jeanette Thompson said over the phone. "You can expect to receive a check for $5,000 for the educational benefits you should have received this past year, and you will get your VA benefits every month in the future as long as you are in school."

In spite of the pain of being wrongfully accused and discharged unjustly, now I knew God had put me in seminary and was going to keep me there!

CHAPTER 5
THE STATION WAGON AND THE BLACK, WHITE, AND YELLOW CHURCH
(Glen Kehrein's story—2)

I met Malcolm Little, better known as Malcolm X, through his book *The Autobiography of Malcolm X.* He was one of several authors who opened my mind to black rage. Reading such books as *Black Rage, Crisis in Black and White, Native Son,* and *Soul on Ice* was both painful and powerful. Slowly I was learning about both the history of the black American experience and the feelings of being black and angry. Like many white readers, I felt politically correct sympathetic guilt, even as I listened to the black power movement's demand for reparations for past sins.

During the development of the black power movement, a faith perspective was largely missing. Evangelical Christians remained largely disconnected from the struggle; their critical analysis reflected apathy or ignorance. Even as black leaders and writers were reflecting the black experience, genuine white concern seemed unwelcomed in an age of black empowerment and militancy.

Upon graduation from MBI, I realized I could not return to Wisconsin. Socially and spiritually, I was "a man without a country": too theologically conservative to be a liberal, too socially liberal to be a conservative. During this period of drifting, I married my high school sweetheart, Lonni, and we settled in Humboldt Park, a neighborhood on Chicago's near northwest side that was changing from a Norwegian to a Puerto Rican community. We found an apartment for $90 a month. Around the corner, Salem Evangelical Free Church held services in both English and Norwegian while Hispanics slowly engulfed the neighborhood.

Rod's Station Wagon

Soon Salem hired a young, energetic Christian education director, Bill Dillon, and he began to recruit us for the new youth club. At this point I was too cynical about the church for any kind of professional ministry position, so volunteering in a club program three days a week was just right, while a job at American National Bank paid the bills. Lonni and I jumped in with both feet —our first two wedding anniversaries were spent coaching our respective teams at the AWANA Olympic competition. From that point until the present Lonni has walked beside me, fully invested in every aspect of the ministry path to which God has called us.

A few white kids from the church came to the program, but most of the children were either Puerto Rican from within walking distance or black kids driven by Rod Thompson. Rod was one of those white people Raleigh talks about who sold insurance in the black community. He sold inexpensive burial policies to ensure that poor people could give a loved one a decent five hundred dollar funeral. Every week he went around collecting a few bucks from his regular customers.

But Rod also was on a mission. Like the fabled pied piper, kids flocked around as Rod passed out leftover Sunday school material. Soon he began piling the children into his car and bringing them to club. When the sedan became too small, he bought a station wagon.

Rod was the first white person I'd met who seriously tried to cross racial lines and reach out to black people. He acted like a father to many of the kids he brought to club, and they loved the guy. The club program grew to a six-day-per-week activity with a Bible and basketball program on Saturdays, four club programs for different ages during the week, and Sunday school on Sundays. Rod's kids never missed a regular day or special event. His station wagon was like a clown act at the circus: open the door and fifteen kids would tumble out.

One weekend a long-awaited father-and-son retreat arrived. Rod's son came, but Rod could not join us, as Friday was the best night to find his customers at home. That decision proved deadly. Upon our return Sunday night friends told us the shocking news: Rod had been killed in a robbery attempt, shot to death on Warren Avenue for the cash he'd been collecting. The police had arrested someone for the murder (who later was convicted), but it was a terrible loss—to his family, to the kids, and to me.

As with many youth of the '60s, I had been caught up with making an impact and bringing change. There was a kind of romantic appeal to being socially significant, denying anything "establishment," becoming radically different from our parents' generation and moving into the inner city as an "urban pioneer." We thought our efforts would totally transform society. But when Rod died I realized that ministry in the inner city was not a romantic, youthful adventure. The inner city was a place filled with the cold reality of life and death.

Other cold realities awaited, too. When Rod was killed, members at Salem Church voiced the opinion that Rod should not have been venturing into the black community in the first place. They didn't say he got what he deserved, just that he'd been foolish. I was disappointed to discover that Salem's commitment to the club programs was a concession to Bill, who was let go soon after Rod's death for "budget reasons." Rod's death and Bill's departure reinforced my feeling that evangelicals had little commitment to the people of the city.

Lonni and I decided it was time to look for a church with a greater commitment to the kids, a church where they would feel more comfortable. (Later the members of Salem Evangelical Free Church would engage in a period of soul-searching and struggle of their own. Eventually they decided to stay in the city. Salem became a bilingual church, with Hispanic and English services, and the leaders developed a strong neighborhood ministry, which now includes a quality Christian elementary school.)

But where would Lonni and I go? We were starving for spiritual relevancy in a church committed to the inner city. Now we had thirty spiritually "orphaned" kids who also needed a church home. We hungered for a church interested in what interested us.

Welcome to the Circle

The first Sunday Lonni and I visited Circle Church on Chicago's West Side, we felt like two parched, desert travelers who had finally crawled to an opulent oasis. On that Easter Sunday 1971, all the members were signing a "Declaration of the Open Church," Circle's vision of different races and classes coming together, not to assimilate into the culture of the majority, but to appreciate and celebrate in Christian harmony their differences in culture, class, and race.

It was exhilarating! Senior pastor David Mains led a dynamic team, including a black associate, Clarence Hilliard, and a Chinese associate, Ka Tong Gaw, all powerful preachers. This group of evangelical Christians seemed truly committed to bridging the gap between the races in the context of dynamic preaching, exciting worship, and active social concern. While whites were still the majority, skin colors spanned the rainbow, as attenders mingled together in one common faith.

We looked no further; Circle was the church for us. The leaders swallowed hard a few times when they found out this young married couple would come complete with thirty kids. The members were mainly young professionals without children, and the church had only a small Christian education program. But within a few months they set up a structure to welcome those kids, including people who took on the kids as surrogate parents, driving them to all church functions. We couldn't have asked for more.

The Black and White of It All

Circle Church was populated mainly by highly educated young adults—about 15 percent black, 5 percent Asian, and the rest white. Almost everyone agreed that education was the key to solving the problems of race relations. For instance, a black module (our name for ministry groups within the church) was formed, its purpose to "blacken Circle Church" (i.e., make it more attractive to black people). A major task became black awareness training of the majority white membership.

With all the black awareness reading we had done, Lonni and I decided to link with this group, and we became two of the most committed whites involved in the black module. Though we wanted the blacks to "tell it like it is," we soon were not very comfortable. (But then, was slavery comfortable?) We stewed in our guilt and then would dump on less enlightened whites by telling *them* "like it is." It eased our pain to be one of the enlightened few.

As I began to face our country's racial history and our ancestors' past behavior, before long I began to hate the fact that I was white. No matter how educated I became, I could never escape the blight of my whiteness. I might become one of the "good guys"—less ignorant and racist than other whites—but I could never have the black experience. (I was reminded of that a million times.) Part of the black identity at the time typically made it a requirement to exclude whites from the brotherhood; to admit that a white person really understood was to surrender power.

While enlightening and educational, the process was deeply painful and personal. I now feel there also was a destructive aspect to it. Because the church was committed to racial education rather than racial reconciliation, our actions had a philosophical rather than a theological foundation, and that led to basic inconsistencies. For instance, I understood the need to develop black pride, but it took on an unhealthy expression when it created a barrier between blacks and whites in the church. Even the black pastor seemed to maintain a subtle social distance from whites, a gap that no amount of commitment on my part could bridge.

One time André Crouch was scheduled to sing at Malcolm X University, just down the street from the union hall where Circle Church met; so several of us from the black module—three or four whites and Circle's black associate pastor, Clarence Hilliard—went over to Malcolm X University together. But as soon as we entered the auditorium, which was filled with blacks, Clarence separated himself and didn't sit with us. It was obvious that in a black setting he didn't want to be identified with us. That was hurtful, but with the "proper" white guilt I had assumed, it was acceptable.

In all fairness, I must say that I did not have the courage to confront Clarence and hear his explanation. It was easier to hold the unresolved feelings inside.

Another example of how philosophy superseded theology arose when we faced disagreements. Blacks were the only ones permitted to define what was right for blacks. As a result, at times it seemed that the "black experience" became more important than asking "What does Scripture say we should do?" It did not always seem like the Bible was the final authority to settle a dispute.

We wanted so much for this experiment of integrating the church to work that we failed to see that education and confrontation were not leading us toward the most basic need: racial reconciliation.

Building on Sand

One thing we did realize was that we needed to translate all our talk into action and develop an actual neighborhood ministry that lived out our social and spiritual concerns. *That* got my blood going! In the fall of 1971 I enrolled at Wheaton College, studying for a sociology degree. During this time, two groups were forming within Circle Church: one wanted to focus on a neighborhood outreach strategy under the black module's leadership, and the other was interested in developing intentional Christian community. Many of the white members were interested in both community and outreach, but none of the blacks were interested in intentional community living.

This was disappointing because several of the white members wanted to develop something similar to John Perkins's Voice of Calvary in Mendenhall, Mississippi, which combined intentional community living and outreach in the context of a multiracial church. Voice of Calvary included a health center, a gym, a tutoring program, an elementary school, a farm, a summer camp, an evangelism training program, a co-op housing development, and a Bible institute. About half of the thirty staff members were white and the other half black.

Upon graduation from Wheaton, I began to work for Circle Church under Clarence's supervision to develop specific neighborhood programs. The vicinity around the union hall where the church met was not a suitable residential neighborhood. (In fact, Circle was a commuter church, with people driving in from all over the city and suburbs.) I began to search for a location for a new community center, and concluded such a center should be in a racially changing, residential neighborhood; here we might have a stabilizing effect before the neighborhood deteriorated badly. The Austin neighborhood a few miles to the west (which at that time had the second highest crime rate in Chicago) fit the bill.

To have an effective ministry in the city, most of us believed we needed to *intentionally* live in the neighborhood in order to serve it. That required some *sacrifice* of people's lifestyles (Principles 2 and 6; see chapters 9 and 13). That's where we felt the vision of Christian community intersected with the vision for outreach.

The church members eventually accepted my proposal to start a community center in Austin, with medical, legal, and family counseling resources. The original staff—doctor, nurse, lawyer, family counselor, director (myself)—and our spouses all bought the dual vision of ministry and fellowship.

Lonni and I were the first Circle members to move into the Austin neighborhood in June 1973; in September others joined us in a large two-flat, and we called ourselves the Austin Community Fellowship, a subgroup of Circle. Together with Circle Community Center (CCC), which was located just a few blocks away, the whole project was gaining momentum. It was a very exciting and energizing time. We thought we knew all of the right ways to do cross-cultural ministry; all we needed was the time to put it into action.

What we didn't realize was that the whole foundation was built on sand.

Another analogy for our venture is a Hollywood set. When people came to visit Circle Church on Sunday morning, the multiracial congregation, the energetic worship anchored by dynamic preaching and music painted an impressive scene. But behind the scene, it was all propped up with two-by-fours. There was insufficient substance when it came to the most critical of elements necessary to its success: committed relationships (Principle #1).

I've since come to realize that racial reconciliation among Christians requires solid relationships. There are no substitutes. But at Circle, from the top down, the relationships weren't built on trust. Everyone was bound to a vision but not deeply committed to each other. Without solid, committed relationships, building the vision was more like building on sand.

The Funky Gospel

Whenever blacks and whites try to get together, differences must be hammered out. Clarence Hilliard (black) and David Mains (white) certainly had their share of differences. I was one of the elders as well as director of the outreach program, so I was involved in many meetings, where the two men disagreed strongly. Each man meant so much to my spiritual growth that it was like watching parents argue. Sometimes we would spend hours discussing an issue that, in the end, would terminate in compromise just to end the debate. But the issue was not truly resolved, and residual feelings of discontent remained below the surface.

—□ ■—

Some of the disagreements reflected personal preferences; others reflected cultural differences. For instance, David was very time-oriented. (He now directs *Chapel of the Air*, a radio ministry where things are timed to the second, and he is both both comfortable and effective.) Since this dynamic church was growing through David's vision, Clarence was expected to conform to this preaching style. But that was not Clarence's style, and in general, that kind of structure is not attractive to many African-Americans. In looking back, I realize now that Clarence needed to work in a much more flexible arena.

Worship planning also carried its times of tension. There was a clear definition of worship: attributing worth directly to God. Therefore songs shouldn't just talk about God; they should attribute praise directly to God, as in, "Holy, Holy, Holy! Lord God Almighty! Early in the morning our song shall rise to Thee." However, many gospel songs that blacks feel indispensable to "having church" don't speak directly to God. Clearly cultural expectations created unresolved racial tension.

The three pastors rotated preaching responsibilities, but each sermon required at least four meetings to refine it. This resulted in the most dynamic, powerful preaching we'd ever heard. David's precision in doctrine and word choice was an effective communication style, but Clarence's natural style, nurtured in traditional black churches, was also effective, though quite different. David and Clarence were much closer friends than typical church staff, yet their relationship included more issues than a homogeneous staff would normally deal with. Some of those issues, left unresolved, began to build a kettle of tension.

When the explosion came in 1976, it was over a sermon that Clarence wanted to preach, titled: "The Funky Gospel," and David's authority over the Sunday serice. David said the sermon had serious doctrinal problems and wouldn't allow Clarence to preach it. Clarence claimed David was denying a black preacher full and free expression and destroyinbg the principle of the open church. In the eyes of some people, that sermon and David's response to it were the sum of the problems. But, in my opinion, that event only triggered an eruption that had been building for a long time.

Theory Rather than Relationships

Circle had a vision of being a multiracial congregation. It

was a noble pioneering experiment that had no scout riding ahead and pointing out the dangers.

Relationships deeply committed to the principles of racial reconciliation might have weathered these conflicts. But as it turned out, the relationship between Pastors Mains and Hilliard, like many relationships at Circle Church, were not deep enough to withstand the explosion. When the fissure opened between David and Clarence, the whole church split down racial lines. Racial camps emerged, each justifying their position in the conflict. As whites who had aligned ourselves with the "black movement" within the church, we felt blacks defensively retrenching and closing us out. We retreated in response. Humpty Dumpy had fallen from the wall.

I'm sure blacks also felt that the white leadership was making self-serving decisions that forced them out. In response, all the black members rallied around Clarence.

In an attempt to be fair and not blame one more than the other, the elders removed both David and Clarence from the pulpit; neither could preach until we had resolved the problem. But the black community calls that "silencing the pastor." We had no idea of the significance of such a move. As for David, the elders' action was an insult that did not take into account his role as senior pastor, publicly humiliating him without cause.

The elders tried to patch things up, but it just got worse. In one leaders' meeting it was acknowledged that things were so bad that Clarence couldn't possibly work under David anymore. But David asked, "How can I be the senior pastor if a staff person can't work for me?"

"As a black man," Clarence responded, "I can no longer have a white person tell me what to preach and how to preach. I won't be throttled; I must be allowed to speak prophetically."

Finally David proposed a solution to Clarence, "Look, this thing has fallen apart. Let's put the best face on it we can. You can rally all the people who are interested in the Austin neighborhood—the Austin Fellowship and Circle Community Center. We'll commission you to be the pastor in planting a new church, and that will be our solution. It will be a church split but with all the positive potential of Paul and Barnabas going their separate ways."

But Clarence wouldn't buy it. He was not willing to let us sweep the issues under the rug. Neither could he offer any acceptable alternatives that would resolve the conflict. [1]

The Missing Ingredients

Even now, as I look back at the situation, I don't know what else could have happened because of the ominous breakdown in relationships. Everyone involved, beginning first with Clarence and David but certainly not limited to them, was deeply wounded. The distrust, always festering under the surface between the blacks and whites, finally destroyed us.

I can hardly describe the pain I felt as the dream crumbled around our feet. As a high profile church, often pointed to by homogeneous church growth critics, the humiliation was publicly reported in *Christianity Today* magazine. It was like watching a loved one die an agonizing, public death.

The time to install fire extinguishers is not while the house is burning. We learned the hard lesson that the time to work out racial differences is not in the middle of conflict. In a cross-cultural tinderbox setting, we have to be building relationships and working on the issues of trust, sincerity, and openness—key principles of reconciliation—all the way along. If relational depth is not there, a crisis will only expose it and cause everyone to retrench to their most defendable positions: blacks mistrusting whites and whites mistrusting blacks.

Once the confrontation occurred, we never really dealt with the content of Clarence's "funky" sermon. Were there doctrinal problems or not? If so, how serious were they? If it was heresy, then it was right for David to block its presentation; black heresy is no more sacred than white heresy. Or was it biblical truth in cultural garb? But we never discussed the content, for the dispute had gone far beyond the point where reason would prevail.

Instead there was a proposal to place Clarence under direct accountability to the elders. But the perception of blacks was that Clarence was being placed under a restriction that David was not. The elders thought the change would remove Clarence from under David's authority and place the two men on equal accountability. However, several of us soon felt this last ditch effort to save a sinking ship could push David to resignation. What the elders felt to be a significant concession, the blacks charged as racist. Amid the charges and a growing rejection of the proposal, communication between the white elders and the black leadership quickly and completely broke down.

With this final tailspin in communications, it did not seem to the elders that there was any hope of resolving the situation, and we asked for Clarence's resignation. Clarence refused to give it, so he was terminated.

Because this controversy was so public, the elders decided to schedule one final service on a Sunday evening where Clarence was invited to preach his sermon so everyone could hear what was in it and to allow the black members to say and do whatever they wanted. The whole church plus many outsiders turned out for that service. It was an excruciating evening, sort of the last hurrah, peppered with many accusations.

Then it was over. Clarence Hilliard and all the black members left the church immediately. A year later, David Mains and his family left. The heart had been cut out of the vision of the open church.

At the time of the Circle Church split, Circle Community Center, with its legal aid clinic, counseling center, and youth program had been operating for one and one-half years. But because most of the staff were white, our ties to the evangelical black community had been through the black module at Circle Church, and especially through Clarence Hilliard.

When all the black members left the church, the center staff was orphaned. We felt very insecure living and working in a nearly all-black neighborhood without black support or leadership. Other black churches who heard of the split were suspicious. We couldn't process this loss effectively because there were no blacks left at Circle to act as sounding boards. Yet we really leaned on each other, and a larger circle of individuals still supported the Center and the general outreach in the Austin neighborhood.

My greatest loss was that not even one personal relationship with a fellow black believer survived the holocaust. In my gut I knew that as whites we could never do ministry in Austin alone; we needed our black brothers and sisters. I was desperate for a black friend who would believe in me—someone who would trust me. I needed somebody black to say I was OK. It was a void no white person could fill.

Tyrone's Story
Then a new black family came to Circle Church. I immediately got to know the husband, whom I'll call Tyrone. He was intelli-

gent and a good Bible teacher. As our relationship deepened I shared my side of the Circle Church saga and he basically said, "Sounds like those black folks did you dirty."

I was astonished. *Could there be someone who would trust me again?* Here was a thread to hold onto, and I grabbed hold of this new relationship, spending time with Tyrone.

Clarence had been my pastor and was about fifteen years older than I, but with Tyrone I had a peer relationship. He, too, had been wounded in a couple of previous church situations, so we felt drawn together to commiserate. Soon he and his family moved into the Austin neighborhood, and both he and his wife began working at the Center—he with the youth program, she as the receptionist. It was great to have black folks involved again!

Tyrone was a good worker and a good friend, but there were some red flags I should have seen early on, including severe tensions within his extended family. He had once been part of a cult-like group that had left a lot of scars. But who was I to expect reconciliation? I was happy to let the past be the past. Although Tyrone shared some things with me, he said very little about his marriage. But from observation and hints dropped here and there, I knew he was deeply unhappy in his personal life. Still, things would be OK, I rationalized.

As time went on, I began to realize that his personal struggles left him full of rage. That rage had begun to find a "politically correct" outlet as black militant anger at white oppression. But I prided myself on being one of the good guys as I amazed Tyrone with my knowledge of the black struggle and ability to accept appropriate white responsibility.

As we spent many hours together, our relationship grew closer for about two years. We even shared a mutual passion, fishing trips to the north woods. But Tyrone's anger gradually deepened. Finally we attended the National Black Evangelical Association conference together, and the moment we walked in the door, Tyrone refused to spend time with me or even be seen walking around with me. As Yogi Berra said, it was dejá vu all over again. Something was seriously wrong.

Our wives picked us up from the airport after that conference, but the atmosphere was so cold between Tyrone and his wife that Lonni and I could hardly talk during the drive home.

The next day Tyrone's wife came to work in tears: Tyrone

had walked out last night, leaving her and the kids, she believed, for a woman who was the principal of a nearby school and a militant black activist. Incredibly, Tyrone came to work as though everything was normal, even though his wife worked at the front desk of the center as the receptionist. I had to act, but I literally shook at the prospect.

Predictably, when I confronted Tyrone, he roared, "How can you as a white man understand the pressures on a black man? You'll never understand; you have nothing to say to me."

Tyrone accused me of being racist even to question him. We never had a chance to talk about what the Bible says or what was really happening. He just started swinging the "racist" club at me immediately. Of course, he knew all my vulnerable buttons to push—I'd pointed them out to him when I opened my inner personal pain and insecurities from the church split.

The Fellowship tried to support me, but when you're being accused of racism, white folks can't do you much good; talking to them just made me feel worse.

The center's steering committee was most concerned about how the whole confrontation would appear to outsiders. On the heels of the Circle Church confrontation, could we afford to fire another black leader? We were all paralyzed.

A Beacon of Light

About that time John Perkins stayed at our house while on a trip to Chicago, and I asked for his counsel. While he acknowledged the sticky situation, the issue was clear to him: What Tyrone was doing was sin, pure and simple; he had to go.

What I appreciate most about John, one of evangelicalism's elder statesmen, is that even though he is a high profile black leader, he holds to the Word of God above everything else—even race. Sin is sin whether committed by a black or a white person.

I longed for a ministry partner with that courage. Perkins freed me from the confusion, and the next day I called Tyrone into my office and fired him. Exploding in anger, he threw me across the room and nearly broke my arm as I crashed into the door. (I'm not a small man, but he weighed a good hundred pounds more than I did.)

But worse than the bruises he gave me, Tyrone's rage destroyed me emotionally. How could this breakdown in a relationship have happened again? What was wrong with me? My insecurities made me question all that I had done to contribute to the problems both with Tyrone and with Clarence at Circle Church. I couldn't be innocent. Was I racist? Was I so weak or naive that I couldn't deal with problems? All the accusations Tyrone had yelled at me drove deep.

I Could Not Quit

Within the next few years, most of the whites who helped start Circle Community Center moved on. The pain had been so great and the burnout so total that their hearts were no longer in the struggle. Eventually, I think that would have happened to me, too; I was certainly burned out. But deep down I could not shake the belief that God had called me to racial reconciliation and urban ministry.

The main reason I didn't leave the city or the center was the grace of God. In addition, my wife, Lonni, was a major source of support during a very bleak time. She shared all that pain with me, understood my call, never failed in her encouragement, and even nursed me through chest surgery to remove a tumor in the middle of it all! Still, I continued to feel incomplete. Perhaps the damage between blacks and whites was too deep to heal in only one generation. I began to believe that the best I could do was leave a heritage that perhaps my children could actualize.

Scripture left a glimmer of hope, however. As Peter wrote, "The God of all grace, who called you to his eternal glory in Christ, after you have suffered a little while, will himself restore you and make you strong, firm and steadfast" (1 Peter 5:10). God finally did send me a black partner, a friend strong as a rock.

NOTES

1. The Circle Church story is much like the story of the blind men describing the elephant by which appendage they are touching; each man has a different perspective. As I showed Clarence a draft of this chapter, it became apparent that we have some significant differences in our perspectives. I want to emphasize that this chapter represents my conclusions, as drawn from my reflections of eighteen years. This account should not be taken as the definitive word.

   It has been difficult to be transparent and honest to my conclusions without airing some dirty laundry. All of the parties, including myself, made mistakes. My intent is that we learn from the past, from both our successes and mistakes.

   Each of us stands upon a foundation built by others. Circle Urban Ministries and Rock Church are built upon the pioneering work of Circle Church and its leaders. To them I owe a deep debt of gratitude for much of my early spiritual growth and ministry guidance.

CHAPTER 6
BRINGING IT TOGETHER

*T*wo wounded men, one white, one black, unknown to each other, lived only a few miles apart in Chicago in 1983. Glen Kehrein, white, lived in a black community on Chicago's west side. Raleigh Washington, black, was attending a white seminary in the northern suburbs. One was emotionally bloodied from cross-cultural relationships that had blown up in his face, shattering his dream of true racial reconciliation in the church. The other had been unjustly stripped of his career by jealous whites who couldn't stand to see an "uppity nigger" climbing the ladder of success ahead of them. Each had a need to reconcile to his God and to a seemingly hostile race.

A man named Jim Westgate, a professor at Trinity Evangelical Divinity School who once served as family life pastor at Circle Church, became the link that would profoundly change their lives. Kehrein and Washington were about to learn the first steps of true racial reconciliation as they began to develop a new vision together.

A New Relationship

Raleigh Washington: All through seminary, Paulette and I had talked about going back to Jacksonville, Florida—my old stomping grounds as a kid. We had even been asked by the southeastern district of the Evangelical Free Church to consider planting a new church. Starting a church in Jacksonville would fulfill our dreams, yet for some reason the prospect did not excite us much.

As graduation loomed near, Jim Westgate, one of my professors and a part-time director of urban ministry for the Evangelical Free Church, took me aside. "Raleigh, I want to talk with you and Paulette about planting a church in the Austin community in Chicago. There's a neighborhood outreach there called Circle Community Center that needs a church to partner in ministry."

Ministry in Florida had been attractive for many reasons, and weather was not last on the list! However, that very week Paulette and I had separately become unsettled about ministry in Jacksonville. Now Jim was speaking to us about planting a church in Chicago. As he talked we felt God was giving us clear direction. Our unsettled feeling turned to peace; we were convinced of our call to Chicago.

I recruited six seminary students (two black, four white) to help pioneer this new church. In our small apartment in Waukegan, my family selected its name: Rock of Our Salvation Church (based on Psalm 95). The name would fit our hybrid nature and relate to both the black community and the mainly white Evangelical Free denomination. "Rock Church," if in name only, was born.

Then one night I had a vivid dream in which I was preaching to five hundred white people. Frankly, I'd had few thoughts of preaching to white folks; I didn't fully understand the dream, but it made me think. I felt God was saying that somehow whites would play a role in my ministry call.

A few months later, after my graduation from Trinity seminary and a visit with family in Florida, Jim Westgate finally took Paulette and me to visit Circle Community Center. Here we met Glen Kehrein, the director.

This fellow Glen seemed reserved, yet friendly, as he gave us a tour of the center and Chicago's Austin area, but I was impressed with the grasp he had on the neighborhood. And I was impressed by Circle's ministry in the 'hood—Christian doctors, lawyers, family counselors, and youth workers all helped the residents. I began to see how a church could begin where Circle had plowed.

We drove around, looking at several possible sites, but I had a strong bias against a storefront location. "No way!" I sputtered to Glen and Jim. "In the black community the storefront church has the wrong image. Too often the pastor is just a hustler, preying on poor people."

Glen was thoughtful. "Well, I think we might be able to arrange some way for you to get started in the center for the first few months. Then we can see what happens."

I looked at Glen as if seeing him for the first time. *He would do that for me?* I wondered, amazed. *He doesn't even know me, and he's practically inviting me to share space with the center!*

When the meeting was done, Paulette turned to Glen and asked innocently, "Are there any homes for sale in this neighborhood?"

Glen Kehrein: When Jim Westgate mentioned that there was an interesting black student at Trinity seminary he thought I ought to meet, I was not impressed. After my Circle Church experience and the blow-up with Tyrone, the black staff member who broke my heart (and almost broke my arm), I had come to the depressing conclusion that I wasn't going to see any significant black and white reconciliation in my generation. Circle Community Center was doing some good things, providing needed services to the poor. There were even blacks on staff, but a ministry springing from committed and reconciled black/white relationships apparently was a pipedream.

Still, out of deference to Jim, I agreed to a meeting. Raleigh was genuinely passionate about his call to preach. But, frankly, I could not determine whether he was a true godsend or a disaster that I would be gullible enough to let happen once again. After the meeting I imagined trying to explain it to my wife, and in my mind I could just hear her moan: "Oh, no! Here we go again. Glen, won't you ever learn?"

Besides the old wounds, I had other reservations. Was this Washington guy really our style? How would a former lieutenant colonel fit with a center staff that regarded being nontraditional as a badge of honor? Products of the '60s and '70s, the founders and most people in Circle Church and the center prided themselves on being "new wine in new wineskins." We had rejected old-fashioned evangelism for "living our faith" in serving the community.

But I had to ask myself, *Where has all that pride and progressiveness gotten us?* Although our programs helped people in the short run, I had to admit few lives were permanently changed for the better. Not many were becoming Christians, and we could point to only a few who were now being discipled in a local church. Though we denied it, I wondered if we had evolved into ministers of a social gospel. If so, Raleigh's energy and call would fill a big vacuum.

Still, I wondered whether he was for real. Would his seemingly boundless energy and enthusiasm last for the long haul, or would he use his platform as a stepping stone for bigger things and leave us just as our hope was renewed? Though I was uncertain about Raleigh, his wife seemed genuine. When Paulette asked about houses for sale, I quickly told her about the sign that had just gone up across the street from our home.

Raleigh Washington: I thought Paulette's inquiry about homes for sale was ludicrous. Seminary had left us in debt. We were living in a government-subsidized apartment and struggling to provide for our five children.

But when Glen showed us the house and then offered to speak to the neighbor so we could view it right then, Paulette jumped at the chance. I wanted to refuse to go, but what could I do? It was a beautiful home, ideal for a family our size, and all the way back to Waukegan, Paulette talked about which room would suit which kid.

"Look," I said, "there's no way. We couldn't even come up with a down payment! Let's just be satisfied with a small apartment that we can afford."

"If God wants us to be in Austin," said Paulette, "He wants us to have a house. I think we should pray for that one. We can't adequately minister to people out of a cramped apartment."

That was Paulette, always moving out in faith. "You're right," I sighed, and so we started praying.

At that time I was working with a Jewish attorney named Jeff Strange, who had volunteered to represent me—without charge—in attempting to get my discharge from the Army reversed. The day after we visited the Austin neighborhood, I was talking to Jeff on the phone about my case with the military, and the prospect of us moving to Austin came up. "Raleigh," he said, "I don't know how you got through grad school [meaning seminary], but I believe you're gonna do some good in Chicago. So, if you see a house you want to buy, don't do anything until you call me. I'm a broker, and I'll give you my broker's fee for your down payment on a house."

In less than twenty-four hours we had our down payment. Then, based on the $20,000 salary the denominational district had approved for me (which I still had to raise) and the $8,000 Paulette was scheduled to receive from a teaching job she took in a nearby Christian school, we qualified for a VA loan to cover the rest of the cost of the home. It was an unmistakable sign that God had led us to this place.

Glen Kehrein: I had been worried how Lonni would respond to this new relationship, but the first time the Kehreins and Washingtons got together as couples, our wives hit it off famously. In little time Paulette's compassion freed Lonni's hurt and pain, and Lonni was crying like a baby on her shoulder.

Arrangements were made for Raleigh to begin his church in the conference room at the center. His pulpit was two cardboard boxes with a cloth draped over them. Because it was a small room, the arrangement was obviously temporary, and that suited me just fine. I was not willing to make any kind of commitment that didn't have a built-in testing period, feeling still fragile from the wound of the Circle Church split.

Every time Raleigh and I talked, the excitement grew within me. However, I remained intentionally reserved. Yes, the center could give the new church a jump-start, but the success of the church and its relationship to the center would have to live—or die—on this pastor's shoulders. *If it works, who knows what God might do*, I thought. *If it fails, let it be as painless as possible.*

Raleigh Washington: When I asked for office space at the center, the best Glen could offer was an old desk in the basement three days a week; a volunteer used it the other days. But I didn't mind, because on the other two days I just hung out in other people's offices, getting to know what the center was all about. But I was disturbed that there was no overt evangelism of the people being served by Circle. "How about making me a volunteer chaplain?" I suggested. It would be a good way to round out the services offered by the center, and an even better way to contact potential people for the church.

But the center staff had a different agenda. They were solid professional people, Christians who loved the Lord and were committed to providing quality service for the poor. The center's ministry slogan expressed it well: "God's love made visible in the city"—not to be confused with being made *verbal*. Overt evangelism embarrassed the staff's professionalism. Some leaned back in their chairs and looked at me over the top of their glasses as if to say, "Who is this fundamentalist, cold turkey evangelist coming in here to ruin our reputation in the neighborhood?"

But Glen remained cautiously supportive and reminded his staff that the original vision of Circle Center was to be an outreach of a local church, not separate from a church. He pointed to the strength we would gain by having a chaplain to follow up with people's spiritual needs. I could see our friendship was building, and our hearts began to knit together. *Maybe this partnership between a spiritual and social ministry, and between black and white, has a chance*, I thought.

Glen Kehrein: Things were changing. As a pastor, Raleigh brought an energy and presence that helped us sharpen our purpose and mission. Slowly, we were evolving from a Christian service agency supported by four "affiliate" churches into a wholistic ministry that genuinely combined faith and works. The other affiliates could not be involved much beyond the board level, and Raleigh dove in fully. He sought my advice on every step he made and asked me to school him about the neighborhood and the city of Chicago.

A Mutual Commitment

Glen Kehrein: My relationship with Raleigh was deepening into a true friendship, sincere and interdependent (Principles 3 and 5). He was not afraid of being seen with me as a white man; he went out of his way to identify with me. Secure in his black identity, Raleigh had little need to express independence and to distance himself from me. This was too good to be true.

A real marriage between our two ministries seemed possible. But that would logically mean sealing the relationship with Rock

Church by Lonni and I joining as members. The two ministries could not really join in partnership unless we as leaders made a mutual commitment.

I believe one's personal life and ministry should be consistent; that's why I live in the community where I minister. Thus, if God were drawing the center and Rock Church together in ministry, I knew my family needed to join the church. Anything less would be hypocritical.

Lonni's gut reaction to my suggestion that we join was, "But I feel at home in the Fellowship." Then she took a big breath. "But I know you're right. Being comfortable and homogeneous is one of Satan's weapons against racial reconciliation." We later understood that she was expressing another reconciliation principle: sacrifice. Had my wife not been willing to sacrifice her comfort with a homogeneous church, we would never have experienced what God had in store for us.

It took a few months to complete our ministry commitments with Austin Fellowship, but in December 1984 we joined Rock Church.

Raleigh Washington: One day Glen said to me, "Raleigh, I want you to know that if you and Paulette had not come, I don't know if I would still be here. I was nearer the end of my rope than I admitted. But when you and Paulette embraced me, encouraged me, and supported me in this ministry, I came alive again. God sent you here, and I'm glad to be your partner."

I didn't know what to say. This white guy really respected me. He had spent ten years building this ministry, then he invited me in, recommended me to become chairman of the Circle board of directors, and, with his family, joined Rock Church. That is trust and commitment! Through his openness to us, Glen challenged Paulette and me to consider some of the convictions and concerns he and Lonni held. During this time God was teaching us several of the principles crucial to racial reconciliation: commitment, openness, sincerity, interdependence, and sacrifice. (See chapters 8–15.)

The Kehreins displayed a deep commitment to the poor, the oppressed, and the needy. Paulette and I had never felt particularly called in that way. In the military, we had learned how to live among upper-middle-class folks, and we liked it. Even in seminary we had been in an upper-middle-class community, and I was

taught upper-middle-class values by upper-middle-class professors. (I remember one professor recommending that whenever we
felt stressed in the ministry, we ought to have the church board
give us a three-month sabbatical and go on a cruise!)

But Glen and Lonni cared more for the needs of poor people
than for their own comfort. When they experienced stress, a cruise
wasn't even an option. Choosing to go back and identify with poor
people was contrary to my competitive nature. But we saw something in this couple that moved us deeply. Paulette and I were
challenged by their commitment. "If they can love these people so
much," we said, "how can we love them any less?" God's call to us
to serve the poor and the oppressed was first experienced by seeing needy people through the loving eyes of Glen and Lonni Kehrein.

A New Facility

*Rock Church and the center both grew, and the 8,500 square feet
building became crowded. At one point the congregation packed in
the conference room on Sunday and spilled into the hallway. Clearly
a new facility was needed.*

*One day Glen grabbed Raleigh and said, "I found something I
want you to see." "Something" was a former public school, Austin
High Annex, composed of three buildings. At its height the school
had 3,000 students, but the school's quality and enrollment had fall-
en in the racially changing community; then unhealthy asbestos was
discovered in the building. With enrollment down and the cost of
maintenance up (asbestos removal alone would have cost $300,000),
the Board of Education closed the school. The building was for sale.*

Glen Kehrein: By this time the whole community was in decline,
and no one wanted the huge facility. In 1983, the school board just
walked away from it. Within a year and a half, the building had
been totally vandalized, stripped, and left for dead like so many
other buildings in the inner city.

Even though the building was in utter ruin, I had a feeling of
excitement as we walked through it. Austin High Annex had once
been a Catholic convent and high school, and as we came to a
room the nuns had used as a chapel, Raleigh's eyes lit up. "This
would be the perfect size to develop an emerging church. God
wants us here! We could put 50 in this room and it wouldn't feel
empty—but we could squeeze 150 in here, too."

The whole complex provided about 150,000 square feet of space. But the old school consisted of three buildings; could we do the renovation in stages? "Even if we were only able to restore one of the buildings," someone commented, "we'd have 38,000 square feet—almost five times what we have now."

I was groaning inside just thinking about shoveling out all the debris, getting electricity to the different rooms, and replacing the heating plant, but Raleigh was starting to get excited. "Think what it would say to the people of the community to see this building restored! Just occupying this location would take it out of the hands of the drug dealers and gang bangers, and that in itself would bring hope to the neighborhood."

After we finished our tour, we went to a nearby greasy spoon restaurant for a cup of coffee, overwhelmed with the challenge and the opportunity. We talked and then covenanted in payer: "God, if you open the door, we'll walk through."

The next day I called the Board of Education and found out the school was indeed for sale. I wondered what exorbitant price this complex, complete with gym, forty classrooms, a 1,100 seat auditorium, and two parking lots, would command. "You could probably have it for about $100,000," the negotiator finally revealed.

Only $100,000! Suddenly, we were talking about a figure I could get my mind around! I called up a business friend who had been very supportive of CCC already and told him about the opportunity. I even drove him around the place (but didn't want to take him inside fearing what we might encounter there). That night, he phoned back. Business had been good, he said, "even better than our wildest dreams. My wife and I agree that God has blessed us, perhaps for just such an opportunity. We feel the Lord wants us to give you $100,000 for the building."

When the appraisal was finally set at $80,000, that left us enough money to board up the windows and even begin the clean-up.

Final approval of the sale in July 1984 had to go through the Chicago City Council, which was in the middle of the infamous "Council Wars"—the racial standoff between Harold Washington, the black mayor, and almost all of the white council members, led by "Fast Eddie" Vrdolyak. Almost no city business was being accomplished during those months, but the sale of our new property passed without a hitch. Then the Lord helped us navigate the zoning approval. To our amazement, two black ladies from south Austin showed up at the hearing to say, "We've been checking out this

Circle Community Center, and we're here to make sure that absolutely nothing gets in the way of these people getting this building, because we want them to be there."

Before the renovations of the first phase were completed, the price of repairs soared to $750,000, even with waves of volunteer crews helping with the work. I had estimated the cost at less than half that, but God provided. For instance, Circle Church, which owned the old center building, voted to donate 100 percent of its sale to the new center.

Rock Church had its first service in the new chapel on Sunday, June 2, 1985, with seventy-five people. Circle Community Center relocated to the new building later that September, at which time we adopted its new name: Circle Urban Ministries.

By the time Rock Church outgrew the chapel, the second building—Phase Two—was ready and we moved into the gymnasium. We're now trusting that when we max out the gym, Phase Three will be accomplished, enabling us to move into the 1,100-seat auditorium.

Working It Out—Together

Raleigh Washington: Conflicts are inevitable, but one of the things Glen learned from his Circle Church experience was that cross-cultural relationships could not survive if differences were left unresolved. He had discussed with me the tension that existed at Circle Church; when the leaders struck a spark, the whole congregation had exploded.

I rarely let issues lie around unresolved, mostly because of my personality: I've never been afraid of conflict. Sometimes Glen and others did not understand my motives and would be blown away when I charged in like a bull in a china shop. We had to diffuse that kind of tension at Rock Church or we would experience the same breakdown in relationship. But how? It wasn't going to happen spontaneously. Glen and I had committed ourselves to spending time with one another, getting to know the person underneath, daring to be vulnerable, learning to be sensitive to each other's weak points. In this way we hoped to model for the church a way to keep our racial and cultural (and personality) differences from becoming barriers.

But we also knew modeling was not enough. As a whole church we had to be intentional about resolving differences and diffusing tensions. That's when we came up with a wild idea: "Fudge Ripple Sundays"; that is, quarterly meetings in which all the white members—the "vanilla" in the Sunday—meet together to talk freely about any feelings or problems or tensions in our cross-cul-tural setting; the black members—the "chocolate" in the Sunday—do the same thing. Then we come together in a "fudge ripple" meeting to talk about the issues that had come to light. (We'll talk more about Fudge Ripple Sundays in a later chapter.)

Glen Kehrein: But conflicts can begin subtly. Personal tensions arose in our relationship. Suddenly Raleigh began to get a lot of high-profile exposure as an "expert" on urban ministry—when six months earlier he didn't even know where to find Austin on a city map! White Christian groups were always on the lookout for a "safe" black speaker—that is, a black evangelical who spoke their language—but I felt he was exploiting the opportunity, overlooking the person on the team with ten years of experience in urban ministry.

At these speaking engagements Raleigh first talked about planting a cross-cultural church. Only twenty or thirty people were involved at that time, however, so he would soon be describing Circle Urban Ministries, especially once we began developing the new building.

As our exposure broadened, I began to hear reports of "what a marvelous work Raleigh Washington is doing." When we attended conferences together, I'd sit at a table with five or six other people while he talked about Chicago politics or Mayor Daley (things he knew comparatively little about). Finally someone would lean over to me and ask politely, "Where did you say you were from?"

"Circle Urban Ministries."

"Oh, you work for Raleigh. What is it you do?"

Of course, I recognized Raleigh and I had different gifts, but it didn't take long for Satan to convince me I didn't deserve being slighted and to suggest that Raleigh was on an ego trip. From time to time I expressed my irritation in off-handed comments, but I never really laid it out. One of the things that hurt most was when Raleigh began getting invitations to speak in chapel at Moody Bible Institute. As an Moody alumnus, I felt I had something to say, but Raleigh was always getting the platform. That burned me! But envy wasn't very spiritual, so I just tucked it away and said nothing.

———□■———

Then, about five years into our relationship, I came across a paper from the Christian Community Health Fellowship (CCHF), a national association of health centers like ours, which announced Raleigh Washington as a key speaker at a conference on community development. The subject: "Urban Community Development." I couldn't believe it. *Raleigh Washington an expert on community development? He couldn't even figure out how to buy the vacant lot next to his house, while I have spearheaded a housing ministry that has rehabilitated two hundred units of housing!* I fumed. *What an ego he has to accept such a speaking assignment!*

Then Raleigh got another speaking invitation from Moody, and suddenly I couldn't keep quiet. "You just gotta be up front all the time, don't you? You accept these speaking engagements whether you know what you're talking about or not."

Raleigh's mouth dropped open. "What do you mean?"

Pulling out the CCHF conference invitation, I charged, "You shouldn't have accepted that. What do you know about community development?"

Raleigh scratched his head. "Well, they called my secretary asking me to speak, so I agreed. I didn't know they had a theme in mind. They asked me to challenge the doctors and nurses on wholistic ministry—and that's my forte."

It got emotionally bloody as we battled back and forth. I accused Raleigh of having an ego problem; he accused me of having a wounded ego. "What do you want me to do," he asked, "turn down speaking engagements just because other people haven't offered you equal time? People come to me looking for a preacher, and that's my primary call."

I was struggling to deliver the knockout punch, to put my accusation into convincing words. Then I suddenly realized my problem: jealousy. And the problem wasn't his, it was mine. Until I accepted my responsibility, our relationship and ministries would be crippled. In reality, Raleigh's speaking engagements had helped raise funds and awareness for Circle Urban Ministries in ways I never could have.

When I was able to confess my problem as jealousy, our relationship moved to a deeper level. My confession also helped Raleigh see his weakness, a lack of sensitivity. Most important, we affirmed our willingness to do what is best for the ministry, no matter who gets the bouquets.

As painful as it was, this situation helped us clarify the principles of *sincerity* (the courage to be open and honest with each other) and *sensitivity* (understanding what creates the feelings and fears behind the tensions between us). Similar experiences over the years have also refined and developed other principles of racial reconciliation: our deep need for *interdependence* between black and white in ministry—we really do need each other. But that interdependence will mean *sacrifice*; we may have to work behind the scenes while someone else gets the stage; or we will need to sacrifice our "comfort zones" in order to worship or minister or be friends together.

And of course, we fail. But the process of repentance and forgiveness can actually *empower* one another to minister in cross-cultural situations. As we move into the second part of this book, we want to explore each of these principles in depth, providing tools for making racial reconciliation in the church a reality.

One More Day

Raleigh Washington: As the '80s neared an end, our ministries and relationship were becoming firmly established, but there was one major issue that remained unresolved: the conclusion to my military career. I had forgiven most of my accusers, yet I was to experience once more a deeper reconciliation between blacks and whites.

Jeff Strange, the attorney, had been working on my case with the military for nearly eight years. With Jeff's urging and the financial support of a close, concerned couple, I finally secured a specialist in military law, Mike Gaffney of Washington, D.C., to try to speed up a drawn-out process. Gaffney recommended a long shot: get the Army Board of Correction of Military Records to reconsider my case. The chances of getting a personal hearing were slim, 1,000 to 1, as the board grants only twenty-five personal audiences out of the twenty-five thousand cases it reviews each year. When the board agreed to give us a personal hearing, I knew that God was in the plan. Even the new attorney was in awe of this development.

The board told us we would have no more than one hour to present our case. But board members listened for three hours; then we returned home to await the decision. Days later Mike called with the news. "Raleigh, we got a reversal!"

That sounded great, but the attorney and I were unsure what it meant. Paulette and Jeff joined me in one final trip to Washington to meet with army and Justice Department officials. I'll never forget the first words out the officer's mouth, "Colonel Washington, I want you to know that my job is to make you whole." After all those years, the army finally was admitting its injustice. I was vindicated! Paulette and I were ecstatic.

Then we called Glen and began marveling together at God's plan. With my loyalty and drive, I would not have retired early from the military and entered the ministry. On the plane ride home, the Scripture kept running through my mind, they "meant it for evil . . . but God meant it for good" (Genesis 50:20 NIV).

Once the army processed the decision, I was called to active duty at Fort Sheridan, Illinois, in May of 1989 for one day. After going through processing, all I was required to do was be there in uniform for a retirement parade. "Invite any of your friends and family to the ceremonies," I was told. So seated with me during the parade were two busloads of friends from Rock Church, professors from Trinity Seminary, my entire family, including my mother from Florida, and of course, Glen and Lonni.

A couple days before the event, Glen Kehrein's father called me and asked how I was going to get there. "I suppose I'll just drive up," I said. (Fort Sheridan is less than an hour north of Chicago.)

"No," he said. "I'll drive you. What time do you need to leave?"

When Mr. Kehrein arrived to pick me and my family up, he was driving a classy, black limousine from the funeral home where he worked. I was in my full-dress, green uniform including the officer's cap with all the "scrambled eggs" on the bill.

When we arrived at the gate, I noticed the military policeman stationed at the gate salute an officer in the car in front of me. Suddenly, I was overwhelmed with the realization that, after nine years, he was going to have to salute me. "Pa Kehrein, when we get to the gate and the military policeman snaps a salute, don't drive past him, hold it there—it's been nine long years, and God will grant me thirty seconds of carnal joy."

The guard saluted, and I savored each moment, allowing myself to be the lieutenant colonel on active duty once more. In a few seconds, I returned the salute and asked Pa to drive on—immediately praying, "Forgive me, Lord." That small gesture somehow salved years of hurt and humiliation.

The parade field was dazzling in the warm spring afternoon as I stood on the reviewing stand with my family. When the band marched by, it turned and gave me a salute before playing "Auld Lang Sine." Then a colonel gave a speech applauding my military career. For one final, glorious time the Washingtons were a military family. We drank it all in as we moved on to the reception.

On Friday of that same week I was given a retirement celebration at the officers' club. Major General (retired) Elmer Pendleton flew in from Washington, D.C., and Sergeant Major Joe Frith and his wife, Josie, flew in from Florida. (He had worked for me when I was in recruiting.) Good friends came from great distances, both childhood friends and those who fought with me for justice: Charlie Williams and his wife, Fran; Jeff and Carol Strange; Jeff's brother, Howard; Mike Gaffney; and a special friend, Martha Berg.

I wore my formal blue uniform for the celebration, and all my family came formally attired. Attendees were not required to dress formally, but the women from Rock Church came in long, formal dresses. Most had never been to a formal event before . . . but every single one was beautiful.

PART TWO

TOGETHER

CHAPTER 7
WHERE ARE MY
AMBASSADORS OF RECONCILIATION?

When south central Los Angeles went up in flames in April 1992, the glow lit TV sets across America. Angry blacks and worried whites were tense. Would the sparks ignite racial tensions in cities all over the United States?

The backlash in other urban areas, however, was minimal, and many Americans breathed a sigh of relief. Soon the L.A. riots were as old as yesterday's news. What happened there was someone else's problem.

But the embers in urban America glow just beneath the surface. The fire has lost its heat, but the smoke can still suffocate us. The fumes are fed by hopelessness and powerlessness on one side, and indifference and insensitivity on the other. We have a crisis in our cities, a crisis that is draining the lifeblood from the black community. Ominous statistics read like a medical chart in the terminal ward:

• Homicide is the leading cause of death for black males and females ages fifteen to thirty-four.

- Blacks account for 44 percent of all homicide victims, even though they make up only 12 percent of the population.
- Ninety-five percent of black homicides were committed by black perpetrators.[1]
- Infant mortality among blacks is twice as high as for white infants.[2]
- In the ten largest urban cities, the high school dropout rate for black males is 72 percent.[3]
- The 1991 unemployment rate for black Americans was 12.9 percent—more than twice the rate for white Americans.[4]
- At the end of the 1980s, more than half of African-American children were born to single mothers.[5]
- In 1960, 78 percent of black families with children were headed by both a mother and a father—a figure that dropped to 37 percent by 1990.[6]

So why are we surprised when young black men with low self-esteem, few positive role models, and little hope for making it out of the ghetto join a gang for a sense of belonging, identity, power, and protection? Using drugs is a way to dull the pain, and the young men accept selling drugs as the only road to success in a community where too few fast-food jobs are the only alternative.

But statistics don't really tell the story. The real story of urban grief and despair is the lost lives. A sniper's bullet cut down little Dantrell Davis, age seven, as he and his mother crossed the street from their home in Chicago's Cabrini Green public housing project. Dantrell was on his way to school during an autumn day in 1992 in a location where gunfire from gangs was common. As of this writing, investigators are unsure whether Dantrell was the unintended victim of a bullet meant for someone else or actually sought by the sniper, killed to spite his great-uncle, a leader of the notorious Black Disciples. It matters little. Young Dantrell was gunned down, an innocent victim of gang-related violence.

Unfortunately, Dantrell's death is not an isolated incident. He is the third child in Jenner Elementary School (and the twenty-seventh child in Chicago) to die a violent death in a single year.[7] Can you imagine that happening in your neighborhood?

A whole generation is at risk in our inner cities. They are mainly African-American and Hispanic children, and the cancer is spreading. Gordon McLean, who ministers to many young gang members as director of the juvenile justice ministry of Metro Chicago Youth For Christ, often intones ominously to complacent whites, "Gang violence—coming soon to a neighborhood near you."

A Fragile Peace

McLean is right. The riots in L.A. were only a foretaste of the racial tremors rumbling beneath the surface in our country. On one hand we have Louis Farrakhan, the charismatic black muslim who used to rant and rave about "white devils" while he plucked black men off the street, gave them dignity, and got them off drugs. On the other, we have David Duke, former Ku Klux Klansman and one-time Louisiana legislator who once paraded in a white sheet, preaching hate. Today, Duke and Farrakhan both dress in pinstripe suits and speak calmly, but their message is still the same: race-baiting, alienation, and separation between black and white.

Satan loves that. Ever since creation, Satan has been working overtime to alienate people from their Creator and from each other. And he's still at it.

Jack and Jenny Oliver live in Evanston, Illinois, just north of Chicago, a community that prides itself on being ethnically diverse and racially sensitive. The Olivers were shocked to discover that their next-door neighbors—the only black family on the block—had recently received several anonymous "hate letters" enumerating various complaints and telling them to get out of the neighborhood. Suspicions and accusations regarding who had sent the letters broke apart the fragile racial peace of that city block. Up to this point, except for "hi" across the fence, there had been very little relationship between the black family and the other white neighbors. Most of the whites gave as their reason certain irritations, such as late night noise, as well as the hostility of the black grandmother, who wouldn't even say hello.

What they didn't know—until the hate letters started the white neighbors talking with other members of the black family— was that, as a child, the grandmother had seen her own brother lynched by the Klan. Suddenly a glimmer of understanding broke through some of the judgmental attitudes in the neighborhood. Without knowing who had written the letters, Jack and Jenny wrote a (signed!) letter inviting all the neighbors to use the incident as an opportunity to build relationships between black and white and work out problems person to person, rather than letting them breed further distrust and alienation. It's only a step—but it's a step in the right direction.

Reconciliation: Part of Daily Living

Separation and alienation between people is nothing new. During the first century, people faced the same barriers of race, class, and sex that we have today. In fact, before Christ died, Herod's temple divided the people in all three areas. The Holy of Holies, set off by a heavy curtain into which only the high priest could go once a year, divided the people from God. The Court of Priests divided the "professional clergy" from the "lay people." The Court of Israel divided the men from the women. The Court of Women divided Jewish women from the Gentiles. Last but not least was the Court of Gentiles. Josephus, a first century theologian, informs us that a cornerstone of the fifth partition read: "Any Gentile that goes beyond this partition only has himself to blame for his ensuing death."

But when Jesus cried out from the cross, "It is finished!" the curtain that separated the Holy of Holies was torn from top to bottom. The people were confused and astounded. What did it mean? They didn't yet understand what Christ's ministry was all about: the reconciliation of all people with God and with each other.

In a letter to the Corinthian church, however, Paul the apostle spelled it out clearly:

> Therefore from now on we recognize no man according to the flesh; even though we have known Christ according to the flesh, yet now we know Him thus no longer. Therefore if any man is in Christ, he is a new creature; the old things passed away; behold, new things have come. Now all these things are from God, who reconciled us to Himself through Christ, and gave us the ministry of reconciliation, namely, that God was in Christ reconciling the world to Himself, not counting their trespasses against them, and He has committed to us the word of reconciliation. Therefore we are ambassadors for Christ, as though God were entreating through us; we beg you on behalf of Christ, be reconciled to God. He made Him who knew no sin to be sin on our behalf, that we might become the righteousness of God in Him. (2 Corinthians 5:16-21)

The Word of God is not just saying that reconciliation is a good idea. Rather, Paul informs us that the ministry of reconciliation is a *mandatory* part of every Christian's daily living. This passage outlines, first, the act of God in creating us anew, from the inside out; second, the purpose of God to reconcile the world unto Himself; and third, the method of God in calling all Christians to be ambassadors for Him, giving them the ministry of reconciliation.

Reconciliation has a twofold reality: it has already happened, and yet it is still in process. We have been reconciled to God through conversion; we are a new creation (v. 17). This is an accomplished fact. But this reconciliation must continue to work through us, crossing racial, social, and sexual barriers by means of the ministry of reconciliation empowered by God through Christ to work in and through us.

The result should be a newly created body of believers who no longer look at people as the world sees them (v. 16)—as potential threats or the dregs of society. We acknowledge that it is God who alone can accomplish reconciliation across the barriers of sin and separation (v. 18). We accept the responsibility not only of the message of reconciliation (v. 19), but the ministry of reconciliation (v. 18) as well, becoming Christ's ambassadors, pleading with others to be reconciled to God (v. 20).

Racial Reconciliation: Priority of the Church

With materialism, secular humanism, New Age cults, disintegrating families, perversion of sexual mores, and abortion battling for the soul of the church today, don't Christians have enough to wrestle with? Why make racial reconciliation a priority in the church? We see three reasons to urge such a reconciliation.

First, Christ made it a priority. "For [Christ] Himself is our peace, who made both groups into one . . . that in Himself He might make the two into one new man, thus establishing peace" (Ephesians 2:14–15). The apostle Paul was referring to the historical alienation between Jews and Gentiles, which was creating conflict in the church in Ephesus. With love and compassion, Paul made the bottom line abundantly clear: Christ's purpose was to bring the two together, creating "one new [people]" in the body of Christ.

Second, the apostle Paul made it a priority. In writing to the Colossian church, he described the Christian's new being as undergoing "a renewal in which there is no distinction between Greek and Jew, circumcised and uncircumcised, barbarian, Scythian, slave and freeman, but Christ is all, and in all" (Colossians 3:11). In one fell swoop Paul extended the priority of reconciliation in Christ beyond the Jew/Gentile issue to include all people groups regardless of race, nationality, ethnicity, class, religious tradition, or status. He assumed that all of these alienated or separated people belonged together in this melting pot called the church.

Third, the theological foundation of our faith is reconciliation. When our relationship with God was broken, God brought us back —reconciled us—to Himself through a personal relationship with His Son and our Savior, Jesus Christ. Now He has called us to be His ambassadors and has given us the ministry of reconciliation. This means, first of all, reconciling people to God through the power of the cross, and then reconciling people to people across racial, class, and gender barriers.

To be ambassadors for Christ, then, is to be reconcilers wherever relationships are broken, in whatever situation God has placed us. We believe Satan has exploited the sin of racism throughout the centuries, and certainly in this country, to alienate people from God and from each other. Small pockets of valiant believers,[8] men and women, black and white, have been "living out reconciliation" in the name of Christ against all odds, but the battle continues.

Our Benign Neglect

The ministry of reconciliation can never be mere passive acceptance of a theological truth, but must include active participation. Unfortunately, the Christian church at large—to state it in the most favorable way—is guilty of benign neglect. At best, we have been standing quietly on the sidelines while racism continues to wreck havoc on our society. Most Christians—white, black, Hispanic, and Asian—have not directly attacked the problems of racism. True, most of us wouldn't march with the Ku Klux Klan or hurl epithets at a minority child integrating our schools. But few of us, churches or individuals, have made it a priority to heal the divisions between black, white, brown, or yellow by deliberately and intentionally building relationships across racial lines.

Historically, through its neglect in not confronting the problem, the white segment of the church has allowed itself to unwittingly become a co-conspirator with the enemy. Scripture has been used, the church has been used, tradition has been used, social convention has been used to support every form of prejudice and oppression of ethnic minorities, including Hispanics and Asians. Consider these actions, inactions, and poor theologies used by many in the American Christian church.

- The "curse of Ham" (Genesis 9:25) was used for centuries to justify the white race subjugating the black race.
- The Southern church's tacit approval of Klan activities is well documented.
- The American church, for the most part, accepted the World War II imprisonment, denial of civil rights, and unlawful confiscation of property of Japanese-Americans because of their ancestry. Most Asian-Americans were feared as traitors while white European-Americans were honored as patriots.
- In recent times, homogeneous church-growth principles, espousing the maxim "people feel more comfortable with people like themselves," are used to justify continuing separation of believers on the basis of race and class.
- Churches have eagerly sent thousands of missionaries to dark-skinned peoples in distant lands while ignoring the plight of the inner-city immigrants at their doorstep.
- Inner-city mission programs (like foreign missions several decades ago) have too often embodied a condescending "white Bwana/ignorant blacks" attitude.
- Clapping, syncopation, or other "emotional" musical forms— qualities typical of black music—have been characterized as "of the devil."
- Where integration has "worked," it often means that blacks have assimilated white culture (a denial of black cultural strengths).
- Interracial dating and marriage—even between born-again believers—have been discouraged, forbidden (even on Christian college campuses), and feared.

Satan has used race to divide believers and make a mockery of our faith, and we as Christians have not stood against it. We sing, "They will know we are Christians by our love," but as black, white, Asian, and Hispanic Christians we harbor fear and mistrust, anger and hatred in our hearts toward each other.

Christ is holding out His nail-pierced palms: "Where are My ambassadors of reconciliation? I died on the cross to heal the divisions between you; I have given you the ministry of reconciliation! Why are My children still alienated from one another? Why is the wound of racism still festering in My church? Where are My ambassadors?"

As ambassadors for Christ, we must bring the ministry of reconciliation specifically to the area of racial alienation. Our consciousness has been raised; many laws have been changed; it is even "politically correct" to be racially tolerant. But that isn't reconciliation.

After the Rodney King verdict and the riots in south central L.A., author Kurt Vonnegut was quoted in *The Chicago Tribune* as saying: "We can actually hate blacks if we want, so long as they have a fair shot at the American dream. To hell with love and everything else." That's an incredible statement, a very humanistic worldview of the problems that we're experiencing. He's saying, we've talked about love (the '60s version: "All we need is love, love, love") and it didn't work.

But Vonnegut's statement represents absolute sin, for Jesus made very clear that hate is murder. Murder and violence and destruction of the human personality and spirit begin in the heart. Vonnegut's statement is also a practical impossibility. No one is going to give African-Americans a "fair shot" at the American dream if "we can actually hate blacks if we want." In God's economy, justice and love are always inextricably linked.

Black people in this country are perishing from lack of knowledge of the saving grace of Jesus Christ. We are letting the Louis Farrakans of the world tell them that Christianity is a "white man's religion." By our actions—and our inaction—black and white Christians are saying to each other, "I have no need of you." And Satan is having a heyday.

The Key: United in Christ

We believe the body of Christ holds the key that can unlock the stranglehold of racism in our society. That key is the ministry of reconciliation. Christ has given us a mandate. It is high time the church as a whole, and individual believers, answered the call of Christ and became ambassadors of reconciliation in our homes and churches, neighborhoods and cities.

We must go beyond "why," of course. How do we bring together all races—black, white, Hispanic, Asian—so that unity in Christ is not just a spiritual theory but a visible reality?

The eight biblical principles of racial reconciliation we shall discuss in the following chapters have been developed out of our life experiences and measured with the Word of God. Though they grow out of our personal experiences as black and white leaders, they apply to all racial groups in this multiethnic, multicultural nation called America.

Each principle is important. If we take each one seriously and bathe our responses in prayer, we too will be able to say confidently with the apostle Paul: "There is no distinction between Greek and Jew . . . [black and white], but Christ is all, and in all" (Colossians 3:11). The apostle believed that the gospel of Christ could eliminate any wall of racial division in his day, and he reminded Christians of their common bond in Christ. As we shall see, the good news is unchanged today. Christ "has destroyed the barrier, the dividing wall of hostility" (Ephesians 2:14 NIV).

NOTES

1. The first three statistics are from Carl C. Bell with Esther Jekins, "Preventing Black Homicide," *The State of Black America 1990* (New York: National Urban League, 1990), 143–55.

2. LaSalle D. Leffall, Jr., "Health Status of Black Americans," *The State of Black America 1990,* 131.

3. Mark S. Hoffman, ed., *The World Almanac* (New York: Pharos, 1992), 169. Based on the first six months of the year and projected forward.

4. Marvin McMikel, "Black Men: Endangered Species," *Club-Date,* August/September 1989, 29.

5. Andrew W. Edwards, "The Black Family: A Unique Social System in Transition," *The State of Black Cleveland 1989* (Cleveland: Urban League of Greater Cleveland, 1989), 187.

6. Andrew Billingsley, "Understanding African-American Family Diversity," *The State of Black America 1990,* 89–90.

7. "Special Report: Dying Young," *Chicago Tribune,* October 18, 1992, sec. 2, 1

8. Two examples of such believers and churches are Cary Casey and Wayne Gordon and their Lawndale Community Church in Chicago's impoverished West Side community.

CHAPTER 8
PRINCIPLE 1: COMMITMENT TO RELATIONSHIP
*Racial Reconciliation is built upon
the foundation of committed relationships.
(Key verse: Ruth 1:16)*

Time alone doesn't heal. It never has, and it never will. Racial alienation in this country goes back for centuries and affects everyone. Effort is needed to bridge the pain of past experiences. We who are Christians need a *deep commitment* to cross the chasm and build significant relationships across racial lines.

An old proverb says, "If you have a hammer you see all problems as nails." In other words, we tend to create a solution that fits our strength. In American society that strength is education. In this country, most people see education as the answer to racism and separation. Education is an important tool, but it does not provide a solid foundation for reconciliation. African-Americans have had to "study" white people just to survive in a predominantly white society, and yet that education often leads to mistrust and separation. Sometimes whites embark on black awareness programs in an attempt to become more familiar with the African-American culture and the Euro-American misperceptions that lead to prejudice. That's a step in the right direction, because ignorance does breed prejudice. But education by itself does not lead to reconciliation.

The first principle of racial reconciliation is not education but relation. Committed personal relationships are the foundation of racial understanding and acceptance (key verse: Ruth 1:16). To begin the process of reconciliation, each of us must get involved personally in a friendship.

Lonni Kehrein, Glen's wife, was working for a very progressive couple in Oak Park, a city long famous as a "model" integrated suburb of Chicago. (About 75 percent of Oak Park is white, 18 percent is black, and 7 percent Asian, Hispanic, and other.) The Thompsons had been involved in civil rights for many years and had all the "right" books on their shelves—books by Eldridge Cleaver and other writers in the '60s who articulated black rage. But when hearing about Lonni's deep friendships in the black community and significant involvement in cross-cultural ministry, they spoke with pain in their voices. "You know, we don't have one black friend, not one. What went wrong?" Education alone didn't bring real change to their lives.

Many folks would welcome friendships with people of other races if those relationships happened easily and were automatically filled with joy, peace, and success. But the fact is that cross-cultural relationships require effort; they often break down over misunderstandings and disappointments and sometimes defensive attacks. Misunderstandings are hard enough to settle with people who are like us. But in this country, every disappointment between blacks and whites reminds us of centuries of bad history. It's normal to want to avoid pain, so most people, both black and white, walk away from interracial relationships, saying "I don't need this hassle."

We believe, however, that true racial reconciliation won't happen among Christians unless we commit ourselves to developing relationships across racial lines. We can't stop with a commitment to the concept of racial reconciliation; it must be put into action. Genuine reconciliation happens only between people who make a commitment to relationships and who consider the relationships so important that they won't let them go, even when the going gets tough.

But where can we find the courage to make such a commitment?

"Keep Yo' Han' on de Plow"

"Keep yo' han' on de plow, hold on!" goes the traditional Negro spiritual. Jesus once described the quality of lasting commitment using the image of a farmer plowing a field. Jesus had called people to follow Him. Sometimes they responded in the first flush of enthusiasm with "I'll follow you wherever you go, Master!" But when He challenged them to put their enthusiasm into action, He received a lot of excuses: "After my elderly parents die, then I'll follow you"; "I've got a lot of family responsibilities. Let me wrap up the family business; then I'll follow you."

To this second excuse Jesus responded simply, "No one, after putting his hand to the plow and looking back, is fit for the kingdom of God" (Luke 9:62).

Jesus was saying, "If you want to follow me, you can't stand on the sidelines. It's going to take effort and hard work to plow up this field. Be sure you count the cost, because once you grab hold of the plow, you have to keep going. Anyone who looks back when the going gets tough isn't worthy of the kingdom of God." Jesus was very clear that the way of the cross isn't easy; it takes commitment.

This is the kind of commitment needed for all serious relationships: husband/wife, business partners, deacons in the church, and cross-cultural friendships. It's like plowing virgin sod—four feet deep and never opened up; conflicts are inevitable. But when you keep your hand on the plow, the end result is a deeply enriched relationship. This is the first step you must take for racial reconciliation to occur: be committed to any relationship you begin to develop.

Breaking Down the Wall

The way of the cross isn't easy, but it is the cross that leads to racial reconciliation. For the cross brings people of different races together. Only through the cross can we break down the wall that divides us as races.

In Ephesians 2, the apostle Paul zeroed in on the great wall of hostility that had existed for centuries between Jews and Gentiles. Ever since Abraham, the children of Israel had the promise of a relationship to God through the law, and they had the mark of circumcision to prove it. The Jews had been taught that they were not only God's chosen people, but God's only people. Therefore, all other peoples (lumped together as Gentiles) were inferior, despised, and to be avoided.

In fact, bigotry and prejudice were socially acceptable, tightly woven into the religious fabric of biblical Palestine. A mutual relationship between Jews and Gentiles? That seemed impossible, both spiritually and socially. But Paul wrote:

> Now in Christ Jesus you who once were far away have been brought near through the blood of Christ. For he himself is our peace, who has made the two one and has destroyed the barrier, the dividing wall of hostility, by abolishing in his flesh the law with its commandments and regulations. His purpose was to create in himself one new man out of the two, thus making peace, and in this one body to reconcile both of them to God through the cross, by which he put to death their hostility. (Ephesians 2:13-16 NIV)

The dividing wall applies not only to the alienation between Jews and Gentiles (still alive today), but between black and white, Asian and Hispanic. That wall is high! That wall is wide! There's animosity on both sides. But Christ, in His voluntary death on the cross, broke down the wall of hostility between us so there could be real relationships between all people who accept Him, regardless of race.

The good news is that the road map for achieving racial reconciliation has been given to the body of Christ. Racial reconciliation is more than intellectual assent to a theological concept; it's putting rubber to the road. We—Glen and Raleigh, white and black—are committed to each other as brothers in Christ for a much longer time than to our natural relatives because when we die our human familial relationships will end, but we are spiritual brothers for all eternity. All Christians can and should have such relationships with believers of other races.

"All right, Glen and Raleigh," you say, "that's fine theologically. But living it out is a different story. What does that kind of commitment look like in everyday life?"

Like a Marriage

When a man and a woman marry, they vow to not quit when the going gets rough ("until death do us part"). That is the kind of commitment needed to accomplish racial reconciliation. Why? Because as certain as a marriage relationship will be tested, efforts at racial reconciliation will certainly be tested as well. Only when "divorce" is not an easy option will the relationship have a chance.

Obviously, there are things unique to marriage that cannot apply to racial reconciliation. But because most people ask, "What's the bottom line, what's the minimum I have to put out to achieve reconciliation?" we believe marriage is a realistic analogy. Commitment and hard work, crucial to marital success, are essential for solid personal relationships with members of other races.

Cross-cultural conflict carries a heavy stick that drives people apart. We have found that our relationship requires regular conflict-resolving "summits." At least once a month we set aside a morning and "rent" a secluded booth at the Original Pancake House. (We've often wondered what the waitress must think this relationship is all about!) We each come prepared to show the other just how off-base he is. Often we start on opposite ends of an issue, hang in there to hear each other out, and don't stop until we end up with a common mind. What does it take to build that unity? Keeping our hand to the plow, taming the knee-jerk reaction to cut and run, the old "I don't need this" response. Our commitment to the relationship pledges that we will not throw in the trump card—announcing grandly, "I quit!"

A recent summit involved feelings about a fund-raising event, a golf tournament. I (Raleigh) felt that Glen didn't support the event; he wasn't as invested and involved as he should be. Glen just didn't seem to care if things weren't falling in place, and he wasn't directing his staff to get things done. Because the golf outing was my idea, I was hurt by Glen's response, which seemed to be if it wasn't "his thing," he didn't care.

From Glen's point of view, I was playing my old lieutenant colonel role, asking him to "Snap to it, sergeant!" Once we both fully vented our feelings, however, Glen was able to express his full support for the event. His lack of involvement came entirely from a lack of knowledge of the game. Not being a golfer, Glen just didn't know what to do. Hearing this, a light went on for me; as a passionate golfer I had taken a lot for granted. His motives and intentions were no longer suspect or experienced as nonsupportive.

From that point we could finish the plans—and the event came off as a great success.

Without our commitment to resolve the conflict, our relationship would have sustained damage; instead it was strengthened by having a summit.

When Conflict Comes

Making a commitment to "hang in there for the long haul" acknowledges that a cross-racial relationship is not going to be a honeymoon. Problems will come; it's not a matter of if but when. And when they come, we need to seek a resolution that benefits both parties so that we can coexist in peace, happiness, and joy.

That's why Principle 1 is critical to racial reconciliation. No matter how well people get along with or understand each other, inevitably there is going to be a tiff, a conflict. A committed relationship will endure the threat.

Glen and I experienced a deeper threat to the ministry when the inevitable occurred: conflict over money. As pastor of a missionary church, I have to raise support. Likewise, Glen raises even larger amounts for CUM. But contributors usually do not designate whether their giving should go to the church or to CUM.

Soon we became protective. Was my ministry getting its "fair share" of the pie? We wrestled for months and months, each strongly emphasizing the importance of his own efforts and arguing his case. Should the money be split 60/40, Rock Church/Circle?

"Very fair," Raleigh said.

"No way," Glen replied.

"I'm always on the road, speaking and challenging folks to give," Raleigh said.

"Yeah, but look at everything Circle is doing while you're out bragging about it," Glen answered.

"Yeah, but without the church you'd be just another social service agency."

"Yeah, but without Circle you'd be just another storefront church."

Tempers rose and blood cells raced every time. Each conversation drove us further into our own corners. Conflict-resolving summits were not bringing resolution.

This time the light came on for both of us at the same time. We don't even remember who threw up the first white flag of surrender. But suddenly we both realized this civil war was going to destroy us and bring down the ministry with it. Scripture speaks of truth as a light. When exposed to light, sin is ugly. We finally recognized our ugly sin; then we both confessed, sought forgiveness, and put the issue to bed.

Since then (several years ago) we have had many occasions to put Philippians 2:2–3 into action: "Make my joy complete by being of the same mind, maintaining the same love, united in spirit, intent on one purpose. Do nothing from selfishness or empty conceit, but with humility of mind let each of you regard one another as more important than himself."

This is why the apostle Paul says, "Do not let the sun go down on your anger" (Ephesians 4:26). If a fight doesn't get settled in a marriage, what happens? That night the husband and wife sleep as far apart as they can in the bed. A similar thing happens when you let unresolved conflict smolder in a cross-cultural relationship. It creates distance; it goes into the memory bank and creates a grid that colors future interactions. Resentments build up and finally explode—maybe over a minor matter.

Before I (Glen) met Raleigh, most of my experience showed that there was not enough commitment between blacks and whites to work through racial and cultural differences. For instance, a black woman comes to the relationship saying to herself, *Underneath the smiling exterior of this white woman is probably a raging racist. She says she's "color blind," which means she's going to ignore the fundamental issue of race in this situation.* And she is not committed to confronting her white friend with those feelings.

Meanwhile, I have talked with white men who are thinking, *Underneath the friendly facade of this black guy is just another militant. Every time he sees a problem, he sees racism.* He is not committed to knowing this black man and developing a friendship. He simply assumes that the person is hostile and avoids him.

It doesn't matter what the conflict is. When conflict is seen from a black perspective or a white perspective, the racial dynamic crosses all issues. Assumptions are made, often based on stereotypes about racial attitudes. But if we acknowledge this and commit ourselves to hang in there and work through it, we'll have taken a giant step toward racial reconciliation.

Going for Help

If you are committed to a genuine relationship, you and your friend must be willing to confront each other and express your disagreements. For instance, Raleigh and I are both strong-minded, and we have given ourselves permission to really go at each other no-holds-barred. "Hey," we said to each other, "we're both big boys; we can take it." After all, the proverb says, "Iron sharpens iron, so one man sharpens another" (Proverbs 27:17). But sometimes we hit a seeming impasse. What do we do then? And what should you do when your friendship is threatened by conflict and one of you wants to end the relationship?

We found that we needed a mechanism of accountability to resolve issues we couldn't work out between ourselves. For Circle Urban Ministries we have a board of directors, and for Rock Church we have a qualified group of elders that meets every two weeks. Both groups understand their spiritual role in keeping us accountable, and they're not hesitant to do that.

You may benefit from accountability in your cross-cultural friendships as well. When you establish a committed relationship, ask other friends or a family member to be available to give advice, and when needed, to help you resolve issues. Someone removed from the two friends can give a fresh perspective.

We have learned that sometimes an issue needs a broader arena than the two of us. This was the case when Raleigh was asked to direct a master's degree program in urban ministries for Trinity Evangelical Divinity School, his alma mater.

"It feels like just another white organization co-opting black leadership out of the black community," I complained to Raleigh. For years white organizations did nothing for the black community. But as soon as it became popular to be involved, they wanted to recruit a high-profile, dynamic, token black person so they could say, "Look at what we're doing! Send us your money." That's what I was afraid would happen to Raleigh.

"Hey, I don't think so," Raleigh said. "After all, I graduated from Trinity. It makes sense to give something back to my alma mater."

"Just take the practical logistics," I argued. "Rock Church needs you, Circle Urban Ministries needs you, but now Trinity would get a big chunk of your time and energy. You know what it takes to develop a program and raise the funds to get it going."

Jim Westgate, the professor from Trinity who had encouraged Raleigh to come to Austin in the first place, gave input from Trinity's point of view. If the seminary was going to train pastors in urban ministry, they needed someone like Raleigh. Given the strong feelings on all sides, we agreed to submit it to our board of elders, who with their wives helped bring a resolution.

Their counsel helped bring out both how much this opportunity to help urban pastors meant to Raleigh and how detrimental Glen feared it could be at home. It took the objectivity of others to solve the dilemma. It was decided that Raleigh would work for several years to help get the program running and then gradually bring someone else into an ongoing role. That's exactly what happened, to the benefit of both ministries.

Is Divorce Ever an Option?

Perhaps you have already developed a relationship with a Christian of another race. But it's been a struggle. At this point you may be thinking, *We just don't get along at all. Is it really helpful to grit my teeth and gut it out, no matter what?* Whether the relationship is a personal friendship or ministry partnership, the question is valid. Let's rephrase it: "Can tenacity actually damage people or a ministry, when it might be better to say, 'This isn't working, let's gracefully bow out; we can each serve the Lord in another place'?"

Yes, there are some circumstances where that may be the most loving recourse. But, whoa! Before you take off running, have you really given reconciliation a chance? Have you done your best to apply all eight principles we're recommending? (Keep reading for the other seven.) Have you submitted yourselves and your relationship to others who are committed to helping you make it work? And, if you still conclude that it won't work, are you equally committed to try again until you find a cross-cultural relationship that does work?

As mentioned earlier in the book, several attempts I made to establish peer relationships across racial lines—at Circle Church and elsewhere—broke down. But it didn't alter my commitment to racial reconciliation. Yes, I felt like I wanted to cut and run, but because of my commitment, I didn't have the option of doing that. Even though I failed in those situations, it didn't change my call to be reconciled to my black brothers and sisters through relationships.

What About a Separation?

In Acts 15:36–41, Barnabas and Paul went their separate ways after a "sharp disagreement" over whether to bring John Mark on their next missionary journey (he had earlier deserted them in Pamphylia). However, references to John Mark (Colossians 4:10; 2 Timothy 4:11) as a coworker during Paul's prison years indicate that either they parted amicably, or they experienced significant reconciliation.

At some point you may decide that God is calling you someplace else, or that it's best for you to separate (for whatever reason). Remember, a separation is not necessarily a divorce if you preserve the relationship in the process. Look at what causes a divorce: misunderstanding, mistrust, resentment, anger, vindictiveness. Even though Paul and Barnabas were said to have had a "sharp disagreement" (Acts 15:39) over what was best, there is no indication that mistrust, resentment, or vindictiveness were the motives. Divorce, on the other hand, is the destruction of a relationship!

If God at some point would lead the two of us in different ways, our relationship should be just as committed and just as loving, even though we may be 3,000 miles apart and not able to keep it at the same level of communication. If God calls us to go different directions, reconciliation says that we need to arrive at that decision with the same principles we would employ in staying together. We would work it through together and come to a clear, committed agreement that God was calling us each to a new place.

Unfortunately, what happens all too frequently in cross-cultural relationships is that people arrive at the "need" to separate, independently and much too soon; separation becomes the answer to conflict, the replacement for working through differences, thus masking the pain.

Levels of Relationship

It's important to acknowledge, however, that the levels of relationship can vary. Some will develop a deep commitment to partnership that will affect where they live, what they do, who their friends are; others will have everything in between, including fairly superficial, on-the-job friendships.

But even at the very beginning of a relationship, if it's going to be real, you must apply these same principles to move toward the goal of reconciliation. What about those relationships where you are thrown together willy-nilly? That white person at work may have gotten the promotion you wanted; the black family in the apartment upstairs plays their music too loud; your kids' teacher seems to play favorites with the white students. Your first reaction to the would-be friend may be, "That jerk! We may have to live or work together, but reconciliation isn't possible." To be truly committed to a racial friendship, we need to move beyond our initial, self-centered response.

If you're a leader in a church or ministry, remember that not everyone needs to have the same depth of relationship we have, or the same kind of partnership we've developed between Rock Church and Circle Urban Ministries. That would be an unrealistic expectation. However, Christians who are called to be in the forefront of urban ministry, who are called to the ministry of reconciliation between black and white, had better be in a committed personal relationship. You are the leaders. You are setting the pace. If you don't have that kind of relationship, you're not being equipped the way you need to be. Racial reconciliation must begin on the personal level. It is out of that kind of relationship that ministry will grow.

■   □   ■   □   ■

Applying the Principle

Our society and even some in the church say, "Stay with your own kind; you'll be happier." We doubt it. Building cross-cultural relationships can be an exciting adventure. Of course, like any adventure, it has pitfalls along the way. But adventures also have excitement and fulfillment, and (as is certainly the case around Rock/Circle) there is never a dull moment.

But any adventure involves risk. Don't be afraid of it. Don't be afraid to reach out and seek someone who is racially different from you.

Commitment is a combination of attitude and action. Here are three ways to increase your level of commitment to a cross-cultural relationship:

1. Take risks. You must be willing to reach out to someone who is racially different, even if you risk misunderstanding by that person.
2. Discover opportunities. Look for people of different backgrounds at your work, in the neighborhood, where you shop.
3. Move beyond saying hello. When you meet someone, try to initiate a conversation that moves beyond a superficial greeting; take time to know the person. It could be the beginning of a great friendship.

On a recent speaking trip to my childhood church in Ripon, I (Glen) was startled to see several black folks in the congregation. The sight reminded me that most of us no longer live as I grew up, in total racial isolation. Our paths cross, even in small-town America, with Asians, Hispanic, or African-Americans. But we don't choose, usually out of discomfort, to pursue that contact into a relationship. Instead, we often ask ourselves, *What will that person think?*

Stop at this point. Take inventory. Where do those people cross your path? The Hispanic person on your job? The Asian family that moved into the neighborhood one block over? The black family visiting your church? Each represents an opportunity to build a cross-cultural relationship.

What will it take to build that relationship? Ask yourself that question. Then turn to the next chapter for one of the answers. That answer is Principle 2: Intentionality.

CHAPTER 9

PRINCIPLE 2:
INTENTIONALITY

*Intentionality is the purposeful, positive, and
planned activity that facilitates reconciliation.
(Key verses: Ephesians 2:14–15)*

nn, a white woman, had moved from the suburbs into a
Southern black community because she felt called to racial
reconciliation and to minister to the poor. She had sacrificed to put herself in the middle of the situation and become involved in a Bible study with some African-American Christians.
But she discovered that people were not all that excited to have
her there. She followed the principle of commitment fully, yet
friendships did not develop.

What went wrong? Ann asked herself the same question, and
she wrote us a letter.

"I couldn't understand why people didn't like me," she
wrote. "One day in our Bible study I expressed my frustrations.
One of the black women spoke up and said, 'Do you want me to be
honest with you? The fact is . . . we hate you because you're white,
and you hate us because we hate you.'"

Ann was shocked. "But when I came to grips with what she'd
said, I understood that was really the case," her letter continued.

"In our society, that's the bottom line for blacks and whites. But now that I've been told the truth, I can deal with it, because I know that God's love can break down the barriers of hate."

That's blunt talk. But alienation between blacks and whites has been fomented by hundreds of years of racial agony in our society. If we expect it to break down by itself without our being doggedly intentional about it, we're naive. Commitment by itself is not enough. We must be intentional, pursuing a relationship even when it is uncomfortable. That may mean planning for our involvement.

Racial reconciliation doesn't happen spontaneously. Blacks and whites can work side by side, live side by side, even go to church together, and still not be in a meaningful relationship with one another. The reality of the 1990s is that most blacks and whites are still separated and alienated from each other, and eleven o'clock on Sunday morning is still the most segregated hour of the week.

Even those who are pained by this don't know how to do or be any different. We drift downstream in the direction society is going; the current is strong. We are born into that stream, and our culture and traditions and prejudices carry us along—unless we make an conscious effort to do something different. If we are going to address separation and alienation between races we have to be intentional about it.

But what does it take to go upstream against the flow?

"Git on Board, Little Children"

In the lexicon of Negro spirituals, there is frequent reference to "de gospel train." In fact, one spiritual, "Git on Board, Little Children," tells us "de gospel train is coming" and it's time to "git on board." For the sake of analogy, the only way to keep from being swept downstream with the rest of society is to get out of the water and board the train that runs back up the other way.

We may agree that God has given Christians the ministry of reconciliation. We may recognize that developing relationships across racial lines is the key to true reconciliation. But all too often, our beliefs and good intentions sit dead on the tracks. That is where intentionality comes in. Intentionality gives priority to purposeful, positive, and planned activity that facilitates reconciliation (key verses: Ephesians 2:14–15).

Intentionality is the locomotive that drives racial reconciliation. It must become part of our attitude. We must want to know the other race, to contribute to the other person's spiritual, social, and emotional growth. Our attitude must be: *I will be intentional in pursuing a relationship with this person.* Paul wrote: "Have this attitude in yourselves which was also in Christ Jesus" (Philippians 2:5–8). What attitude? Christ, who was "in very nature God" and equal with God, nonetheless humbled Himself, took on the nature of a servant, and was obedient even to the point of death. Not just any death, but death on the cross! *That* took intentionality. He intended to be involved with sinful, inconvenient people. So He entered their lives by coming to earth.

Why did Jesus do such a thing? Let's look at Ephesians 2:13–16 once again:

> But now in Christ Jesus you who once were far away have been brought near through the blood of Christ. For he himself is our peace, who has made the two one and has destroyed the barrier, the dividing wall of hostility, by abolishing in his flesh the law with its commandments and regulations. His purpose was to create in himself one new man out of the two, thus making peace, and in this one body to reconcile both of them to God through the cross, by which he put to death their hostility. (NIV)

Jesus intentionally left heaven and took up residence in human form on earth, even though He knew it would lead to the cross. It was the only way to accomplish the work that the Father had given Him: to reconcile men and women to God by becoming the sacrifice for their sin. In that same act, as these verses clearly show, Christ also broke down the barrier of hostility between people of different races, making peace possible.

On the way to the cross, Jesus broke down a lot of barriers between people as He brought the good news of God's redemption (and it got Him into a lot of trouble). He shocked the healthy by touching the "unclean" lepers; He bewildered His power-hungry disciples by telling them they had to become like little children; He embarrassed the self-righteous by refusing to condemn the adulterous woman; He offended the "righteous" by associating with sinners; He shamed the rich by praising the small gift of a poor woman who gave sacrificially; He provoked the "ethnically pure" Jews by inviting half-breed Samaritans to become children of God.

These barriers didn't come falling down by accident; Jesus intentionally went out of His way to make a point: "If you're going to follow Me, the barriers need to come down. In fact, those barriers are keeping the people from seeing who I really am."

Today there are many barriers separating people, even people who call themselves Christians. And one of the most alienating is the barrier of race. Two thousand years of history show us just how firmly this barrier is in place; it will only come down if, like Jesus, we become intentional about it.

Going Out of the Way

After graduating from Moody Bible Institute, I (Glen) worked in the mail room at a bank for awhile. I noticed for the first time a phenomenon that is common in such "integrated" settings as college campuses and the workplace. The white employees all sat together in the lunchroom and the same with the blacks. That's what felt most comfortable to people. But I decided to sit at the lunch table with the black employees. I wanted to know them better and figured the best way was to spend more time with them. So I planned to sit with them and did so.

The other whites looked at me very strangely; maybe the blacks did too! But even after I was transferred to another department, I still made a point to spend time with the black employees and talk to them. I was drawn into the enjoyable opportunity to cross into another culture. We always seemed to have more fun and laugh more than the quiet, reserved group of whites that surrounded us.

Both the Kehreins and the Washingtons have had numerous people live in our homes. When Clyde Dooley, an older black man, came to live in the Kehrein home, it was an exercise in intentionality. Besides having spent decades in a homosexual lifestyle, Clyde had been a heroin addict for twenty years, but as a new Christian his life had miraculously changed. He had lost his small apartment because a new owner was charging more than he could afford. Clyde was on disability and could not afford another apartment. He was homeless; we had an extra room. But accepting him might require extended lodging. Were we prepared to have him

Raleigh Washington and
Glen Kehrein at Circle
Urban Ministries
headquarters.

Raleigh, age 17 and today (top); Lt. Cdr. Robert Aubuchon and Lt. Col.Raleigh Washington present final American flag to fly over Fort Brooke to Puerto Rico Secretary of State Chardon.

Glen, ages 9 and 17 (top); Glen looks at courtyard of CUM headquarters in Chicago.

Raleigh makes a point during a seminar on racial reconciliation and urban ministry with forty church and parachurch leaders (top); Glen and Raleigh share a laugh in a growth group meeting.

Congregation of Rock of Our Salvation church in prayer; members Lonni Kehrein and DuRohonda Grant talk about the Sunday message.

Wendell Synder of Kearney (Nebraska) Free Church assists Calvin Blackwell during CUM workday (top), while two volunteers help CUM worker Clarence Watkins (bottom left); Paulette Washington and Lonni Kehrein enjoy a laugh during Harvest Fest Barbeque.

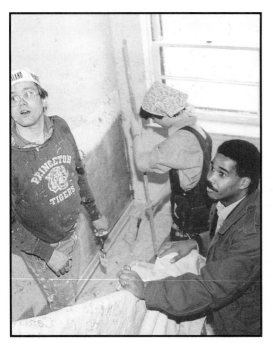

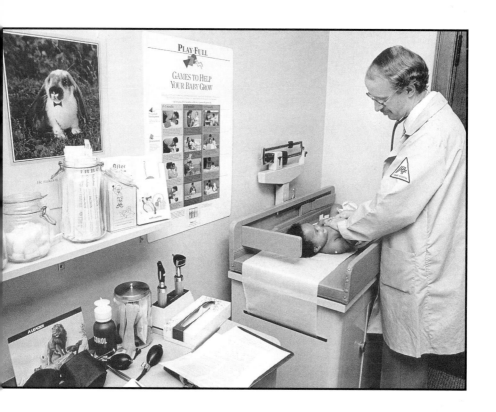

Dr. John Beran examines an infant at the CUM medical clinic (top); two women move down CUM hallway, arm in arm.

Workers helped convert an empty classroom into modern reception area at CUM (top); Chicago Mayor Richard Daley listens as Raleigh explains the programs of CUM and Rock Church during a recent tour of the area.

for a very long time? Yes, Lonni and I decided. Intentionality requires risk.

But several of our children were not excited by the possibility. They did not make Clyde feel welcome; in fact, quite the opposite. Tension built; the road was rocky. But intentionality means you don't throw in the towel when things get rough.

"Brother Glen, I think the children don't feel comfortable with an old man in the house," Clyde said after a week. "I think I need to just stay in my room until I can find someplace else. I don't want to cause any trouble."

"That's not the right solution," I told him firmly. When people who are different from us come into our space it's natural to feel discomfort at first. Our kids were reacting. I encouraged Clyde to hang in there, and Lonni and I spoke to the kids more intentionally about why we felt God had given us this opportunity. We reminded them how the innkeepers had turned away Mary and Joseph when they were looking for a place to stay in Bethlehem; in effect they were turning away Jesus, the Messiah, who was born homeless, in a stable. What was our family going to do when a homeless, poor person needed a place to stay? They finally agreed to give it a shot.

As the days went by Clyde won the kids over (especially when he did their turn at the dishes). Dinner table talks included the old man reminiscing about moving many times as he was growing up. Perhaps the most touching moment came at Christmas. Our tradition is a fondue meal and warm family time on Christmas Eve, concluding with a time around the tree. For gifts we are limited to only one per person, but each of the children had bought Clyde a gift.

It seemed like a touching scene out of a Christmas movie when Clyde opened his gifts. At sixty-nine, frail, his life almost spent, he said with tears streaming, "I've never had a real Christmas before. Never a real family like this. Never had a tree. I remember as a boy seeing Christmas trees in other folks' houses and dreaming about what it must be like. Now I know. This is wonderful." It was as if Christ himself—not old St. Nick—was peeking in our window.

God continues to grace our life with "Grampa Clyde," as the kids call him. Because he was homeless, in six months I was able to get him a newly rehabbed, subsidized apartment just blocks from Circle. He calls us his family and we still spend holidays together when we can. Our lives have been deeply enriched by being intentional about crossing the barriers.

Our Isolated Communities

Dealing effectively with the racial issues that separate us requires intentionality. This principle cuts both ways. Many whites in this country, Christians included, live in isolated communities with very little contact with blacks. But the black person, who lives in a white world and may rub shoulders with whites every day, can be isolated as well. If he or she doesn't choose to cross racial lines—in ways that other African-Americans may not like—he or she will remain as isolated as any white person.

During the years of intentional Reconstruction (1865–77) after the Civil War, blacks achieved more advancements than have happened in more than a century since. Before state legislatures reacted and intentionally implemented Jim Crow Laws and other hurdles to separate blacks from whites, the black community's ownership of capital grew from virtually nothing to 1 percent of the capital in this country. Today it's somewhere between 1.5 and 2 percent. Both the initial rapid development, followed by the deliberate squelching of black initiative, is a testimony to the power of intentionality—first for good, then for ill.

The sad truth is black churches developed out of necessity, as blacks were not welcome in white churches. These black churches, however, became important institutions, not only for passing on the faith, but for leadership development and preserving the culture. But what does this say to the world? That Jesus can reconcile us to Himself, but He can't reconcile us to each other? If so, we are distorting the gospel message, even as we ignore the Scriptures' call to be reconciled.

Today, those attending many white and black churches would say they have an "open door" policy: anyone who comes is welcome. When someone of another race occasionally attends, some people say, "This is great!" But blacks and whites worshiping together won't happen in a serious way unless it's intentional. Circumstantial integration doesn't last because it cannot survive the first racial clash—whether it's a misunderstanding or a struggle over style or leadership. Unless the church leaders and the people intentionally go out of their way to include people of other races, and intentionally address the barriers that stand in the way, the cross-cultural, committed relationships will not happen.

Chocolate, Vanilla, and Fudge Ripple

At Rock Church, we are very intentional about becoming a cross-cultural church. In fact, our church constitution declares it, and our mission acronym "CALLED" reinforces it. "CALLED" means Rock Church is a:

C — Cross-Cultural Church
A — in the Austin community
L — under the Lordship of Christ
L — building Leaders
E — through Evangelism
D — and making Disciples

Almost 70 percent of the church is black, and 30 percent is white. Whites obviously have to be very intentional about coming to our church and becoming members since we're located in a largely black community. Whites do not take quickly to the idea of being a "minority," but those who are willing to put themselves in that position find it tremendously educational. (We expect key leaders, black and white, to move in and become part of the community.)

But blacks have to be intentional, too. Historically, the black church has been the primary place for blacks to express their culture free from white dominance. When black visitors wander into Rock Church, they are taken aback by the significant presence of whites. Some will respond with a quick exit. Others take the risk and discover Rock to be a loving atmosphere of blacks and whites living together in sincere relationships. Months later, feeling secure and a part of things, individuals have revealed, "Man, when I walked in and saw all these white folks, I thought, 'I got to deal with the white man all week long, and now in church too? No way!'" Underlying these thoughts is the often unexpressed feeling that when whites are present they must run the show.

We are also intentional about tackling cross-cultural problems. Our Fudge Ripple Sundays are specific meetings intentionally planned to address problems and deepen black-white relationships in our church. On the Sundays designated for these quarterly meetings, all blacks get together during the Sunday school hour in a "chocolate" meeting and express whatever concerns them. Following the church service whites do the same—the "vanilla" meeting.

After lunch we all get together in a combined "fudge ripple" meeting where we serve fudge ripple ice cream and Oreo cookies.

When we come together in the two-hour fudge ripple meeting, we talk about all the issues that came up in the earlier meetings. Our goal is to be preventive rather than prescriptive. The issue may be directly related to race (for example, whites show up right on time for a meeting, blacks dribble in), or it may be a personal or church issue (for example, "I volunteered for the committee, but I felt my suggestions were ignored . . .") where race colors the dynamics (". . . because I was the only black/white"). At other times these sessions are built around a topic like interracial marriage, the L.A. riots, or the legacy of Malcolm X.

Contrary to popular assumption, we don't outgrow the need for these meetings, any more than a married couple gets to the point where they never have to do problem solving any more. But it's amazing how just taking the wraps off diffuses a lot of problems. Why? Because evil cannot thrive in the light. This spiritual principle is articulated in 1 John 1:7: "If we walk in the light, as he is in the light, we have fellowship with one another, and the blood of Jesus, his Son, purifies us from all sin." Notice that bringing things into the light not only "purifies us from all sin" but also creates fellowship between us. However, if we keep things hidden (i.e., walk in darkness), Satan magnifies those things into conflict because we don't understand what's going on behind the other person's reaction. We don't realize that if we do this or say that, the other person may read a negative meaning into it. The power of darkness intentionally keeps things hidden. Our antidote is to create an atmosphere that intentionally sheds light.

Whether we are black or white, yellow or brown, criticism and resentment can lead to sin. Being intentional about addressing problems in our fudge ripple meetings every three months is one way we work at racial reconciliation in our church. A similar kind of intentionality will work in any church, whether the disagreements are between members of the same race or different races.

In the end, we must trust the Spirit of the Lord that whatever is brought into the light can be dealt with through the body. One reason church or individual conflicts get so brutal is that so much has been kept in the dark. When people get triggered into responding, all the things they've been holding back for years explode. We have all seen the result of a lesser degree of intentionality—it's called a church split.

That's why once a quarter at Rock Church we unload. We don't want to allow issues to build to an explosive point. And then we celebrate our honesty and openness with cookies and ice cream. Oreo cookies and Fudge Ripple Sundays really help you enjoy the differences and celebrate the common bonds of care in Christ.

Intentionality Is Not Color Blind

People wonder why we are always talking about race. Most whites think we shouldn't make such an issue of it; then maybe people would behave as though race didn't make any difference. Well-meaning whites have moved into an integrated community thinking racism won't be an issue. But we have rarely heard a black person say, "I am color blind; I don't see color." Blacks live with the effects of racism every day.

It is a common contention by whites that, yes, racism is a historical fact, but has little current impact. Rare instances of some "redneck" response might occur, but discrimination is no longer the norm. But that perspective occurs because whites have experienced racism only intellectually and not empirically.

"Prime Time Live," ABC's newsmagazine show, once broadcast a stunning destruction of the myth that discrimination is now rare. Two TV investigators were similar in every way—except for the fact that one was white and one black. The plan was simple: both men would do everyday activities in a white community (it happened to be St. Louis) and see if they were treated differently. In a dozen instances—buying shoes or a car, applying for a job or apartment—the young men were treated in nearly opposite ways. While the white man was welcomed, the black man was ignored or insulted. Such covert racism is never experienced by whites, who sometimes view blacks as being "overly sensitive" about racism.

Recently a mixed group of men from our church held an overnight meeting in a hotel in a white Chicago suburb. Free popcorn and drinks were set up for the taking in the hotel's atrium. But when several of the black men from our group—dressed as well (or better) than the white guests—picked up the popcorn, hotel staff confronted them with, "This is for hotel guests only." Our friends got the clear insulting message: "You are black; this is not a place for you." Was their conclusion overly sensitive, or were they victims of covert racism? Your response probably depends on your life experience, which depends on your skin color.

Intentionality acknowledges that race *is* an issue. John Perkins, the founder of numerous ministries committed to racial reconciliation and justice, says, "We are all damaged by the evil of racism which Satan uses to separate us." The damage to blacks has resulted in feelings of inferiority; the damage to whites has promoted feelings of superiority. Intentionality says, "I recognize this damage. I recognize the hurt you have received. I not only don't want to cause more hurt, but I want to make the extra effort to help heal the wounds."

This cuts both ways. The hurt in the black community is historic, systemic, and crippling, but practically every white person who has tried to relate cross-culturally can identify individual hurts of being accused, rebuffed, or misunderstood by things black people have done or said.

If we're not intentional about dealing with these hurts, if we say that all we have to do is act in Christian love and the problems will go away, we are engaging in denial, a mere scab covering a deep wound. The healing must happen from the inside out, or infection will set in and fester until it destroys the body.

Salt Brings Pain Yet Preserves

Jesus told us to be salt and light in the world. As "salt," we are the preserving agent of society so it doesn't get rotten. As "light," we shine God's truth on our relationships; we open up our lives, cutting through the darkness. Even God the Father was intentional as He planned for our reconciliation by sending Christ to earth. God sought to rebuild the relationship with us that had been broken by sin. To do that, Jesus suffered agonizing pain and rejection. But that's what it takes for reconciliation. As salt, we can expect to feel rejection, but we also can help to restore a society threatened with rot.

When we are intentional, there will be pain. Not long ago, a young white woman who attends Rock Church burst into the pastors' offices, weeping uncontrollably. "What's wrong?" we cried. Lynn and her husband wanted to be part of racial reconciliation, and they pursued it an intentional way. They had adopted two children, one black and the other mixed racially, and they attended our church to be part of a racially diverse environment. We listened intently as Lynn told us her story as she quickly moved through a box of tissues.

For two and a half years Lynn had been trying to establish a relationship with Diane, a young black woman in the congregation and a single mother. The relationship seemed to be going well and the two women were enjoying each other.

"Then she started playing games with me," Lynn said. "We would make plans, and she wouldn't follow through. But I decided to keep trying." Lynn invited Diane to a movie, and Diane agreed to meet on Friday. Lynn decided to return from a business trip a day early "so we could go to the movie together."

On Friday, Lynn arrived at Diane's apartment at seven o'clock and rang the doorbell, but nobody answered. She came back forty minutes later; still no answer. Frustrated and angry, she realized she'd been stood up. But she tried again at a time Diane should have been home and rang the bell; still nobody was home.

Finally she went to a neighbor (also a church member) who lives a floor below and said she'd been trying to reach Diane but no one seemed to be home. "Oh, somebody's there," the neighbor said. "We can hear the kids running back and forth. Try knocking on the door." So Lynn knocked and one of the kids opened the door. As she walked in, the young mother she'd been trying to see walked into the bathroom and turned on the shower.

"Are you taking a shower now, or did you just turn it on?" Lynn yelled through the door.

"I'm taking a shower!" Diane yelled back. Lynn tried to wait patiently; but then the kids, one at a time, starting going in with towels to take a shower. By that time, Lynn was fed up, so she left.

As Lynn poured out her frustration and anger and hurt, she cried, "I don't know how long I can keep going in this relationship!"

As Arthur Jackson, the associate pastor, and I (Raleigh) talked with her, we said, "Don't you know this is characteristic of Diane's behavior? She's a baby Christian; she goes up and down, and a lot of times when she's down, it's because of sin in her life. Then she's uncomfortable being with you, so she shuts you out."

Yes, Lynn knew this. We talked together for another fifteen minutes, helping her see that she'd been giving but not receiving in return. The relationship was not mutual; Lynn had been making allowances when she needed to challenge.

Lynn had needed a place to vent her feelings, but now she was making herself accountable to us, asking whether she should continue the relationship. We didn't require her to go on; we just helped to clarify the issues and review the principles of reconciliation. But when we finished, Lynn was determined. "I'm going home right now and write Diane a note. I'm going to tell her we're going to meet, we're going to talk, we'll deal with this issue whenever she's willing to deal with it—but I'm not going to give up."

As Pastor Jackson and I held hands with her and began to pray, I couldn't hold back the tears. I realized that the weekend in question was the weekend just after the Rodney King verdict and the Los Angeles riot. Even as the nation was gripped in the frenzy of racial conflict and left gasping by the injustice of the system, we were joining hands with a young white woman who was in tears because her efforts to develop a relationship with a black member of the church had been rebuffed. But she was determined to hang in there and even take abuse in order to make it happen.

Unless we're intentional to that degree, it's not going to happen. "Whew!" you're saying. "That's really above and beyond the call of duty." Is it? Jesus tells us to take up our cross and follow Him. The cross is going to mean rejection; it's going to mean pain. We can't just talk about it; we can't just sing about it. We have to live it! But on the other side of the cross, there's reconciliation and resurrection glory.

Spread the Net

We've said that racial reconciliation begins with developing at least one significant relationship across racial lines, and being very intentional about it. But the question always arises, as we mentioned in the last chapter, "What if I try to develop a relationship and it just doesn't click?" Increasing the number of cross-cultural relationships helps to deal with this issue.

As my circle of African-American acquaintances and coworkers grows, I (Glen) am obviously going to develop a deeper relationship with some than others. If we're intentional about wanting to develop a real friendship, getting to know a wide variety of black (or white) folks helps us get beyond the first barrier, race. At least we will not let race be the first door that keeps everything else closed.

You wouldn't usually encourage your son to marry the first girl he dates. Even though the goal is to develop a significant relationship (that is, marriage) with one person, getting to know a wide variety of women helps your son recognize the kind of person most likely to sustain a long-term relationship.

It works much the same way with cross-cultural relationships. The first or most convenient person you meet, white or black, may not be the right one. But if you're willing to take the risk and cross over the barrier of race, you will soon begin to recognize key qualities—that person is an acquaintance, this person is a spiritual brother or sister, that person is off the wall, and this person is a kindred spirit, a real friend. The more relationships you establish, the more you will realize that people don't fit as neatly into a "white box" or "black box" as it might first appear.

Three Key Questions

When we go to churches or conferences to talk about racial reconciliation, pastors and church leaders always come up afterward and ask, "We want to establish a relationship, but how do we get started?" A second question is, "What if the other person is off-base theologically?" And a third question is, "I believe I'm where God wants me right now, but there are very few people of another race in my community [or work or church or denomination]. How do I get involved?"

Questions like these came up after I (Raleigh) spoke in a suburban church in Michigan. Their community had very few blacks, except for some middle-class executives who worked for a large pharmaceutical dealer. "How can we live out these principles?" they wanted to know.

"Have there ever been any black or Hispanic or Asian families who came to the church for a little while but then left?" I asked.

They all agreed that had happened.

"Did you ever wonder why those families didn't stay?"

Heads nodded.

"The point is, if someone in the congregation had intentionally developed a personal relationship with them, they'd be here now. You know, inviting them home for Sunday dinner, including their kids in a family trip to the zoo."

Then I asked, "Now, do all of you work and play 365 days a year with no contact at all with anybody except people who are exactly like you? No? Then, how intentionally will you try to establish a relationship with one or more of those people?"

The challenge is this: be proactive in initiating a relationship with a person of a different racial or ethnic group. How do you do this? Once every two weeks be committed to have breakfast or lunch with that person. What's the purpose behind these meetings? Just to talk to one another. Do this for six months with no other agenda. Be open, be transparent. If the person asks you why, say, "Hey, I believe God wants me to get to know and understand people different from myself." But it takes intentionality.

If things go well, pretty soon the person may invite you to his or her house, or vice versa. If you're white, and a black person comes to your house, what are your neighbors going to think? Some may think, *He's a nigger lover.* If you're black and you invite a white person to your house, what are your friends going to think? Some may think or even say "He's an Oreo." Many times I (Raleigh) have been aware of black brothers watching me with Glen and not saying a word; but their eyes, full of innuendo, have implied strongly that I am just a lackey for a white man. That kind of response from people we care about doesn't feel good.

The test is, will you persevere in this relationship in spite of opposition? When you do, you reap the benefits that the relationship brings and laugh at the supposed "price" you thought it would extract.

Relationship Leads to Ministry

Many times white Christian leaders—especially seminary professors and pastors—will express an interest in establishing a cross-cultural ministry. We tell them the same thing: "Find yourself a soul brother minister—or a deacon or an elder—and have lunch or breakfast with that person once every two weeks. Don't try to find out what you can do for each other; don't make plans for how your churches can exchange services; don't set up a black awareness program. Just get to know each other for five or six months. If things click and a relationship develops, then ministry will grow out of what you have established between you personally."

Both black and white Christians were sobered by the explosion in south central L.A. after the Rodney King verdict. A large part of the tinder was that whites, blacks, Hispanics, and Asian-Koreans were shoe-horned together in a large, urban community —you might call it "integrated"—but very little effort and energy had been spent developing understanding, communication, and relationships across those racial lines.

If we're going to be ministers of reconciliation (2 Corinthians 5:18), we first need to know how to establish cross-cultural relationships. If we want to be used by God in a multiracial environment, especially in urban arenas, we have to learn how to relate to people different from ourselves.

When does cross-cultural ministry take place? When personal relationships take root and have some real meaning and validity. You won't have to wonder what people are thinking; you won't have to ask what you can do. Barriers will break down as intentional relationships are built one on one.

■   □   ■   □   ■

Applying the Principle

Intentionality is a planned activity; it requires purposeful strategies. Here are some positive activities that churches and individuals can consider to develop relationships with those of another racial group.

For *churches,* intentionality might be:

1. If you are in a homogeneous neighborhood, establishing a "sister church" relationship with a black or white congregation. In a sister church relationship, the pastors/leaders develop relationships with one another and provide opportunities for their congregations to fellowship and share experiences with one another.

2. If your neighborhood is changing or already diverse, recruiting ethnic leadership rather than moving the church to a "better" place.

3. Submitting to minority leadership when you are white.

4. Changing worship and music to include several cultural styles.

For *individuals*, intentionality might be:

1. Inviting a church member or neighbor or coworker who is racially different to dinner in your home, adjusting however necessary to make them comfortable.

2. Developing a continuing friendship with a person of another ethnic group.

3. Visiting a black church or other ethnic congregation as a family at least four times a year.

4. Expecting and accepting pain in the early stages of a new cross-cultural relationship.

CHAPTER 10
PRINCIPLE 3: SINCERITY

*Sincerity is the willingness to be vulnerable,
including the self-disclosure of feelings,
attitudes, differences, and perceptions, with
the goal of resolution and building trust.
(Key verse: John 15:15)*

When Jerome, a young black man, first began attending Rock Church, he was typically suspicious around the white members. Either he stood back and avoided direct encounters or, when an interaction couldn't be helped, his friendly but distant greetings seemed to say, "OK, you can come this far but no further."

As we got to know Jerome bit by bit, we realized what a risk he was taking getting involved in a cross-cultural church. "My old man used to tell me, 'Don't trust the white man; one day he'll turn around and do you in,'" Jerome admitted.

"[My dad] told us stories of what white folks had done to black people he knew, like job and housing discrimination. And it wasn't just something he said; we kids saw how he acted around different people. He was on guard around white folks, but with the 'brothers' he could relax and be himself."

Paranoia? No, just the cautious instruction of a father who loved his son and wanted to prepare him for life in the real world.

This kind of counsel passes from generation to generation in the black community, complete with stories of how supposedly friendly whites turned around and betrayed them. With that background, a black person needs only one bad experience to keep the lesson fresh.

Given the history of black people in America, mistrust between the races is intrinsic. Even at Circle Church, which was trying to bring the races together (see chapter 5), several black members had feared all along that it was just a matter of time before the whites stabbed them in the back. The black associate pastor, Clarence Hilliard, often received caution from his peers (leaders in the National Black Evangelical Association) that he was being too naive, too trusting to believe in the promises he got from whites at the church. Certainly that fear—left unresolved—set up the African-American members at Circle to expect such a betrayal, and without intentional countering measures (such as fudge ripple meetings) possibly became a self-fulfilling prophecy.

When a confrontation arose between the black pastor and the white pastor, the blacks felt the whites were out to get them—or at least out to get the black pastor—and so they rallied around to protect him. Whether or not their posture hindered resolution is hard to tell. But from the black members' perspective, when push came to shove, the elders (who were all white by this time) sided against Pastor Clarence—exactly as the blacks expected.

Unfortunately in most black/white relations, even well-intentioned ones, an important ingredient is missing: trust. There's only one way to build trust; we call it the principle of sincerity. Principle 3 declares that people must genuinely open their lives to one another, sharing who they are inside, taking the time to know the other person behind the "front." The principle of sincerity requires being honest and transparent about our thoughts, feelings, disagreements, disappointments, and negative perceptions. (The principle is rooted in Christ's definition of friends in John 15:15.)

That's a tall order! In fact, it's downright scary—but not impossible. Today, even Jerome has developed a good relationship with several white brothers at Rock Church. But it took time to get beyond the mistrust that had been ingrained since childhood. His father still thinks Jerome is crazy to trust me (Glen), to go on fishing trips with me, to spend time at my house, and vice versa.

What does the Bible say about the kind of relationship that builds trust? Jesus and His relationship with His disciples provides the key.

"What a Friend We Have in Jesus"

Even though Jesus devoted much time to preaching to the multitudes and healing the sick, He also spent a lot of time alone with His disciples. For three years they walked and talked, ate and slept, laughed and cried, got dirty and tired, prayed and sang hymns together. Many times they didn't understand why Jesus did what He did or said what He said, but nonetheless He was investing a lot of time in the relationship.

Then they came to the Passover meal, which they ate together in a borrowed upper room. At this meal, commonly called The Last Supper, Jesus opened His heart as He never had before. "These things I have spoken to you in figurative language," He said, but "an hour is coming when I will speak no more in figurative language, but will tell you plainly . . ." (John 16:25). Among other things, Jesus defined the kind of relationship they should have with each other:

> This is My commandment, that you love one another, just as I have loved you. Greater love has no one than this, that one lay down his life for his friends. You are My friends, if you do what I command you. No longer do I call you slaves; for the slave does not know what his master is doing; but I have called you friends, for all things that I have heard from My Father I have made known to you. (John 15:12–15)

Notice that Jesus was not calling them disciples or followers or servants at this point, but friends. In fact, Jesus spelled out what the difference is between a servant (an unequal relationship) and a friend (a mutual relationship). "A servant," He said, "doesn't know His master's business. But a friend is someone with whom I share everything (*all things*)."

Notice also that Jesus took the initiative. He not only called them and led the way in demonstrating godly love, He also opened His heart to them and let them see Him in His most vulnerable moments. In fact, one of His inner circle used this intimate knowledge to betray Him. But Jesus never flinched; He had come for the purpose of reconciliation, so that these very disciples—and every single one of us who call on His name—could be friends with God and with one another in the deepest sense.

Sincerity Means Openness and Honesty

One thesaurus uses the following synonyms to define "sincerity": candor, frankness, honesty, truthfulness, one's true nature. In other words, to be sincere in a relationship means the masks have to come off, unspoken thoughts must be spoken, honest feelings must be revealed. Sincerity is entrusting everything to the other person! It is the ultimate in transparency. Consider the following five aspects of sincerity.

First, sincerity means investing time in the relationship. It takes time to share the many layers of our lives with each other; it's not going to happen overnight. But it's not going to happen at all if we only get together once a year.

Second, sincerity means taking the initiative to share my own life—being willing to go first. It's tempting to lean back and say, "Tell me about yourself," or, "What do you think?" We may even convince ourselves it's good manners to let the other person do the talking. But in a relationship where trust has not yet been established—and we need to assume that mistrust is an issue in cross-cultural relationships—we need to be willing to reveal something of ourself first. Then, when we have made ourself vulnerable, the other person has the option to respond in kind. It's a little like playing leapfrog: initiative on our part will lay down a little layer of trust, enabling the other person to risk sharing something of himself or herself. As trust grows, so does the ability to open our lives to each other, back and forth.

Third, sincerity means being open and honest. To achieve racial reconciliation, two people—one black and one white (or brown or yellow)—must be willing to share their lives in an open and honest way on many levels: background, home life, strengths and weaknesses, relationship struggles, thoughts and attitudes, dreams and goals, reactions and feelings. Any interaction qualifies as an opportunity to practice sincerity, as openly and honestly as we know how. And if we later realize that we were just putting a good face on it, or stuffing our real feelings, we may need to go back and try again.

Much of the tension between whites and blacks stems from people's inability to express how they feel honestly. At Rock Church Glen and I had concluded, "If our members were free to get their complaints off their chests, they wouldn't experience so much tension, and could possibly work together toward mutual solutions." That's one of the reasons for our Fudge Ripple Sundays. We seek open, honest, and free communication. We wanted to create an atmosphere that encouraged black people and white people to be open with their inner thoughts. In our society that usually happens only in guarded, racial seclusion.

We are very candid in these meetings, trying to create an environment in which it's OK to say, "When white folks start coming to the church, pretty soon they're in leadership because they've got all that education." Or, "It upsets me when black parents yell at their kids." We ask people to write their comments anonymously so the real feelings can come out. It is a spiritually acceptable gripe session! People can gripe, complain, or ask a question about anything in the chocolate, vanilla, and fudge ripple meetings, but we tell them, "If you go outside and make the same complaints in the parking lot, it's a sin" (because one is designed to bring resolution, while the other only creates strife). Seven years of Fudge Ripple Sundays have prevented racial gridlock and built a foundation for the continuing process of racial reconciliation at Rock Church.

Fourth, sincerity means a willingness to be vulnerable. To share one's life means exposing some things in our personal closets. If a black person feels safe in a church testimony time, he or she will tell the "scuzzy" stuff, the secrets of who they really are; white people are often more reluctant to do this. It's scary to be vulnerable; we might get hurt. But the only way to never get hurt is to keep the barriers up. Racial reconciliation is about removing the barriers that stand in our way.

For example, Clyde (see previous chapter) was an active homosexual for nearly fifty years before coming to the Lord at a friend's funeral held at Rock Church. It was the power of God unto salvation, because we've seldom seen by human effort a genuine change in a homosexual spirit. To avoid getting caught up in the gay lifestyle again, Clyde spent thirty to forty hours a week volunteering at the church so he could be around Christians and learn.

One day a group of fifteen white youths and their youth pastor visited the church from the suburbs, and Clyde spoke during Sunday morning worship. "I just want to praise the Lord," he said. "I had my AIDS test and it came back negative. I don't have

AIDS." Clyde was vulnerable, willing to risk the rejection of those teens. The kids were so shocked their mouths flew open. Clyde's revelation reflects just how open blacks can be when they feel safe, and he feels safe in Rock Church.

Fifth, sincerity helps establish trust. The issue of mistrust is a barrier that many whites don't fully understand. Though they often conduct their own lives in a more reserved, private manner, they wonder why black people don't trust them fully. But the life experience of blacks, the stories that pass from generation to generation, build a survival mentality that whispers, "You just can't trust white folks; sooner or later, they're gonna betray you." But when a person sincerely opens his or her life with a person of another race, that builds a foundation of trust, which leads to honest communication and meaningful relationship between black and white.

The goal of sincerity is to develop a baseline of trust on which a cross-cultural relationship can be built. As the principles of racial reconciliation build on one another, it can even be described as an equation: Commitment + Intentionality + Sincerity = Trust.

WWB/BBW

One of the greatest hindrances to the principle of sincerity is what we call the "Kehrein-Washington Law of Racial Dynamics." The law can be described as follows: "Whites know how to talk to whites about blacks" and "Blacks know how to talk to blacks about whites," or WWB/BBW for short.

In its most basic form, Whites Know/Blacks Know is whites talking among themselves about blacks and blacks talking among themselves about whites, creating a common body of "knowledge" (stereotypes) about the other race that fortifies the feeling of "us" versus "them." That's racism.

"Wait a minute!" a black brother or sister will protest. "For blacks, that's just survival." But in the sight of God, it is also racism.

The practice of WWB/BBW is a common cause of the breakdown in cross-cultural relationships, inhibiting the kind of openness and honesty that could lead to understanding between the races. Even in our well-meaning attempts to build relationships across racial lines, WWB/BBW pops up soon enough. At the first bump in the road, we tend to fall back to a "safe arena" (other whites if we are white; other blacks if we are black) to talk about the problem. But when we talk to one another about the other race, it reinforces our negative stereotypes and distrust.

In the first few months of Rock Church's existence, a white women came as a missionary to Circle Urban Ministries and joined the Rock Church, then a small band of about thirty people. Joan, a sincerely committed person, worked at Circle to establish the education program and volunteered in several areas of the church, including playing the piano on Sunday morning. Having an extra room in our house, we (Glen and Lonni) offered it to Joan until she could get more established. Lonni and I were still "checking Raleigh out." He appeared too good to be true and we had learned to let time test relationships. So Joan became a conduit of information about Raleigh's leadership, preaching, and ministry style within the church context. Very natural, right? But a good example of WWB, live and in living color!

Soon we began hearing criticism. Raleigh was too dominant. The volunteer interns from Trinity seminary were very discontent, the service was too long, and many parishioners were unhappy—those kind of things. Listening to Joan, Lonni and I found our hopes fading that Paulette and Raleigh would be the ministry partners we had been looking for.

Then Joan came to me all upset about a Bible study she and Pastor were co-leading in one of the apartment buildings owned by Circle. "The Bible study is supposed to go from 7:30 to 9:00 P.M., but Pastor often arrives late, and other people come late because he's late," she complained. "Then by 9:00, everybody's antsy; they want it to be over and done with but Pastor goes on and on. It's really destructive to the Bible study."

Whew! It sounded really bad, so I decided I'd better talk to Raleigh. "That's an interesting reflection," Raleigh said, "because some of the folks in the Bible study were just talking to me, and they're very disgruntled with Joan. The black people are not that time-conscious; they get there when they get there, and then we get the Bible study started. But just as a good discussion gets going, we hit the magic time—9:00—and it doesn't matter what we're talking about, Joan wants to cut it off. Some of the folks in the Bible study are starting to wonder why Joan is trying to control everything." Raleigh's point was driven home when I learned that talk was going around the apartment building that Joan was trying to destroy the Bible study. Very natural, right? But a good example of BBW, live and in living color!

It was a classic case of WWB/BBW. Instead of talking directly to Pastor Washington about the problem she perceived, Joan took her complaints to another white person (just as the black people took their complaints to Pastor). And I bought into it, since as a white person I understood those expectations about starting and ending meetings.

The Kehrein-Washington Law of WWB/BBW is a symptom of the disease of racial alienation. Raleigh calls the whispered conversations that increase the distrust between us "bad rap." Remember the analogy to a marriage relationship? It's as if somebody tells a husband, "Hey, I saw your wife having lunch at the cafe with this good-looking man and they were pretty warm and affectionate, I tell you." When the wife comes home the husband has already made an assumption and blows up. A terrible fight ensues —and then he finds out it was the wife's brother.

The cure for WWB/ BBW is to avoid making assumptions and to talk directly to each other across racial lines about problems or different perceptions between us. The Bible instructs us: "If your brother sins, go and reprove him in private; if he listens to you, you have won your brother. But if he does not listen to you, take one or two more with you, so that by the mouth of two or three witnesses every fact may be confirmed" (Matthew 18:15, 16). The issue mentioned here is sin, but the principle is the same in other areas, such as misunderstanding, hurt feelings, or frustrated expectations. Jesus was talking about using sincerity—speaking directly to one another in an open and honest way—to reconcile a strained relationship ("you have won your brother").

The Matthew 18 blueprint is important in all relationships, of course, but even more so when the relationship dynamic must also cross the boundaries of race and culture. Only then will we be able to increase our understanding, resolve conflicts, and break down the wall of hostility and distrust.

The Importance of Withholding Judgment

"People of color"—from many cultures, including African-American—typically handle time and structure differently than whites do. Our ethnocentrism primes each ethnic group to make judgments. Goal-oriented whites often value "getting it done."

This they see as "good"—a job needs to get done, the sooner the better. Although people of color understand the job must get done, they aren't willing to sacrifice time for relationships.

While visiting missionary friends in Mexico City, Lonni and I (Glen) one day decided to go sight-seeing. On the way to the pyramids outside the city, our friends dropped off a package for a friend of theirs. In the U.S. the encounter would have lasted thirty seconds—tops. In Mexico it involved extended conversation and refreshments. Our friends, Rick and Diane, had never met the recipient and would, most likely, never see him again. Two hours later we were back on the road.

As whites we often see such encounters as "a waste of time," rushing to judgment rather than attempting to understand the culture. The Mexican value of relationships is often viewed as laziness. As whites often rush to judgment, they miss the positive nature and value of that culture. If a person does not withhold judgment long enough to realize that getting the numbers on the board is not the only way to do God's work, racial and cultural rifts develop.

Withholding judgment long enough to understand earns the right to be heard. Without it WWB/BBW kicks into high gear. Criticism almost always will be communicated down racial lines; because we have the same cultural mind-set, judgments get reinforced.

Pastor Washington is an energetic, enthusiastic kind of guy, and other people in the ministry have to cope with the results of his high-powered personality. Once a CUM staff person came to me (Glen) in a panic: "Another volunteer group is coming! Pastor Washington said they could come, so they announced they're coming—next week." Another muttered, "There goes Pastor again, making all these promises and we've got to live with the consequences."

I got all excited and charged in to confront Raleigh (Matthew 18, right?). "Raleigh, stop inviting those volunteers! In your enthusiasm, you are overcommitting, but it's not your staff that has to do the work; it's my staff that has to do the work. So cut it out."

"Glen, that's not the way it happened," Raleigh protested. "I never make a date commitment with volunteers. As a matter of fact, I tell them, sure, we want you to come but I have no idea what would work. You need to call CUM and make arrangements."

There were other instances, too, when I came to Raleigh in an accusing manner. "Why did you do that?" And he'd say, "Glen, I wish you would ask me what I did instead of hearing it from someone else, making a judgment, and then coming to me with your mind all made up. I feel like you automatically trust the input from white people more than you trust me."

I soon began to realize, *I'm going to create a rift in our relationship if I don't listen to my friend's side of the story before I make a judgment.*

There is a fine line between withholding judgment and leaving things unresolved that are irritations or resentments. Withholding judgment doesn't mean we can't talk—openly and honestly—about the things that frustrate us. But let's be direct and honest, and let's avoid the WWB/BBW trap. Each of us brings our own background and perspective into a cross-cultural situation, and sincerity means being honest about what we think and feel. The timeliness issue is a great example because that rubs white people the wrong way a lot. We can say, "It bothers me that the service goes so long; why is that so common in the black community?" But we shouldn't come into the situation saying, "That's wrong; you should do it this way."

Richard and Pat Lord—he's a medical doctor, she's a Ph.D. in chemistry—are two high achieving, structured white folks who came to Rock Church, not because they felt a call to cross-cultural ministry or the black community, but because they had friends here who said, "This is a pretty good church." They fell in love with the church, began to get involved, came to all of the fudge ripple meetings, and were eager to learn.

One day Pat said to Raleigh, "Pastor, don't say your target to end the service is one o'clock because we never stop at one. Your target isn't really one o'clock or we would hit it once in a while. I'd rather you'd say two and let it end at one-thirty. But I get frustrated when you go beyond the expectations you've set up." I appreciated her openness, and I felt motivated to work on our ending time on Pat's behalf because she said what she wanted, yet I also knew she was willing to give me some flexibility. It's important to have those kind of conversations, to get our frustrations and feelings out so we can deal with them—but in an atmosphere that says, "This isn't an issue of right or wrong; let's find God's mind for this situation." If we can be transparent while withholding judgment, it builds a phenomenal foundation of trust.

Another time we had a black awareness program that went until 2:30—nearly four hours. Everybody was talking about how great it was, but it just went too long. I said, "We've got to figure out what to cut out when we do it next year."

But Richard and Pat had an idea. "Why don't we just scrap Sunday school that day and start at the Sunday school hour? Then we could keep all the different parts of the program and still finish at the normal time." It was an excellent suggestion from two time-conscious individuals who nonetheless were committed 100 percent to understanding why all that we did was so meaningful. Their sincerity was developing their sensitivity—the topic of our next principle.

Pat and Richard's ability to withhold judgment while investing their skills made them much-beloved sponsors of the junior high youth group. They deeply empathized with the plight of the black community; when they moved at the end of Richard's medical training, they set up a college scholarship fund for our young people.

The Test: Attitudes About Money

Before we end this chapter on the principle of sincerity, we need to mention a ticklish area that often challenges the level of trust between blacks and whites: money.

Attitudes about money are an Achilles heel that can hobble attempts at racial reconciliation. The white stereotype is: blacks and Hispanics can't manage money. The black stereotype is: whites and Asians want to control the money. Merge these stereotypes in a cross-cultural situation and blacks are convinced that whites don't trust them with money.

Remember the parable of the unrighteous steward in Luke 16:1–13? The steward was about to lose his job because he had mismanaged his master's assets. To protect himself, he called in each of his master's debtors and canceled part of their bill. The dishonest rascal made a lot of people happy (at his master's expense), and even his master had to admire the shrewd way his servant used money to make friends.

Jesus pointed out that the people of the world were, even in their dishonesty, wiser in the use of money than the people of the light, who often play down the significance of money. Then He said, "I tell you, *use worldly wealth to gain friends for yourselves,* so that when it is gone, you will be welcomed into eternal dwellings" (v. 9; italics added). A few verses later Jesus challenged, "If you have not been trustworthy in handling worldly wealth"—that is, *making friends with it*—"who will trust you with true [eternal] riches?"

You cannot serve two masters, Jesus told us. The unrighteous steward was loving money and using people. The message of this parable is to love people and use money, so that "when it [money] fails, they may receive you into the eternal dwellings" (Luke 16:9b).

Barnabas later illustrated this point when he sold a tract of land and placed the money at the apostles' feet; he trusted them with the money. Later, we are told, Paul collected money from Gentile churches to make eternal friends with the Jews in the Jerusalem church; they trusted him.

When money crosses racial lines, distrust is more the rule than the exception. We tend to trust people who are more like ourselves. Sometimes the distrust is overt; often just implied. When Glen and I (Raleigh) are together at a white missions conference, the offering is almost always given to Glen, even though I may have taken the lead in 75 percent of the matters needed to make the event happen. Conversely, Glen is under great suspicion by blacks in the community. Many who don't know the ministry are convinced that he is getting rich "off poor folks." They see the growth of the ministry and just naturally assume that he is drawing a big salary. It's common for people to even think that he "owns" the ministry—buildings and all!

When my exposure began to grow through speaking platforms in large churches and conferences, some of the leaders in my denomination began to ask among themselves, "What is happening with the money?" (This was WWB at work.) Financial integrity became a concern without even a hint of a scandal and before pursuing factual information. When this happens to blacks (who would readily submit to accountability if asked) more readily than whites, racism is the inference. Recognizing this dynamic, Rock and Circle have maintained membership in Evangelicals for Financial Accountability and have a policy of opening our books to anyone who asks—donor or not.

Our application of this parable is that using money to build relationships is Christ's direction. When you give freely and without suspicion, as did Paul and Barnabas, you build endearment and trust. Furthermore, expect the best from your friend when it comes to money. Love believes the best about the person's motives and actions (1 Corinthians 13:7).

■　□　■　□　■

Applying the Principle

Whether you are black, white, yellow, or brown, take the initiative to reveal yourself to a friend across the color/ethnic group line. Remember, if you are sincere, you will want to make the first move instead of waiting for the other person to initiate.

Of course, trust will not appear immediately in a relationship. All of us need to get to know someone for trust to develop and to risk being vulnerable. If you are white, being open and honest in your conversations (even with other whites) may be difficult because of cultural inhibitions. If you are in the racial minority, you probably will want to withdraw, fearing your sincere efforts will be ignored or, worse yet, taken advantage of by whites.

To whites as well as minority racial groups, here are three ways to open up in sincerity with your brothers and sisters.

1. Spend time together to develop trust. Remember years of abuse, ignorance, and stereotyping have developed a deep layer of distrust. You will need time to overcome it.
2. Be willing to open your "closets," to reveal the hardships and failures in your life. Everyone has failures. Your friend will respect you as a "real person" when you disclose them to him or her.
3. Be on the alert to recognize your (and others') involvement in WWB/BBW conversations. Be ready to confront those involved, in love, including yourself.

CHAPTER 11

PRINCIPLE 4: SENSITIVITY

Sensitivity is the intentional acquisition of knowledge in order to relate empathetically to a person of a different race and culture. (Key verses: Ephesians 4:15–16)

When I (Raleigh) was in seminary, Paulette and I were part of a sharing group with about fifteen white people. Man, those folks loved to play "roots." One woman could go all the way back in her family tree to Sitting Bull; another guy traced his ancestors back to the Mayflower. It was absolutely phenomenal. On the other hand, I could only talk about my grandmother; the first time I saw my maternal grandfather, he was lying in a casket. It was tougher for my wife. Paulette's grandfather is white; she's never seen him in her life and didn't even know his name until a few years ago.

Paulette and I got so tired of being on the sidelines in the roots game that we made up some heavy stuff that went all the way back to Kunta Kinte in Africa. The "folks of the lighter hue" ate it up by the yard—until we confessed it was all a charade. Fortunately, they all burst out laughing.

"Why did you make up such a tale?" one husband asked.

"Because you folks don't realize we can't even get past our grandmothers," we blurted. They were really convicted of their lack of sensitivity.

In general, African-Americans understand the typical white person's attitudes and responses much better than white people understand the black's attitude. It's a skill developed out of necessity. Blacks have had to understand and learn how to satisfy the expectations of white teachers, white employers, white landlords, and white government officials—including the police—merely to survive. Most white people have never had to understand blacks to that same depth, so it is easy for them to make social blunders. And the blunders often come across as insensitivity.

For instance, when getting to know another person, white people tend to ask all kinds of detailed questions about a person's history and family background. Janet, a young white woman, helped me one day years ago by accompanying me to visit a family. Janet was enthusiastic, if not too sensitive. As we stepped inside this small apartment, we saw all kinds of extended family members. In these situations you can't always tell the players without a scorecard, but Janet had a need to know who was who.

Making conversation with a teenager holding a newborn she asked several questions about the baby's father. There was no response. But Janet just had to know this critical information. Finally she blurted out, "Do you know who the daddy is?" Had I been drinking coffee, I'm sure I would have sprayed the entire room. But Janet didn't give it a second thought.

That kind of conversation causes blacks to feel as though whites are compulsively nosey about embarrassing family news. Often the circumstances don't fit the all-American family ideal. In time, this level of disclosure will come out in a committed relationship—after a level of trust has been established. But if used as a conversation opener, such a family focus can actually be insensitive and make the black person feel at a disadvantage in the relationship.

Sensitivity is an important principle when individuals or groups are involved in a process of racial reconciliation. It walks hand in hand with the principle of sincerity in the last chapter. Sensitivity deliberately acquires knowledge that enables us to relate empathetically to a person of a different race (key verses: Ephesian 4:15–16). And the New Testament reveals just how important sensitivity is in building relationships—and eventually ministry—across the barriers of race or class.

A Meeting at High Noon

To reach Galilee in the north from Jerusalem, Jesus had to go through Samaria, the home of the despised half-Jews. On one of these trips, Jesus and His disciples arrived at the Samaritan village of Sychar about noon (John 4). The Middle Eastern sun was relentless, and Jesus sat down by Jacob's well to rest while His disciples went into the village to buy some food.

Soon a lone woman came to the well to draw water. This was unusual; most women came in groups in the early morning or late afternoon when the heat was not so intense. Maybe she had a reason for avoiding the whispers and stares of others. She probably hesitated, seeing a strange Jewish man sitting by the well; after all, Jews and Samaritans weren't exactly on friendly terms. But she needed water, so she came closer to the well.

Then she had one of the strangest experiences of her life: this Jewish man started speaking to her like a real person. Maybe He didn't know she was a social outcast, she might have thought, at first; but as the conversation progressed it became obvious He knew quite a bit about her. Amazed, she began to listen as He revealed the truth about the Messiah, even when He concluded, "I am He."

This is one of the Bible's incredible stories. Such a conversation just wouldn't happen under normal circumstances. The story is rich in meaning, layer upon layer, but one of the things it shows us is Jesus' amazing sensitivity in approaching someone who was not only of a different race, but a despised class; not only a woman, but an adulteress, too. Consider how Jesus displayed sensitivity to someone of another race:

1. *Jesus left His own comfort zone* and met her on her own turf—in Samaria, near her own village. (Some Jews went so far as to go around Samaria whenever they had to travel north or south.)

2. *He chose a time convenient for the other person,* rather than for Himself. The well at high noon was not the most desirable time, but He wanted to meet with this woman, and He knew that she probably wouldn't talk to Him if others were around.

3. *He allowed Himself to be vulnerable* and asked her for a drink. A request from a Jewish man to a Samaritan wom-

an was unheard of! He could be challenged and mocked. The request was also an expression of acceptance and interdependence.

4. *He was sensitive to her point of need and took her to a higher level spiritually* (the gift of living water). Notice that He used a context familiar to her (that is, the daily chore of coming to the well to draw water) to express spiritual truths.

5. *He showed sensitivity in addressing her sin* by letting her reveal her lack of marital status. He then let her know by His response that He was already aware of her condition.

6. *Jesus was willing to spend the necessary time* to exercise a proper level of sensitivity. Little by little He revealed Himself, and drew her out of herself. He used sensitivity to relate to her, even though he was exposing her sin and spiritual ignorance.

Because Jesus was so sensitive, the Samaritan woman allowed the dialog to continue. She was amazed that someone who really knew her past history and present condition was so accepting. When He revealed Himself as the Messiah, she believed—and a great revival started in Sychar that day.

Jesus was the ultimate communicator. As His ambassadors of racial reconciliation, we can take a few lessons. A good communicator knows what to say, when to say it, how to say it, and *if* to say it. That's sensitivity.

A Meeting in the Desert

The evangelist Philip also displayed sensitivity when he met an Ethiopian in the desert (Acts 8:26–40). In this setting, the tables are turned; instead of a Jewish rabbi and a Samaritan adulteress, we now have a Jewish itinerant preacher (on foot) and a black Ethiopian official in the court of Queen Candace (riding in a chariot limousine).

Philip was quite a guy. He was having a very successful preaching ministry in Samaria, accompanied by such signs and wonders as evil spirits being cast out, cripples walking, paralytics being healed. The people were so excited there was dancing in the streets every night.

Then an angel of the Lord told him to hit the road again. *What? Leave when the revival was still hot?* But Philip had an exceptional sensitivity to the still, small voice of God.

First, he had a sensitivity to God's call. Philip was committed to go wherever God told him to go, even if the call was as vague as "Go south to the [desert] road that descends from Jerusalem to Gaza." Most of us probably would have protested, "Why? What's down there? Nothing's down there, that's what! No towns, no villages—just desert!" But Philip got up and went.

Second, he had a sensitivity to God's specific leading. Philip didn't know why God had put him on this desert road, but he was alert; God surely had a reason. When he saw a chariot coming down the road from Jerusalem, he was sensitive to the inner nudge from the Spirit of God: "Go up and join this chariot." Approaching a chariot without permission in those days could result in a sentence of thirty-nine lashes; therefore, Philip was taking a risk to follow the Spirit's leading.

Third, he had a sensitivity to God's people. When Philip approached the chariot, he heard the Ethiopian official reading aloud from the book of Isaiah. This was Philip's clue; the man obviously had an interest in the Scriptures. He didn't assume the man was religiously ignorant, nor did he assume the man had already been evangelized. Instead, with amazing sensitivity he simply asked, "Do you understand what you are reading?"

Look at the official's response to Philip's sensitivity: "Well, how could I, unless someone guides me?" He invited Philip to come up and sit with him. Philip's sensitivity resulted in an evangelistic opportunity as opposed to thirty-nine lashes (which could have resulted if he'd been insensitive).

A Child Shall Lead Them

We can make too big a thing out of sensitivity, and children sometimes can show us how easy sensitivity can be. One summer while standing in the yard, Chelsey Kehrein, age ten, observed a dejected black man walking out of the neighboring apartment building. "Hi, Mister," she called out boldly. "Why do you look so sad?" Indeed he was sad and explained that his mother had just had a stroke and he was on the way to the hospital.

Chelsey expressed heartfelt concern and told him she would pray for his mother. Six hours later the man returned home and rang our bell, looking for Chelsey to tell her that his mom was doing better. He didn't know her but was touched by her concern and returned to tell her the good news.

Quite naturally, Chelsey had been sensitive to a need and crossed class, race, and even age barriers that might have intimidated an older person in order to express her concern.

Sensitivity Builds Respect

When I (Raleigh) was a young teenager, I worked three or four summers for a kindly but firm white grocer named Albert Soud. He taught me how to cut meat, weigh it, and package it, and allowed me to be his unofficial butcher.

One day a girl who lived with her single mom and four other kids in the apartment above us came into the store and asked for twenty-five cents worth of baloney. The family was very poor, so I sliced about three times that much, wrapped it up, and wrote twenty-five cents on the package. When the girl took it to the counter at the front to pay for it, Mr. Soud looked at the package and threw it on his own scale beside the cash register. Then he rolled his eyes at me, paused, and finally said to the girl, "Twenty-five cents, please."

Mr. Soud knew what I had done. *Oh man, I'm going to get fired now,* I thought. About thirty minutes later the shop closed, and I was busy cleaning up—doing a double good job—when Mr. Soud said, "Sit down, Raleigh, I want to tell you something. What you did was wrong. I work hard to try to make ends meet, and you defrauded me. I believe you were trying to help that young lady, but you helped her at my expense. The next time you want to help somebody and you think the reason is valid, ask me, and I will respond to you. But don't steal from me."

I was hurt and humbled; it was a lesson I never forgot. Even though I had wronged him, he was sensitive to the reason for my action. And he had been sensitive at the cash register, not willing to embarrass me in front of the girl.

Even though I had wronged him, Albert Soud had talked to me with respect, like a father would talk to his son. Even though I hated injustice and didn't like what was happening to my people, I developed a real love for that man. Albert Soud was one of the white people who kept me from developing blanket bitterness toward all whites. He was one of the good ones!

We must cultivate sensitivity deliberately. Otherwise, we may say or do things that imply disrespect, even when we don't mean to. During the 1992 presidential race, for instance, independent candidate Ross Perot made the blunder of calling an audience of African-Americans "you people." Speaking to the National Association for the Advancement of Colored People (NAACP), Perot succeeded in offending many in the audience as well as blacks who watched news reports on national TV later that evening. His action was a classic case illustrating racial distance. Consider the response: many white folks identified with Perot, asking in bewilderment, "What did he do wrong?" Many black folks reacted in anger, just as the NAACP audience had.

Perot denied any racism but was ignorant of the historical impact of those words, which have often been used to maintain distance and separation. When a white person says, "It's great to be here with you people today," a black person is likely to hear "you people" as "you poor, ignorant folks of whom I am not a part." To many blacks, it sounds condescending. The term "you people" sets off a little warning: "Watch out; you can't trust whites."

Showing Respect

In the black community, the word *disrespect* is often used as a verb, as in "He disrespected me," or "He dissed me" for short. To *dis* someone is to say or do something disrespectful or arrogant. Among the gangs one can get killed for words or actions that are disrespectful—showing a rival gang's hand sign or wearing a rival's colors. Gangs have taken this to negative extremes, but between races, learning how to be respectful of the other person's traditions is always important.

Education is crucial to learn sensitivity about words of respect and disrespect. When Ross Perot had "dissed" black folks, showing himself to be insensitive, he could kiss their votes goodbye. Avoiding cultural offense is basic to racial reconciliation.

Whites complain, "Why do we always have to walk on egg shells to make the relationship work? I didn't mean anything by saying, 'You people.'" Some say, "One day they want to be called Afro-American, then black, and now it's African-American. It feels like a game to me—one where I always lose."

In a sense, that's true. Black Americans are often testing, testing, testing to see if whites are sincere and worthy of trust. ("Are you sincere about this reconciliation business, or are you looking for an excuse to walk away from it?") The white person's sensitivity is also tested in terms of how seriously he or she tries to understand and listen to black people, thus showing them respect. In his first year in office, President Ronald Reagan stated that he was unaware of a "black problem." Most of black America felt disrespected by their president, and hurt so permeated the black community that they felt unrepresented at the presidential level. Most whites can't even recall that Reagan made this statement, primarily because they were not personally affected by it.

One day Jerome (see chapter 10) and I (Glen) were working at a friend's house doing some plumbing in the basement. I know quite a bit about construction and plumbing, and I knew Jerome had some experience as well, though I was unsure how much plumbing he knew. I also have learned in these situations that whites often (albeit unintentionally) come across with a superior, "know-it-all" approach—something to be avoided like the plague.

Rather than presuming that he didn't know anything, I said, "I'll walk through what I'm doing here, but if I start going over stuff you know already, just tell me." I did that because I knew it could be an issue if I acted like I knew it all.

Jerome didn't make a big deal of it then, but one day I was arbitrating a confrontation between Jerome and Joel, a young white man. Jerome was exlaining how Joel made him feel when he gave instructions. Joel's manner was to talk down to him and seemed to imply Jerome was ignorant. Then Jerome repeated the plumbing interaction and said, "I trust Glen because he respects me. He knows that I know some things." Joel may not have directly shown disrespect, but in his insensitive words and tone of voice, Joel implied that Jerome was ignorant. Jerome's conclusion: "He disses me."

Many whites are driven (sometimes consciously, sometimes subconsciously) by society's assumption that they should know more than blacks. They may even feel they need to instruct and correct blacks, who (according to the news media or politically correct leaders) are "disadvantaged," "dysfunctional," or "deficient." However, without realizing it, whites give off the message that they know it all. This is subtle and often unintentional, but very disrespectful toward blacks. Sensitivity demands that we affirm the worth of others.

Assumptions Versus Reality

Assumptions get relationships into trouble, and both white and black make assumptions about each other. In typical middle-class situations, whites claim to be "color-blind" and assume their black neighbors or coworkers are "just like us" (as our friends who played the "roots" game did). On the other hand, when whites come into the inner city, they tend to assume that most personal and family situations there are dysfunctional, and relate in a patronizing way.

In getting to know one another, of course, we have to deal with reality. Alarming statistics about "the crisis in the black American family" or the "vanishing black male" should generate serious concern. But the assumption that black males have always been absent from the family is offensive. An honest look at history will show great strength in the black family, which has enabled African-Americans to survive in spite of a systematic effort to weaken, isolate, and destroy them. Even more, we can't relate to individuals and families as statistics; each person, each family is a unique creation of God, with strengths and weaknesses, joys and sorrows, gifts and needs.

Meanwhile, among blacks there is an assumption that whites have it all together because they carry themselves well in social situations. Most whites are accustomed by their culture to be reserved. To meet the average white person, one might never guess that the same crisis in the family cuts across all races and classes in America today. The divorce, abuse, and neglect in white families is as painful as for any ethnic group; however, their cultural training often has prepared whites to hold in that hurt.

In contrast, black folks with complex family problems show the hurt. They tend to be more emotional and "tell it like it is." If it's bad, you'll know it. For instance, a black mother may have one child in jail, one on the streets, and one in college—but she'll tell you about them all. If a white mother has one kid in Yale and one on drugs, you'll hear all about the first and never know the second one exists.

Understanding keeps relationships out of trouble. Understanding one another across racial lines can rid us of our faulty assumptions. Such understanding arises when we combine the two principles, sincerity (revealing yourself honestly and openly and spending quality time together) and sensitivity (learning about the other race or person, without making assumptions or quick judgments). When it comes to knowing a person's innermost thoughts, we need to listen to one another, allowing the other person to reveal himself or herself as trust grows.

We have learned first-hand how important these principles are. The difference in our personalities, style, and methodology, for instance, are as great as the difference in our color. Those differences remain even though we are one in heart. When Raleigh and I first approach an issue, the sparks sometimes fly! It has taken many four-hour mornings to hammer out things from our different perspectives, trying to figure out where we each were coming from. It takes great sensitivity to not blow each other away and a willingness to take the time to hear each other out and to understand what the other is saying. On many occasions, we have discovered we aren't in opposition, but simply approaching the same goal from a different perspective or life experience.

Indeed, there have been times when we did not end up in one accord. We continued to hold different perspectives, but we agreed to support one of the two, and we both committed ourselves to it 100 percent.

Good Humor Helps

We often use humor to disarm tension. For instance, after one of us makes an insensitive comment, we sometimes repeat Janet's well-meaning but insensitive question: "Do you know who the daddy is?" That blunder, so hysterical yet sad, has become a catchphrase between us. When we observe others in insensitive encounters, we sometimes turn to each other and whisper, "Do you know who the daddy is?"

Of course, humor also has to be expressed with sensitivity. The two of us make jokes out of racial stereotypes all the time. But this must be done within the context of a secure relationship where trust has been established. In *Black and White: Styles in Conflict*, Thomas Kochman writes, "There still exists a social etiquette that considers it impolite to discuss minority-group differences in public." We use humor as a way to break this social gridlock. Humor can put people at ease and remind us that we should not take ourselves too seriously.

Let's loosen up. Blacks and whites laughing together is a healthy sign of a friendly, genuine relationship.

Is Everything a Racial Issue?

One of the struggles in cross-cultural ministry is the degree to which race figures into every issue. At one extreme are people who think race doesn't figure in at all—it's just a personality conflict, or a disagreement over direction. At the other end are people who see everything as a racial conflict. This presents a challenge to the principles of sincerity and sensitivity.

Not long ago, Glen and I (Raleigh) were struggling over how to resolve a problem with "Bill," a white staff person who would not respond to me but would to Glen. He acted as a different person around me than when he was with Glen. I felt an element of racism was involved, but I saw the problem about four times larger than Glen did and was feeling frustrated because he didn't think it was such a big deal.

In a way the problem wasn't uncommon because a staff person who is black may respond differently around Glen than with me, which illustrates the **WWB/BBW Factor.** But when I pulled that trigger, Glen protested, "Is it really a racial issue or just a personality conflict we have here?"

"I think it's both," I challenged. "Race is clearly an issue because I'm black, Bill is white, and he doesn't seem committed to working on racial reconciliation, which makes the barriers harder to overcome."

We went back and forth on this point and I could feel my defenses beginning to build; I was girding for battle. It's hard to "prove" race is contributing to a conflict, but I was about to try. Then Glen's response changed the whole dynamic of the tug-of-war we had going.

"I think you have a point," he said.

All of a sudden he was no longer my adversary; I no longer had to convince him that racism was involved, or that there was a real problem. We could now get beyond the point blacks and whites never seem to get beyond and deal with the problem. So we talked for the next thirty minutes about how to help Bill relate to me more openly and how I could better respond to him, and it was very productive.

When a black person is willing to be honest and really express what he or she feels, the white person is often shocked at the intensity of feeling about racism. But the reality is that racial discrimination has scarred or touched every single black person to one degree or another; it's alive today, like a burn that has never completely healed, so the "skin" is very sensitive. The black person may not want to risk being honest, fearing another burn.

When tensions arise between a black person and a white, racism may be 70 percent of the problem, or 30 percent, or only 5 percent. But if a white person brushes off the 30 percent as unimportant ("It's only 30 percent"), that 30 percent becomes more like 100 percent to the black person. We have heard white people say, "Black people always talk about prejudice in their experience, but I've never seen anything like that." Of course they haven't experienced it; they're not black! The white person has to realize the difficulty in being totally objective.

Because I've had to deal with racism all my life (such as hotel employees assuming that a black person eating complementary popcorn is not a guest), it meant the world to me when my white brother empathized with my experience by saying, "You have a point." It was not important to me in this situation to determine exactly how much racism figured in, only that Glen acknowledged it was in the mix.

The principle for me was *sincerity*—to be able to come out of my black bag and express what I was really thinking and feeling in that situation. The principle for Glen was *sensitivity*—being able to get beyond his white bag, put himself in my shoes, and accept my experience and how I felt about it—relating empathetically, not merely agreeing with my evaluation.

That the issue of racism can be abused, however, was evident at Circle in Glen's relationship with Tyrone, who would not accept a word of correction about his sin of adultery, calling it "racist" for a white person to even try to address his situation (see chapter 5). Race is used at times as an excuse for inappropriate behavior or to avoid taking responsibility for sin. At that point, the input of another black Christian brother was invaluable in determining what was the core issue.

The whole purpose of the principles of sincerity and sensitivity is to build good relationships based on mutual need, needing the other person's wisdom and advice and not being too proud to say so. Which leads us to the next principle: interdependence.

■　□　■　□　■

Applying the Principle

How do you respond when you make a statement that suggests racial insensitivity? When faced with a racial issue such as Perot's blunder in calling his black listeners "you people," do you opt out by saying, "You're overreacting; it doesn't seem like a racial issue to me"? Instead, intentionally pursue cross-cultural understanding that will increase your ability to empathize.

Another way we can respond when we are challenged for being racially insensitive is to become defensive. Instead, listen and try to understanding the feelings your remarks generated.

Here are three other ways you can increase your sensitivity to other races:

1. Read literature about and by other racial groups. How much black, Asian or Hispanic literature have you read? (White literature is "required" reading for minorities, but whites do not have to touch anything ethnic.) Reading is one of the best ways to build sensitivity.

2. Choose to use your growing knowledge to strengthen your preaching, teaching, and outreach cross-culturally.

3. Do not dismiss unintentional racial insensitivity. Because our comment is unintended, we may think it is unimportant. But it has been heard, and it has an impact. To say it was "nothing" and unintended will be taken as rationalization and justification. Use the opportunity to learn. And if you have offended a brother, apologize for the action. Your humility can pull the two of you closer together.

CHAPTER 12
PRINCIPLE 5:
INTERDEPENDENCE

*Interdependence recognizes our differences but real-
izes that we each offer something that the other person needs, resulting in equality in the relationship.
(Key verses: 1 Corinthians 8:12–14)*

Director Spike Lee's movie *Malcolm X* hit the theaters in 1992,
spawning a revival of the Black Muslim leader's controversial and powerful rhetoric of the sixties (not to mention X
hats and tee shirts sprouting from coast to coast). In one scene in
the movie, a white coed approaches Malcolm X as he arrives on
the campus of Harvard University to give a speech. She assures
him that even though she's white, she's sympathetic to his cause.

"What can someone like me do to help?" she asks earnestly.

"Nothing," he answers coldly.

Part of Malcolm X's great appeal to the black community
was that he stood up for black self-determination. He challenged
blacks to stay in school, get off drugs, get off welfare, get a job, and
take responsibility for their families. But unlike Martin Luther
King, Jr., who walked hand in hand with whites as he challenged
the American conscience, Malcolm's message—at that time—was:
"We don't need whites to make it." Many blacks still believe that.
They desire independence and disdain whites as controllers.

In the realm of Christian fellowship and effective growth in the church, many still believe blacks and whites can go their independent ways and remain effective. In the mid-'80s, C. Peter Wagner of the Church Growth Institute at Fuller Theological Seminary in Pasadena, California, published two books discussing the factors that characterize growing churches.[1] One of the more controversial principles growing out of the Institute's research is the homogeneous factor—that is, people feel most comfortable with people like themselves; therefore, churches must take this human tendency into account if they wish to draw in new members.

Wagner is partially correct; the human tendency is to seek those like ourselves. "Birds of a feather do flock together," and when it comes to church, Christians generally sort themselves out by race, class, and culture. It's not only black and white, either. Most Georgia farmers would feel quite out of place in a highbrow Episcopal service; Cambodian refugees are forming their own congregations under the umbrella of a sponsoring American church; Spanish-speaking and Korean congregations feel the need to preserve their distinctiveness.

Separate but Equal?

Do we need each other? Those who believe in "homogeneous churches" and "niche marketing" or Afro-centrism and self-determination don't necessarily think so. Other than trying to avoid race riots, why should we go through all the grief necessary to achieve racial reconciliation? Why fight human nature? Why not just let "them" have their church, and "we" will have our church?

The real question, however, is do we solidify the human tendency to flock together with our own kind into a "principle" for the body of Christ? Do we accept a "separate but equal" mind-set for Christian fellowship and relationship?

Our answer is no. We cannot get along without each other if the body of Christ is to be salt and light to a world torn apart by racial strife. The principle of interdependence recognizes our differences but realizes that we each bring something to the table that the other person needs, resulting in equality (key verses: 2 Corinthians 8:12–14). Interdependence demonstrates the transforming nature of the gospel and declares that we do need each other if we are to live out the ministry of reconciliation. (Where would the gospel be today if Christ's disciples throughout the centuries had not accepted His challenge to be ambassadors of reconciliation across racial and cultural barriers?)

But don't take our word for it. Let's look at what Scripture has to say about interdependence among the people of God.

Assembling the Body Parts

The apostle Paul spelled out the variety of spiritual gifts given to the church when he wrote to the Corinthian believers (see 1 Corinthians 12:1–11). Different gifts, but the same Spirit. Diversity, but also unity.

Nothing new here. Most Christians recognize that it takes many different gifts within a local church to do all the work: evangelizing, discipling, preaching, teaching, praying, helping, encouraging, and so forth. Then Paul expands his teaching to emphasize the many parts that make up the body of Christ. Here he is not talking about spiritual gifts, however, but differences in race and class and culture: "Even as the body is one and yet has many members . . . by one Spirit we were all baptized into one body, whether Jews or Greeks, whether slaves or free" (12:12–13).

Well, of course, you say. *The worldwide church is made up of many different parts.* "Red and yellow, black and white, they are precious in His sight," goes the children's gospel song. But notice what Paul says next about those many parts (verses 14, 19–21, 24–26):

> For the body is not one member, but many. . . . If they were all one member, where would the body be? But now there are many members, but one body.
>
> And the eye cannot say to the hand, "I have no need of you"; or again the head to the feet, "I have no need of you." . . . But God has so composed the body, giving more abundant honor to that member which lacked, that there should be no division in the body, but that the members should have the same care for one another. And if one member suffers, all the members suffer with it; if one member is honored, all the members rejoice with it.

By naming the different parts of the body as the "eye," "foot," or "hand," Paul makes it apparent that each part has a significant function to play. But even more than that, one part of the body cannot say to another part, "I don't need you" (v. 21). Without each other, we are incomplete. The hand cannot work without the eye. The foot cannot work without the head.

If we apply this to the different parts of the body of Christ that exist within our own cities, the white suburban church cannot say to the black inner-city church, "We don't need you." Nor can the black church say to the white church, "We don't need you." Paul is saying in no uncertain terms: we need each other.

Before I moved to Chicago from Ripon, Wisconsin, it never occurred to me that I needed the inner-city church. What did that have to do with me? I was happy; I was fine. First Corinthians 12 was a nice spiritual thought, but I didn't really feel a need for my black brothers and sisters.

I had not yet opened my eyes to the spiritual reality that "those parts of the body that seem to be weaker are indispensable" (v. 22). But it is true. Many of my black brothers and sisters in the Lord have a depth of spiritual wisdom and character because they know oppression, poverty, and need. Without them, I would be spiritually impoverished, as if I were missing a hand or an eye or a foot.

A Mutual Example

Paul applies this teaching when he encourages the Gentile church to give generously to their fellow believers, the Jewish church, who were suffering in Jerusalem. (See 1 Corinthians 16:1–4.) He mentions the subject in both of his recorded letters to the Corinthian believers. The purpose for sharing their resources, Paul says, "is by way of equality—at this present time your abundance being a supply for their want, that their abundance also may become a supply for your want, that there may be equality" (2 Corinthians 8:13–14).

There is no hint of paternalism here. Paul is talking about *interdependence*, a sharing of resources in a way that is mutually beneficial. In this instance, he requested that the Corinthian believers share their financial resources with the persecuted Jerusalem church. Would the Jerusalem believers share financially with the Corinthian church at a later time? Possibly; but even if not, they had a lot to share in spiritual history, wisdom, maturity, and leadership. Everybody brings something of value to the relationship, creating a relationship of equals.

White Farmers, Black Neighbors

A few years ago during one cold week in January, twenty-five volunteers from the Kearney (Nebraska) Evangelical Free Church worked with us to restore Circle Urban Ministries' facility. At a farewell fellowship in Raleigh's house, a seventy-year-old worker called his time at CUM "the most significant week of my life." Within three months two more groups came from Nebraska, and nearly fifty people from the Kearney Church spent a week giving of themselves to Circle and Rock. Later that year Kearney Pastor John McNeal wrote us a letter saying, "In my sixteen years as pastor here, I have never witnessed a greater moving of the Holy Spirit among [those volunteers]."

We sure needed those white farmers from Nebraska, and their spiritual revival says they sure needed us. That is God's principle of interdependence and equality at work!

Two Are Better Than One

Whether in a church partnership or a personal friendship, blacks and whites can draw strength from each other's gifts and experiences. Consider the call for teamwork and unity in Ecclesiastes 4:9–12:

> Two are better than one, because they have a good return for their labor. For if either of them falls, the one will lift up his companion. But woe to the one who falls when there is not another to lift him up. Furthermore, if two lie down together they keep warm, but how can one be warm alone? And if one can overpower him who is alone, two can resist him. A cord of three strands is not quickly torn apart.

Over the past decade, we have experienced the reality of each one of these reasons why "two are better than one" in a cross-cultural ministry. Let's consider why this is so by looking at the passage phrase by phrase.

First, two are better than one "because they have a good return for their labor" (v. 9).

Ezra and Nehemiah experienced this principle of partnership in the rebuilding of Jerusalem after the exile in Babylon. Nehemiah gets a lot of the credit for actually rebuilding the walls. But years before he arrived in Jerusalem, Ezra had returned to minister to 40,000 exiled Israelites who had been allowed to return years earlier. When Ezra arrived, he was the preacher/prophet who called the sorrowing nation to repentance; he built the spiritual foundation. But Ezra's revival was not completed. The city was still in disgrace and rubble. God then moved Nehemiah to come as the rebuilder. When he arrived and called the people to the task, he found hearts spiritually prepared and a people who had a mind to work. They had been revived spiritually by Ezra, who did a job that Nehemiah couldn't do. Then Nehemiah did a job Ezra couldn't do.

Sometimes I (Glen) have felt that Ezra and Nehemiah's experience reflects our own. For years Circle Community Center (our original name) had been serving people in the Austin community, but we were not seeing people's lives changed from the inside out. Now I realize we had a "church-shaped vacuum" in our ministry. We needed a pastor to minister to the spiritual needs; our social outreach needed to be linked in partnership with a church.

When Raleigh Washington landed in Austin with an unabashed vision for evangelism, he brought to the ministry what we were lacking. Circle had plowed the ground in the community, so the church grew faster than if he had started from scratch in another area. The center's reputation in the neighborhood and the people who were already coming to the center provided fertile ground for planting a growing church. Circle Urban Ministries is stronger today because of Rock Church and vice versa. An interdependent relationship brings the partners a "good return for their work."

For such a ministry partnership to be effective, however, we needed a strong black leader in a key role. Even though the Circle staff was "integrated," we were basically a white-led, highly structured organization. But the black folks are more spontaneous, more relational. The reality is, there is value in both cultural approaches, and there can be excesses in either direction. But when those cultural qualities complement each other under the lordship of Jesus Christ, there is real power.

Second, two are better than one because "if either of them falls, the one will lift up his companion" (v. 10).

Interdependence helps empower us for cross-cultural ministry. We will discuss the principle of empowerment in chapter 14, but let's consider the role of interdependence in strengthening us for service.

Glen and I (Raleigh) can say the same thing. When Glen prepares to meet with some black community leaders, he often asks me to go with him. He has told me, "The fact that you are Circle's board president and my partner in ministry has empowered me in the black community." Similarly, with my humiliation of being drummed out of the Army only a few years behind me, Glen believed in me. When Glen introduced me to the Austin Community, to Circle's board and staff, and the Evangelical Free Church, Glen was my Barnabas. He said, "A church-based neighborhood outreach is what the original vision was all about," which empowered me in an unbelievable way among those board members and program people who were used to running the center without strong, aggressive evangelism. When he put Circle resources and reputation at my disposal to plant a church, he empowered me—a newcomer in the neighborhood.

In the white evangelical community, my partnership with Glen added immediate credibility so that people couldn't dismiss me as "just another jack-leg preacher" with a storefront of twenty people.

Interdependence has enabled us to "pick each other up" when cross-cultural ministry or relationships have left us wounded or under attack, and to support one another when times are tough. That kind of partnership offers mutual benefit to both.

Third, two are better than one because "if two lie down together they keep warm" (v. 11).

How can one keep warm alone? The city is often cold and harsh, but the warmth of relationship keeps us alive and functioning. Cross-cultural ministry can be discouraging, but interdependence lets us encourage each other.

One cold February morning I (Glen) escorted some visitors around our building complex, showing them Phases 1 and 2 of our renovation program. Then we walked through Phase 3, an 70,000 square foot building with a big auditorium, which still lies desolate, in ruin. "This building is an example of what happens in the inner city—a once-thriving institution abandoned to vandals, vagrants, and drug dealers," I explained. "It's a grim reminder of what happens when 'white flight' abandons neighborhoods and the people in them."

As I walked around that bleak, cold, concrete building, I could feel the warmth in my body going out through my feet, leaving me shivering. Suddenly, I had an image of how I felt when I was living and working in Austin without a close cross-cultural relationship: alone and cold, sapped of all warmth.

Working hand in hand, blacks and whites can help each other personally and economically. Maury Kapsner is a manufacturer in Minnesota who wants to encourage people in tangible ways. He approached us with the idea of creating jobs and developing a business in the inner city. His business expertise and willingness to invest resources should mean success, but with no "street" experience, Maury felt he would fail in the ghetto. He was right; the great cultural chasm between white suburbia and ethnic central city dashes many human efforts, especially business ventures. So this committed Christian called on help from the black community with its keen street sense.

Maury sent a young white employee, Steve, to Chicago to seek black help. Steve teamed with two black men, Showen and Bobby, to develop a business in the inner city.

Showen and Bobby had no business experience, though they had worked in semi-skilled manufacturing jobs. Now they aspired to be entrepeneurs, and they brought a zeal for hard work and an expertise in "inner city human relations." As Showen put it, "We know the 'hood." When Steve approached them, he saw their potential, despite their current unemployed status. One year later, Showen/Bobby and Steve/Maury teamed to begin a pallet recycling business, even though the country was in a deep recession. One year after that, the company had more than $200,000 in gross sales, secured a Fortune 500 company as a key customer, and turned a modest profit.

Neither the two black men nor the two white men could have succeeded alone. Each brought distinct skills to their formidable task. Because of the power of interdependence, they succeeded together. Their future is bright.

Fourth, two are better than one because while "one can overpower him who is alone, two can resist him" (v. 12).

Cross-cultural ministry will open you to much criticism. In Chicago politics, for instance, it's often white aldermen versus black aldermen, plantation politics versus black political independence. To be white and active in social outreach and community development in Austin makes Glen suspect. And I (Raleigh) have experienced resistance trying to convince white evangelical institutions to invest in the black community.

In these situations, each of us alone can feel like a fish out of water, but because our ministry is interdependent, we can come to the other's defense. We have seen our two ministries grow because of our interdependence.

Fifth, two are better for the combined value of the new identity: "A cord of three strands is not quickly torn apart" (v. 12).

The Ecclesiastes passage begins by saying, "Two are better than one" and ends with, "[and] a cord of three strands is not quickly broken," affirming the value and strength of intertwined (interdependent) relationships. This principle is true in any circumstance—a marriage, friends, coworkers, brothers and sisters in the church—but it is especially true in cross-cultural ministry.

Glen and I are both strong leaders, with gifts and skills. But as is always the case, we have corresponding weaknesses that leave gaping holes as well. This has cultural dynamics.

Like many task-oriented, European-work-ethic types, Glen has great intensity toward "getting the job done." He is a problem solver, and we surely have problems in the inner city. The heritage and drive that motivated Glen's dad to work fifteen hours a day and not stop until the job was "done right" is a skill we need in the inner city. Now I don't know what end of a screwdriver to use and didn't know how to go about rebuilding any of the abandoned buildings God has given us. But Glen does. Development of the programs and services of Circle Urban Ministries are right down his alley. As we look toward rebuilding our inner cities as African-Americans, we can't be threatened by high-powered whites who want to contribute.

But my (Raleigh's) strength is communication. I can articulate the vision and motivate others to join and invest themselves. I am vigorously pursued for speaking platforms that we then use to generate partners of the ministry. As preacher and pastor and evangelist, I have been allowed to help the church become a cornerstone of Circle Urban Ministries, and this has brought reality to our "faith and works" wholistic ministry. My relational skills have helped to deal with ruffled feathers, suspicions, and the assumptions that always arise in cross-cultural settings.

Together our interdependence produces more than the sum of our individual parts, and the ministry is built up. My style from my culture, military experience, and event-orientation brought exactly what was lacking in Glen, while Glen with his task orientation, analytical mind, and nuts-and-bolts understanding brought exactly what is lacking in me.

Rather than threaten, our strengths complement each other, making an effective inner-city ministry team. We are beyond doubt interdependent upon one another.

Interdependence acknowledges the equal value of the other person in building up the whole body of Christ. It is not tokenism; it must not foster paternalism. Tokenism or paternalism occurs when we try to accommodate people of another race but don't really feel or show that we need them. Accommodation is very different from a commitment to full racial reconciliation.

Today two of the most distinct and separate parts of the body of Christ are black Christians and white Christians. But active interdependence can demonstrate the power of Christ in our fractured cities.

Afro-centrism or Mutuality?

We would be remiss, however, if we failed to acknowledge the real fears and resistance many blacks have to "needing" white people.

One of the strengths of the black church, for instance, has been its function as a significant institution wholly owned and operated by blacks in a white-dominated society. As such, the black church has played a key role in the survival of black people in this country from slavery days to the present. The church was a haven of safety in a hostile world, bringing the black community together. It not only "kept the faith," but provided a social context for mutual support. Even before the development of black colleges, the church was also a leadership school. A person's status did not depend on his or her "job" but on his or her role in the church. Mr. Jones might be a janitor during the week, but on Sunday he was

Deacon Jones, respected and highly esteemed. Those opportunities remain a distinct part of black congregations today.

Well-meaning white people wonder why African-Americans don't flock to their churches when they open their doors. But for many, the feeling is, "Whites control every other aspect in society; at least the black church has been ours."

A positive development is the call for blacks to take responsibility for the problems plaguing the black community. William Raspberry, a black columnist for the *Washington Post*, challenges the attitude that African-Americans must wait for white America to get its act together before blacks can do anything about the crisis in their communities and families. "Suppose that we eventually win the fight [against racism] . . . What would [black leaders] urge we do next? . . . Well, why don't we pretend the racist dragon has been slain already—and take that next step right now?"[2]

For instance, one of the urgent needs in our inner cities is for positive role models for young black men. Spencer Hollis, a black educator, believes radical intervention is our only hope to save a generation at risk. His Project 2000 proposes educating black boys in "immersion schools" (or classrooms) with African-American men as teachers, role models, and mentors.[3] When the proposal was first introduced, a hue and cry arose from women's groups charging "sexism" and from the ACLU alleging violation of civil rights laws. Variations of the plan are being tried. But the point isn't separatism or segregation or sexism. It's practical intervention, giving young black boys a heavy dose of what's missing in their lives: father figures.

Afro-centrism is a big issue today. Black contributions to civilization, culture, history, scientific discoveries, and literature have largely been ignored for centuries; Afro-centrism attempts to rectify this and has become the new rallying flag for black pride and self-esteem. We understand and affirm the need for the black community to develop its cultural identity. Black campus groups have as much validity as the French Club or Asian Student Center. However, Afro-centrism has a negative side when it attempts to rewrite history or becomes a vehicle for black anger, black separatism, and black racism espoused by people such as Louis Farrakhan.

As a black Christian, I (Raleigh) agree that the black community should affirm the dignity of our culture and celebrate our contribution to society. We need to take responsibility for the needs of our families and our community. But as a black Christian working in the impoverished inner city, I will take the risk and say, "I need my white brother. I need Glen Kehrein. And I need him not only because he's Glen, but because he's white." God has called me to the ministry of racial reconciliation, and without Glen as my partner, I would not be complete. He complements me in the ministry.

The Not-So-Homogeneous Household of God

The "church growth" philosophy has endorsed a homogeneous model of the church, and indeed many churches are exploding in numbers because they bill themselves as a "Yuppie" church, or a baby-boomer church. What they're really saying is, "You'll be comfortable here, because we're all the same." But is the homogeneous model consistent with biblical teaching? The household of God, after all, draws from all races, all nations.

The American church today doesn't like to be uncomfortable. It's part of the seduction of the age to equate our comfort level with God's blessing, unlike fellow believers in China and the former Soviet Union. The more comfortable things are, the more we feel blessed. White and black churches in the same city are comfortable in their sameness, and because of that comfort level, there is no felt urgency to cross the barriers that divide us.

Even the church is tempted to measure success by worldly standards—"the bigger, the better"—not whether we are more prophetic, more reconciling, or reaching out to the poor. But is it biblical to develop a strategy of growth around class, race, economic status, age, or stage in life—just because that's our human tendency? On what factors do we base our unity in the church?

Earlier we mentioned Paul's declaration that on the cross Christ "destroyed the barrier, the dividing wall of hostility" between Jews and Gentiles, creating "one new man out of the two, thus making peace" (Ephesians 2:14–16). Remember, the apostle then added:

> Consequently, you are no longer foreigners and aliens, but fellow citizens with God's people and members of God's household . . . with Christ Jesus himself as the chief cornerstone. In him the whole building is joined together and rises to become a holy temple in the Lord. And in him you too are being built together

to become a dwelling in which God lives by his Spirit. (Ephesians 2:19-22 NIV)

Bringing like peoples together proves nothing about the power of the gospel, but when you bring dissimilar factions together in peace—Jews and Gentiles, rich and poor, blacks and whites—you prove God's power.

How do you achieve peace among natural factions? Christ is the answer. We serve one Lord, and we have one hope and faith—regardless of our color or where we came from—and Paul admonishes us to make every effort "to preserve the unity of the Spirit in the bond of peace" (Ephesians 4:3). That is the power of the gospel! That is what the church is all about—not simply accepting our human tendency to be separate and independent, but trusting the power of God to help us be reconciled and interdependent.

Today the church is not complete. Individual believers and churches that remain within narrow ethnic and racial constraints have not experienced how the love of Christ can break down those barriers. But we have lost a significant expression of the body of Christ.

The Goal of Interdependence

This should be the goal of the church: to reflect the unity of the body of Christ in the midst of its diversity; to experience how God has gifted different parts of the body in building up the whole to draw alienated, hurting people to the good news of Jesus Christ.

As I (Raleigh) often tell people, when Jesus came into the world, He didn't come to take sides. He came to take over! When we came into the Austin community, we were competing with the gangs, the slum landlords, the police, and the politicians. So whose side were we supposed to take? But God didn't call us to come in and take sides. He called us to come in and take over in the name of Jesus and reclaim this turf.

Our neighborhood, Austin, had lost 6,000 housing units to urban blight and the wrecking ball when we claimed and rehabbed the school into a ministry complex. Since then we have also rehabilitated twelve apartment buildings, and the work continues. But Raleigh and Glen haven't been swinging those hammers and paying the bills. We can't do it alone. We (Glen and Raleigh) need each other; we also need the many brothers and sisters and churches and organizations—black and white—who have also caught the vision of racial reconciliation and are living out the principle of interdependence.

What Wendell Learned

Wendell Snyder is a most unlikely interdependent partner. Isolated on a Nebraska farm, all he knew about black folks and the inner city came from the nightly news—and it was usually all bad. But somehow he joined a work crew from the Kearney Free Church going to Chicago to volunteer at Circle Urban Ministries. Now, he says, his life has forever changed. "I fell in love with the people and can never be the same. Getting a firsthand view of the need moved me out of my comfortable life." When he returned home he could no longer stomach the racial jokes, because now those jokes belittled his friends.

During these last seven years our lives have enriched each other in laughter and sorrow. Now our roots, black and white, are starting to entwine. Volunteer work crews are always times of joking and fun.

In 1992, when Paul Grant, our music minister and Circle Chaplain, died suddenly at age thirty-one in a canoe accident, Wendell and many other white friends joined us to cry as we buried our colleague.

A bridge has been built, and now literally hundreds of people, black and white, travel over that bridge to each other's community and enjoy the rich benefits of interdependency.

■ □ ■ □ ■

Applying the Principle

Like Wendell, who used his physical skills to help rehab a city center and wound up making friends, you may have distinct skills that can help you make contact and start a friendship with a person of another race or assist a ministry that reaches into another culture. What skills and gifts do you have to that might be useful to a cross-cultural ministry?

Often you will find new friends of another race by helping in a cross-cultural ministry. Therefore, volunteer some time in an inner-city or cross-cultural ministry. Go with the expectation that you will receive as much as you give.

Here are two other ways to prepare for and develop relationships of interdependence:

1. Meditate on 1 Corinthians 12:1–26, the Scripture passage about the interdependence of the different gifts and the different parts of the body of Christ. What insights do you see about how this applies to you and racial reconciliation?

2. If you have a cross-cultural relationship (whether a close friendship, an acquaintance, or coworker), specifically identify strengths that the other person brings to your relationship. Then thank that person for that gift to your relationship.

NOTES

1. Wagner's two classic books on church growth are *Leading Your Church to Growth* (1984) and *Your Church Can Grow* (1976/1985), both published by Regal.

2. William Raspberry, "The Myth That Is Crippling Black America," *Reader's Digest*, August 1990, 96–98.

3. Interview on "Sixty Minutes," CBS television, October 7, 1990.

CHAPTER 13

PRINCIPLE 6:
SACRIFICE

*Sacrifice is the willingness to relinquish
an established status or position to genuinely
adopt a lesser position in order to facilitate
a cross-cultural relationship.
(Key verses: Philippians 2:3–4)*

It's good to have you here! Have you gotten a copy of my latest book?" the senior pastor greeted us. We had been formally escorted into his nice outer office, and now Raleigh and I sneaked a glance at each other while the pastor turned for autographed copies. *Oh boy*, I thought, *we could be in big trouble here.*

By now it had become common for us to be invited to white churches to share the ministry: salt and pepper (Raleigh and Glen) with a little bit of soul (our music ensemble). But this was the biggest church yet, and quite "high brow," too. Could this church really "hang," we wondered?

The pastor continued in his effort to make us feel comfortable. "I haven't had a lot of contact with you people lately, but in the Second World War I made friends with a number of blacks. For that I was known as a 'nigger lover.'"

It's getting deeper, I groaned. But Raleigh, just as nice as could be, responded, "Is that right?"

After giving a brief introduction, the pastor went on to explain that there was "some degree of" (read *great*) concern regarding our "style." Some of the deacons wondered if the people "would respond" (read *be enraged*). "We don't clap too often in service" (read *never*), "and white folks cannot really sit much longer than an hour in a church service." (Later Raleigh whispered to me, "I knew that white boys couldn't jump, but I didn't know they couldn't sit!") Then the pastor concluded, "We begin at 6:30 sharp and end at 7:28." (Not 7:30—seven *twenty-eight!*)

Affirming our understanding of "the ways of white folks" (having been one myself once), Raleigh and I lobbied for another ten minutes with the guarantee that "no one would be bored." Reluctantly he agreed to the brief extension. It was obviously a sacrifice.

Sure enough—and much to the pastor's surprise—we handed him the mike at 7:28. (Not 7:30!) However, he had been smitten; he was caught up in the spiritual excitement that this touch of soul had stirred in his church. Time concerns gave away to "event orientation," and he led the service well into the next hour, seemingly without regard for the time. He was willing to risk the wrath of some church members for the message of the moment.

We later learned that our dear brother had gone out even further on a limb for us. There was no little concern in the congregation about our coming, and he had been willing to take a risk and make the sacrifice in inviting us. For some this might have seemed a small risk. But sacrifice begins by taking the small risks to step out of our comfort zone. Sacrifice then begins to build into reconciliation.

Staying Comfortable

In the last chapter we mentioned the human tendency to associate with people who are most like us. Let's be honest. It's natural; it's understandable. When people have similar backgrounds, think the way we do, use familiar words and phrases and buzz words, worship the same way, like the same music, and aren't too different in looks and dress, it creates a "comfort zone": "These are 'my people'"; "I fit in here, this is where I belong."

But one of Satan's primary tools to inhibit racial reconciliation and cross-cultural outreach is to make us very comfortable with homogeneity—in our neighborhoods, in our friendships and associations, even in our churches.

We understand "sacrifice" is necessary when we think of foreign missions. *Of course the culture is going to be different, and missionaries should make every effort to understand it, respect the way of life, and learn the language. Being a missionary requires special sacrifices,* we think, *leaving family and friends to live in a strange environment.*

But does that excuse the rest of us Christians who stay home? *Of course not,* we agree. *We should share the gospel and serve others in our own neighborhoods and cities.* However, being Christ's ambassadors at home may mean sacrifice—sacrifice that relinquishes an established status or position to adopt a lesser position in order to develop a cross-cultural friendship (key verses: Philippians 2:3–4). That was the situation in the first church, when Jewish believers in Christ began to declare the gospel to Gentiles and became brothers and sisters in Christ together. Yet despite their new relationship, Jews and Gentiles began to struggle with religious and cultural traditions, such as the rite of circumcision (the very cornerstone of Jewish identity!) and eating "unclean" foods. Tensions developed that could be eased only by sacrifice by the established culture.

Knocking down the dividing wall of hostility between the races, between "God's chosen people" and "others," between the oppressed (the Jews) and the oppressor (the Romans) required a great sacrifice: the death of Jesus on the cross. Thus we should not think the Christian life will be a bed of roses for us. Following Jesus means hard work and sacrifice; it means giving up some things we hold dear and that may feel comfortable. For the Jews, sacrifice meant accepting their differences with Gentiles and elevating Gentiles to the same position of respect as their fellow Jewish believers.

We're not going to fool you. To build cross-cultural relationships, to reach out in service and ministry across racial and cultural barriers, we must be prepared to sacrifice. It comes with the definition of Christian love: "This is My commandment, that you love one another, just as I have loved you. Greater love has no one than this, that one lay down his life for his friends" (John 15:12, 13).

The Cost of Sacrifice

Most Christians have at one time or another struggled over this verse in John 15. What does it mean to lay down my life for my friends? We hope we would have the courage and strength to risk death for someone else, the way Corrie Ten Boom did when she hid Jewish men, women, and children in her attic—later to suffer terribly in a Nazi prison camp for getting involved. Most of us won't be faced with such an extreme situation, God willing. But the Christian life is nonetheless one of "dying to self" in countless ways each day for the sake of building relationships in Christ.

If you are married or at college with a roommate, you know some sacrifice is needed; sometimes the "little things" are the hardest. "Sure," quipped one college woman, "I'm ready to die for you; just don't expect me to run upstairs and get your sweater."

One of the "little things" that falls in this category is humility. As the apostle Paul admonishes, "With humility of mind let each of you regard one another as more important than himself; do not merely look out for your own personal interests, but also for the interests of others" (Philippians 2:3–4). That instruction doesn't jibe with the Me Generation. That would take . . . sacrifice.

Paul was very aware of the "cost" involved in relating to others in this way, for he also writes:

> Have this attitude in yourselves which was also in Christ Jesus, who, although He existed in the form of God, did not regard equality with God a thing to be grasped, but emptied Himself, taking the form of a bond-servant, and being made in the likeness of men. And being found in appearance as a man, He humbled Himself by becoming obedient to the point of death, even death on a cross. (Philippians 2:5–8)

It wasn't easy for Jesus to give up His exalted position in heaven and take on the limitations of a human body born to a poor family, a blue-collar man, later to be betrayed by someone He called friend. His cruel execution came because of His threatening message of redemption and reconciliation. But the same attitude that made Jesus willing to die for us is the same attitude of sacrifice it takes to consider others better than ourselves and to look out for the interests of others.

Society's commonsense line is: "Look out for number one"; "Love your friends, but sue the pants off the guy who gives you a raw deal." Biblical commands—such as turn the other cheek, love your enemies and forgive your brother (again and again and again) —are difficult because they're so contrary to human nature. The solution is an attitude of humility, based on Christ's example.

Obviously, such an attitude should affect all our relationships in families, with other Christians, in the workplace. But let's look at what it means as one of the principles of racial reconciliation.

"I Did It My Way"

Frank Sinatra sings that "I did it my way." Sacrifice means not having to have it "my way." Although "my way" may be one way, it is not necessarily the best or only way. In a cross-cultural relationship, we need to be willing to sacrifice certain things that are easier or more meaningful to us in order to incorporate those things which are meaningful to others.

Often this starts with the little things. For instance, if you're black, you may be offered "health food" by your white friend. But you're a "soul food" person and like it greasy, crunchy, and warm. What do you do? When I (Raleigh) am invited to a white brother and sister's home, they're likely to fix health food for me—you know, carrot sticks, crackers, and cottage cheese. Now, I'm a fried chicken man. But I eat it and say politely, "This is lovely."

When they come to my house, they may have to gulp twice and eat greens and greasy fried chicken—at least one piece. It's part of sacrificing to build the relationship. Later, when the relationship has been established and we have sincerely opened our lives to each other, we will know exactly how to cook for each other because we will have shared with complete honesty who we are. Yes, sacrifice means being willing at times to do it his or her way.

Of course, those are only superficial sacrifices. Ultimately, the sacrifices necessary for racial reconciliation go a lot deeper. Maybe one of the biggest sacrifices is our time, because building cross-cultural relationships takes time. You can correct wrong assumptions only by spending time together. Take the time to learn who this brother or sister is, and listen to his or her thoughts and feelings. If there are misunderstandings or setbacks in the relationship, it takes time to work it through. In our pell-mell society, that kind of time means sacrifice.

For those who are called to cross-cultural ministry, it may mean, as it has for us, sacrificing many things involved in the typical middle-class lifestyle, such as having a house in the suburbs with a big backyard, two cars in the garage, the best schools for your kids—the whole American dream. But when God calls us, we need to be ready to lay down our whole life, even a preferred style of living.

This idea of sacrifice may mean ridicule. Whether black or white, you may face the scorn of other people who are adamantly separatist. There aren't many people in the black community who want to reach out to white folks. Separatism is as strong among some blacks as it is among some whites. The black members in our church receive a lot of flack from the more militant blacks in the neighborhood for what is considered "kissing up to whites." They are called "Oreos"—black on the outside but white on the inside. This kind of accusation can cause emotional confusion. Some of our black members ask themselves, *Am I being a traitor to my people by developing relationships with whites, after all we've suffered at the hands of white people? What if my own people reject me?*

This name-calling can extend to whites, who may be labeled "nigger lover"—or just written off as one of those liberal, pinko, social-agitator types. Even closer to home, there may be significant family members who don't understand what you're trying to do. They may caution, "If you keep having these people in your home, you have only yourself to blame if your teenager ends up marrying one of them."

"Nigger lover." "Oreo." That's part of the sacrifice whites and blacks must make to be reconcilers. And if you become intentional about racial reconciliation, you can expect this to occur, no question about it.

Two white women in our congregation have struggled with their extended families because of the call of God upon their lives for the ministry of racial reconciliation. The fathers of both are successful and wealthy businessmen who have given their children every advantage from the cradle through private colleges. Now, after all this has been invested in them, the parents watch as their children decide to become missionaries. Barb has gone, along with her husband, Brian, and children, to a remote village in Zaire, Africa. Amy, a single woman, has come to the inner city, here at Rock and Circle.

The reaction of both families to their choice and sacrifice has been the same, disbelief and struggle. *Why would they give up all this opportunity and choose this? Why "waste" all their education and potential?* But Barb, Brian, and Amy have committed their lives to reconciliation. Sacrifice just goes with the territory because the world will never view this call as prestigious.

Leaving the Comfort Zone

When Lonni and I (Glen) thought about joining Rock Church, it meant leaving Austin Community Fellowship, a local fellowship that had been unable to attract neighborhood blacks. We needed to jump into a ministry partnership with Rock Church 100 percent by becoming church members, yet being part of this heterogeneous church made us feel uncertain, especially Lonni.

"But I feel at home in the Fellowship!" Lonni said the first time we talked about joining Rock Church. Then she took a big breath. "But you're right. We should explore making the change. I know that one of Satan's weapons against racial reconciliation is to make us comfortable with homogeneity or to put us, as husband and wife, at odds with each other."

She was right—and you couldn't get any more homogeneous than Austin Fellowship. We were all white, about the same age, career professionals, all with young families, out of the same church tradition. Our worship was very meaningful: We sang a lot of praise songs, played guitars, and openly shared our lives and feelings. We had no up-front leaders, no hard-hitting sermons, just thoughtful teachings. Our life together was very supportive; changing would mean a big sacrifice.

We talked through all the implications. We were already living in a black neighborhood; we had African-American friends and co-workers; we were ministering to the needs of people in the community. Wasn't that enough? But the reality was, the black people in our neighborhood were not attracted to the Fellowship's structure or low-key style of worship. If we were going to be intentional about racial reconciliation among believers, we were going to have to sacrifice our biggest comfort zone—our church fellowship.

People said, "What's wrong with that? Why give up your source of support? You have a lot to contribute here. I don't understand what you're doing." It was true; Lonni, especially, enjoyed a significant music and worship leadership role in the Fellowship. But we felt God asking us to step out of our comfort zone into something that was going to stretch us.

It was hard for Lonni to let go of the community lifestyle and worship and small group support that made her feel so at home and secure. We felt like we were giving up so much. But God has given us back so much in return. Now she has become the Christian education director of Rock Church (education is her forte; she does it exceedingly well) and couldn't be happier. She is also involved in the music ministry as a "white sister with soul" and is fulfilled to a far greater degree than when she was, in her own words, "so comfortable."

But that doesn't mean it wasn't a sacrifice. Once in a while she'll take out her Austin Fellowship songbook with all the Scripture and praise songs from the Mennonite tradition and charismatic renewal, sit down at the piano, and sing all those songs. "I really miss these songs," she says wistfully (also meaning, everything these songs used to represent). On occasion she introduces one of these songs into the worship at Rock Church. That's part of the mix, bringing who you are and what's meaningful to you into the cross-cultural experience.

What About Worship?

Especially for those brought up in the church, "how we worship" is often a major issue when attempting to cross the cultural barriers. For some, the very format and style they are used to becomes synonymous with the "Christian way" to worship. To an Episcopalian, spontaneous freedom in worship is too free-wheeling and disrespectful. To a Pentecostal, a formal liturgy stifles the Holy Spirit. To the older generation, drums and a synthesizer in worship are downright decadent. To a black preacher, white folks must be asleep because they sure don't respond with any hearty amens.

But worship is at the very heart of racial reconciliation. Can we worship God together? Is it worth the sacrifice to give up some of our pet ways of doing things to make those of a different race or culture feel at home? Or will the world continue to discredit the gospel because Christians don't practice what they preach?

At Rock Church, we start every service with a devotional praise time that's a blend of our black and white church traditions. First, we sing two songs that are hand-clapping, foot-stomping, black gospel songs. Then we sing a couple hymns which have four or five verses of great theology, such as "May the Mind of Christ My Savior"—a beautiful hymn, but many African-Americans have never heard it in the "'hood." And it's not easy for white folks to slow down "Amazing Grace" to about one-fourth the speed they're used to singing it. But in time we forget which songs belong to whom, and soon they all belong to "us." As with Lonni, what starts as sacrifice turns into blessing.

Special programs require sensitivity. In the black community, mommies and daddies who are not regular church attenders show up at Christmas and Easter just to hear their kids give verbal recitations—a real evangelistic opportunity. In the white community, parents often prefer to see a pageant or play. In a cross-cultural situation, it's important to take what's significant in the different traditions into account, even though it means some sacrifice.

What About Leadership?

Developing church leadership also requires a great deal of sensitivity and sacrifice. In our situation, we are concerned about the balance in our church between black and white elders and deacons, and the makeup of our various committees. If we looked at each person only as an individual, we would probably end up having a disproportionate number of white leaders because the whites who attend Rock Church come intentionally, as we are located in a black, inner-city neighborhood. They are generally mature Christians, college educated, committed to reconciliation and cross-cultural ministry. Most of the African-American members come from the neighborhood, often with sketchy Christian experience and few college degrees.

But the message a racially disproportionate leadership would give is that whites are "superior" because leadership is "more natural" for them; we would be reinforcing the stereotype. Without applying *intentional* (remember that principle?) *sensitivity* (and that one) to this dynamic, choosing the "most qualified" leaders (often understood as "most educated") would reinforce the stereotype that whites are "superior" and leadership is "more natural" for them. But our task is to raise up indigenous leadership.

So as reconcilers we sometimes have to say to our white members, "Part of the sacrifice of racial reconciliation is giving up the high profile you might have in another church environment." But that's part of the call to reconciliation, to realize that part of the task is developing leaders and enabling other folks.

This is where we must recall Paul's admonition: "Let each of you regard one another as more important than himself; do not merely look out for your own personal interests, but also for the interests of others" (Philippians 2:3-4). That's empowerment (our next principle). That's investing in people even if it means having to take a secondary role because of the higher priority of reconciliation.

There are many ways we can practice the principle of sacrifice. (See "Applying the Principle" at the end of the chapter for several suggestions.) One specific way is to encourage black males to seek leadership positions, especially those men ages twenty to thirty. When a white person in our ministry understands that problem, a motivating goal becomes: "How can I be used of God to help build up and strengthen the black male?" The answer might be: "I can disciple a black male to replace me in my leadership role in the church or teach him whatever skills I have to share."

We have a paid staff at CUM, and I (Glen) have had to be very intentional getting blacks in key staff positions. I probably could have found some whites who were already trained at the level needed who would have required less time and energy on my part. But if we are going to strengthen the black community in an intentional way, then we have to have black leaders in these particular roles. We must be willing to sacrifice the seemingly easier route and invest in someone who needs to be trained because of the greater call of empowering the black community.

The principle of sacrifice requires a give and take on both sides. But according to God's kingdom strategy, when we lay down our lives to carry out the ministry of reconciliation, there is much more that we gain. Jesus has declared the rewards of a life of sacrifice:

> Truly I say to you, there is no one who has left house or brothers or sisters or mother or father or children or farms, for My sake and for the gospel's sake, but that he shall receive a hundred times as much now in the present age, houses and brothers and sisters and mothers and children and farms, along with persecutions; and in the world to come, eternal life. But many who are first, will be last; and the last, first. (Mark 10:29–31)

■   ☐   ■   ☐   ■

Applying the Principle

As noted in this chapter, sacrifice costs. Yet it is fundamental to building cross-cultural relationships and to achieving racial reconciliation. The following questions will help you evaluate your attitudes and experiences in making sacrifices in cross-cultural relationships and ministry.

1. Which of your "comfort zones" are (would be) most affected by a personal relationship with a person of another race?

2. If you have visited churches of other races or cultures, what did you like most? What made you most uncomfortable?

3. Have you ever been called (for whites) a "nigger lover" (or similar epithet) or (for blacks) an "Oreo"? How did it make you feel? How did it affect your behavior or relationships?

   How would you feel if you were called a "nigger lover" or an "Oreo"?

4. What small sacrifices do you think you would have to make to develop a relationship across racial lines? What are the big sacrifices you foresee to continue the relationship?

5. What areas of sacrifice would your church have to face to commit yourselves to cross-cultural relationships and ministry?

6. What steps would it take to disciple/mentor a young man or a young woman of a minority race to take over some position of responsibility you have right now? Are you willing to make that sacrifice? If not, what are the obstacles for you?

CHAPTER 14
PRINCIPLE 7:
EMPOWERMENT

*Empowerment is the use of repentance
and forgiveness to create complete freedom
in a cross-cultural relationship.
(Key verse: 2 Corithians 8:9)*

The University of Massachusetts, located in the quaint college town of Amherst, is typical of many schools around the nation. At first glance there are many accommodations to the students' racial diversity: integrated dormitories, an Afro-American studies department, a program to help minority students succeed academically, a Malcolm X Center, as well as Hillel House, an Everywomen's Center, and a Third World Cultural Center.

But two assaults on black students, accompanied by racist graffiti splashing the walls of campus buildings, reveal smoldering tensions within. Furthermore, many informal activities, such as parties and meal tables in the student dining halls, are seldom integrated. Most black students say they have not been the object of overt racial slurs, but they also admit to being treated differently in subtle ways. For instance, one white and two black coeds were returning to the dorm after a trip for groceries. A security guard stopped the trio and demanded that the black students produce identification—while ignoring the white student altogether.

Two female roommates—one black, one white—described for a news reporter race relations on campus. "We don't really talk about personal things," said the black eighteen-year-old. "I don't think they [whites] would understand."

"Everybody is so intent on being PC [politically correct]," said her white roommate. "You worry about saying the wrong word."[1]

From the raw passions of south central L.A. to the subtle tensions underlying politically correct universities, the reality is that "Truth, Justice, and the American Way" hasn't worked to bring down the barriers between the races. "Separate but equal" didn't work in the past; "equal rights" isn't working in the present. In the midst of this void crying for answers, the church has largely been silent.

The tragedy of this silence is that we have the answer in Christ, who broke down the "dividing wall of hostility" (Ephesians 2:14). As Christians, we can lamely follow behind society's efforts, or we can accept Christ's call to be ambassadors of reconciliation (2 Corinthians 5:19–20). After all, what message does the church have if it doesn't have the message of reconciliation to God and one another?

Repentance and forgiveness are central to the gospel of Jesus Christ. God doesn't demand repentance so He can make us grovel in our guilt; rather, our repentance clears the path to receive His forgiveness, which sets us free!

Two Empowering Agents

This truth is foundational in the ministry of reconciliation. *Repentance and forgiveness are the primary empowering agents* that set us free—Gentiles and Jews, whites and blacks, Hispanic and Asians—to relate to each other in confidence and without reservation. This is true personally and corporately. An attitude of repentance empowers the other person—or group, or race—to lay aside anger and blame, and it opens the path to forgiveness. Meanwhile, the act of forgiveness empowers the other person (or group or race) to relate and minister freely rather than under a load of defensiveness or guilt. Principle 7, empowerment, begins with repentance and forgiveness to create complete freedom in a cross-cultural relationship and to enable the other person to function with wholeness (key verse: 2 Corinthians 8:9).

But for all its simplicity, the power of repentance and for-giveness remains tangled in a web of confusion over personal re-sponsibility and corporate guilt, blindness to the presence of "institutional" racism (i.e., ingrained in the system), and our hu-man disposition to point the finger of blame at someone else.

True reconciliation only works when both repentance and forgiveness are mutually exchanged. But the astounding thing about the gospel is that a true reconciler must be ready to make the first move—even if there is inadequate reciprocation.

To Forgive Cruelty

Let's put ourselves at the foot of the cross for a few moments. A cruel injustice is being hammered out as Roman spikes are driv-en into the hands and feet of Jesus of Nazareth. Grieving family and friends and followers are in shock. *This can't be happening!* But it is happening. The healer and teacher, the one who had the "words of eternal life," is dying in agony. And then we hear Him say through parched lips, "Father, forgive them, for they do not know what they are doing" (Luke 23:34).

What? Forgive those who screamed, "Crucify Him"? Forgive those Roman soldiers with their barbaric executions? These were the ones who bore specific responsibility for the death of Jesus. Yet the Son of God could forgive such cruelty and injustice. Days later, a resurrected Jesus would empower a friend by forgiving him. Jesus returned to the disciple who in a moment of desperate self-preservation and denial ("I don't even know this Jesus!") chose to stand in the camp of the oppressors. Jesus told Peter, "Feed My sheep," and the disciple went forward, freed and empowered for ministry. Peter accepted Jesus' act of forgiveness.

Usually it's difficult to accept forgiveness, because then we have to own the guilt. But as we repent of our sins and accept His forgiveness, instead of being paralyzed with guilt and defensiveness, we discover we are empowered to have a totally new relationship with God! The principle of empowerment similarly takes the same miracle of repentance and forgiveness to draw together believers who are on opposite sides of the racial and cultural barrier.

Repentance on Behalf of Others

Most of us understand the need for repentance for sins we personally commit against another (though such repentance may be difficult, even for Christians). But many of us struggle with the concept of taking responsibility for the sins of the group of which we are a part—whether that is our family, our nation, our race, or our ethnic group—especially when we feel personally innocent. But we are responsible for such sins, the Bible teaches.

The prophet Daniel, for instance, remained faithful and true to the God of Abraham even in exile in Babylon; yet he confessed sins on behalf of the Hebrew nation. "We have sinned, we have been wicked," Daniel prayed. "Let now Thine anger and Thy wrath turn away from Thy city Jerusalem, Thy holy mountain; for because of our sins and the iniquities of our fathers, Jerusalem and Thy people have become a reproach to all those around us" (Daniel 9:15–16).

Similarly, the prophet Ezra identified with the guilty as he wept and threw himself on the ground, confessing: "O my God, I am ashamed and embarrassed to lift up my face to Thee, my God, for our iniquities have risen above our heads, and our guilt has grown even to the heavens. Since the days of our fathers to this day we have been in great guilt" (Ezra 9:6–7).

Nehemiah did the same, "confessing the sins of the sons of Israel which we have sinned against Thee; I and my father's house have sinned. We have acted very corruptly against Thee and have not kept the commandments . . ." (Nehemiah 1:6–7). Even Moses, pleading with the Lord to forgive the wickedness of the people for making an idol of a golden calf, took responsibility (Exodus 32:31–32).

Notice that none of these leaders was personally guilty of the sin for which he was repenting. Yet each took responsibility for the corporate sin, accepting it as his own. Reconciliation grew out of their godly prayers of repentance. Similarly you and I must accept responsibility for the sins of our group, and then take whatever action is necessary to bring about reconciliation.

After the King Verdict

After the Los Angeles policemen who were videotaped beating Rodney King were acquitted, several of the white members in our church approached me (Raleigh) and other blacks in the congregation and said, "When I heard that decision I was ashamed that I am white." They saw the verdict as evil, and as part of the white race they grieved the jury's decision. They accepted responsibility for the decision, even though they did not participate directly in it. Similarly, when I saw the wanton violence and destruction that followed the verdict—and even reached into our community—I said, "I repent of the rebellion of my people."

There was a spectrum of possible responses to the verdict acquitting the four police officers. Where the emphasis was placed said a lot about a person's attitudes and value system. On one end, people spent all their energy justifying what happened. Some whites said, "Rodney King was a criminal, after all," and, "The jury probably had information we don't have; we have to accept that justice was done." Sister Souljah, a black rap artist, jumped into the headlines after the riots by telling the *Washington Post*, "If black people kill black people every day, why not take a week and kill white people?"

The president of the United States seemed genuinely perplexed by what happened after the Rodney King verdict. President Bush didn't know how to label the obvious injustice of the jury verdict, but he had no trouble recognizing rebellion: "Rioting and looting will not be tolerated!" In the same way, black spokespersons were reluctant to label the obvious rebellion, but they had no trouble calling the verdict racist.

On the other end of the spectrum, people expressed grief and sorrow. Joseph Stowell, president of Moody Bible Institute, declared, "It's not just Rodney King. It grieves me that the justice system in America has for so many years been unfair to blacks." His statement was heartening.

The whites in our church abhorred the rioting and looting of the blacks as much as myself or President Bush. But the whole shocking situation helped them get in touch with the sin of racism, and when they spoke up, they dealt with that and that alone: "When I heard that decision I was ashamed that I am white." For them to repent of the racism that so permeates our society brought healing to the black members in our church in ways that words cannot express. The white members helped create a climate that made it possible for the blacks to respond by acknowledging their own sins. "I, too, am ashamed that I am black," many said as they watched the brutal rioting that followed.

Racial animosity between the black inner city and the white suburbs runs deep in Chicago. A Rodney King incident is just waiting for the spark. Recently more than 650 blacks and whites from our church and neighboring suburbs came to Rock Church for a "solemn assembly," a sacred time of repentance. Clear instructions were mandated: "This is not a time to tell the other person what he or she needs to deal with; this is a time for you to search your soul and repent, both corporately and individually." It was a holy time, lasting nearly five hours. Racial sins, both corporate and deeply personal, were confessed by person after person, black and white alike. It was almost impossible to believe. God broke through our alienation and empowered us to repent of our sins and forgive one another.

I don't think that response would have ever been expressed had those white brothers and sisters not initiated the repentance. It freed the black people to get in touch with the sin that is committed on the black side of the ledger, *because they no longer had to fight to make the whites understand what is wrong and how they feel.*

But we have to understand the corporate disease in order to understand the individual role in bringing about healing. In that regard, let's look at the disease of racism.

Institutional Racism

Carol, a member of Rock Church, told me (Raleigh) that her son was in prison with a life sentence. He had argued with another black man, a fight ensued, and her son killed the other man. It was clearly not premeditated, but he was still given a life sentence. For years this mother was angry and bitter; my own response on hearing the story was that the sentence was a clear case of institutional racism. But after becoming a Christian, Carol said, God helped her give up her bitterness and anger.

Carol later received a letter from a Wisconsin chapter of the American Civil Liberties Union inviting her to meet with several people. They were studying what they felt was a prejudicial application of the justice system. In many other cases similar to her son's, they said, the perpetrator was sentenced to only a few years —not twenty—and was given a chance for parole, which was appropriate in this type of case.

Carol accepted their invitation and traveled to Wisconsin to share how Christ has taken away her bitterness. But it meant something to her that these people recognized that an injustice had been done.

Racism takes many different forms, but probably the most prevalent is "institutional" racism that affects agencies and organizations. Institutional racism occurs in the Christian church when believers operate out of ignorance, tradition, and the status quo, accepting the disparity between the races without questioning why. Institutional racism is often motivated by fear. Fear of the unknown, fear of people different from ourselves, fear of being inconvenienced, fear of losing our budget if we support this black program, fear that the "quality of life" is going to go downhill— all kinds of fears motivate whites to respond in a self-preserving way.

"Don't Blame Me"

Most every African-American has heard a white person say, "Don't blame me for what my ancestors did. I didn't have anything to do with that." Or, "My grandparents weren't even in this country when there was slavery." This is part of the struggle in identifying what responsibility we each have for the state of race relations, not only in the nation, but in the church today.

When a conscientious white Christian says, "I had nothing to do with slavery, but I agree, it was an evil, terrible thing," do you know what I (Raleigh) remember from that statement? *'I had nothing to do with it.'* And my guard goes up. That person is separating himself from any responsibility, and even though he may not say it, what he means is, "Don't put the blame in my lap." That kind of statement colors my perception of everything else he may say. I know he had nothing to do with slavery back then, but emotionally I transfer the *"I'm* not responsible" sentiment to the here and now, and my trust level is going to be guarded.

But if I'm hurting, and you take a repentant stance as a white person, that opens the door for me to forgive you and creates the opportunity for us to have the kind of relationship that will build trust and help us to be reconciled in a deep way.

Black Racism

Some say that "black racism" is a contradiction in terms. A common definition of racism in the black community is based on who has power. To be racist one must be able to dominate another culture and exercise oppression. All white people participate to a greater or lesser degree in the benefits of that racist system; all blacks to a greater or lesser degree are oppressed by it. Therefore, according to this definition, white society (the dominant culture) is racist, but the black community is not, nor could be, racist. When translated to the individual level this means that the actions of the police who beat Rodney King were racist, but the actions of the mob against the white truck driver were not.

As Christians we must categorically reject this conclusion. It denies all levels of personal responsibility. Racism is first and foremost a condition of the heart. This condition, when perpetuated by the dominant culture, leads to oppression and corporate sin. But, like all sin, racism is first personal, and every one of us— African-American, Euro-American, Hispanic, Asian, Native American—must deal personally with this sin in our own lives. And just as repentance and forgiveness are God's way of dealing with any sin, repentance and forgiveness are God's way of dealing with racism. As we are able to appropriate forgiveness and repentance, the chains begin to fall off and we are empowered to relate to each other in a way that leads to racial reconciliation.

Whites must admit reponsibility; but blacks also must admit wrongful attitudes. I (Glen) have found that when I began to take responsibility for racial injustice, many blacks were willing to increase my guilt. Finding a white person willing to admit to racism and "see it like it is" did not always generate reconciliation—it generated more blame. I became a lightning rod for suppressed rage. Thus African-Americans must stand ready to admit to their damage. Blacks feel justified to withhold trust because they have been hurt so many times. Bitterness and anger seethe under the surface for many blacks, but "dumping" on whites who want to change is unfair. Black Christians must have an attitude of forgiveness and stand ready to trust.

No Need to Grovel

Until I met Raleigh, my attempts at cross-cultural relationships were frustrating and discouraging because I could never grovel enough to redeem the past sins of the white race. When Raleigh extended forgiveness and trust, "forgetting what lies behind," we then together began to "press on toward the goal for the prize of the upward call of God in Christ Jesus" (Philippians 3:14).

Christians must take seriously the Scripture truth "If one member [of the body of Christ] suffers, all the members suffer with it" (1 Corinthians 12:26). If I, Raleigh Washington, black pastor and fellow believer, am part of the body of Christ, even if I'm just a little toe, and if I am hurting, then my pain hurts the rest of the body. If the reason I am hurting is because of injustice, then the rest of the body must take responsibility for responding in a way that not only brings healing to me but to the whole body.

Unfortunately, when whites try to interact with blacks, they may be either too defensive or too apologetic. After the Rodney King incident, a white jazz singer said, "If a black guy came up and punched me in the face, I would understand. I wouldn't necessarily dig it, but I would understand because of all that has gone down." Understanding is important, but when whites are willing to be punching bags, they are not free in the relationship.

But when trying to establish cross-cultural relationships, we have to walk through these waters of understanding the pain of injustice and owning our responsibility for bringing healing.

To Repent and to Forgive

The Greek root for forgiveness means "to release from payment of a debt." For me (Glen) to repent of racism and ask for forgiveness of my black brothers and sisters means that I assume my fair share of the responsibility for a debt. And, as a white person, I need to repent whether or not my black brother approaches me with an attitude of forgiveness.

Forgiveness is the other side of repentance. As a black person, I (Raleigh) have to come to the table forgiving my white brothers and sisters for the sins white people have committed against blacks, even though they might not think they are personally guilty of discrimination or injustice. I need to do that for myself whether or not they repent. "Father, forgive them, for they don't know what they're doing." Once I let go of my resentment through an attitude of forgiveness, I empower them to minister freely alongside of me without being defensive or apologetic. If I forgive them, it empowers them with the freedom to challenge me when necessary about any facet of our relationship.

This transaction isn't always said in words. Glen has never said to me, "Brother, I repent of what white America has done to African-Americans." But his position on the issues has said it;

even more important, his actions and the priorities in his life have said it. Nor have I said to Glen, "I forgive you, brother"—not in so many words. But our attitudes and actions toward each other have communicated repentance and forgiveness in an unmistakable way.

In every cross-cultural relationship that leads to racial reconciliation, something happens, an experience of repentance and forgiveness, that empowers the relationship to get beyond the barriers of guilt and blame, suspicion and mistrust, fear and anger.

It's My Responsibility

In _The Content of Your Character_, Shelby Steel challenges both blacks and whites when he says the black community is doing too much blaming, and the white community is doing too much denying. We've got to stop pointing fingers and saying, "It's not my responsibility." Everybody has to take responsibility and work from his own end of the problem in order to bring about reconciliation.

Repentance and forgiveness need to affect our lives on the personal level. We demonstrate our repentance by how we act today. "Yes, I do have responsibility for this state of affairs, and yes, I can do something about it." Acknowledging the wrongs of the past and the present is only the first step; the next step is what we are willing to do to correct injustice and bring healing. As the prophet Micah wrote, "What does the Lord require of you but to do justice, to love kindness, and to walk humbly with your God?" (Micah 6:8).

This is different than the popular form of liberal guilt that publicly denounces the wrongs of the past (where we don't feel too much personal responsibility), followed by the typical liberal response, "Congress should do something about it." They say, "Sure, let's develop a quota system (if it affects somebody else's job) and vote for another entitlement program (but don't ask me to make any sacrifice in my personal lifestyle)."

But the Christian must deal with racial sin and separation the same way he does other interpersonal conflict. When one realizes, "Hey, God is convicting me that this is not right," the biblical response is to go to the other person—not to straighten that person out, but to take responsibility for our own part in the damage. Of course, when you come to me and confess like that, you act as a mirror that helps me see the wrong I have had in the situation. When you lay down your end of the rope in this tug of war, I either have to lay it down, too, or I fall on my fanny! That's the difference between a "guilt trip" or "blame slinging" and a true Christian response of reconciliation.

■ □ ■ □ ■

Applying the Principle

As we have noted, empowering someone else to draw closer to you and achieve reconciliation requires repentance and forgiveness. Depending on our individual experiences, repentance and forgiveness may be difficult. Here are four questions (and suggested responses) to help you prepare for repentance and forgiveness.

1. Do you find it difficult to enter into expressions of repentance (or forgiveness) for the sin of racism? Identify the thoughts, feelings, and struggles you have.

2. Have you been wounded in a cross-cultural interaction(s)? If the relationship is still active, what steps can you take toward reconciliation?

3. If you are black, what changes in your attitude or behavior toward whites would empower them to work side by side with you toward racial reconciliation?

4. If you are white, what attitudes and behaviors do you need to take responsibility for to help bring down the walls of hostility between the races?

Two barriers to repenting and/or seeking forgiveness are feeling heavy guilt or wanting to blame others for your situation. Ask God to show you whether you might be on a "guilt trip" or "blame slinging." Then pray, asking Him to give you the courage to walk in the freedom of repentance and forgiveness in your cross-cultural relationships.

NOTE

1. Karen M. Thomas, "Better Race Relations Challenge University of Massachusetts," *Chicago Tribune*, December 6, 1992, sec. 1:23.

—■□■—

CHAPTER 15

PRINCIPLE 8:
CALL

*We are all called to be involved in the
ministry of reconciliation, but some are gifted
with a special call to be racial reconcilers.
(Key verses: 2 Corinthians 5:17–21)*

A "call" is God's way of impressing upon us what He wants from us. He called Moses from a burning bush (Exodus 3), Elijah out of a gentle breeze (1 Kings 19), and Saul from a flash of light on the Damascus road (Acts 9).

Sometimes His call is dramatic, typically it is not. But there is a definite sensing that God wants the individual involved in a specific task. By His call God instills a desire that cannot be ignored. The prophet Jeremiah endured torture, beatings, and death threats because he had been called to preach repentance to Israel. He expressed it as a fire in his bones (Jeremiah 20). The apostle Paul, likewise, was beaten, stoned, imprisoned, and shipwrecked (2 Corinthians 12).

Have we lost that kind of a call in comparison to the allure of the comfortable lifestyle our world offers us?

The Last Principle or the First?

The reader may be wondering why "being called" is the last principle of racial reconciliation. Doesn't the call come first?

Maybe the best way to understand the relationship of "call" to racial reconciliation is to look at the Christian's call to evangelism. All believers have been given a mandate by Jesus to be His witnesses of the gospel, but some have a special gift as evangelists. We're all called to evangelize but we're not all gifted as Billy Graham, the evangelist, or others who make evangelism their primary ministry. Some evangelists use their gift in their home locales, while others are called to "relocate" to areas around the world where a Christian witness is desperately needed.

Likewise, every Christian has the responsibility to be a reconciler. "Therefore, if any man is in Christ, he is a new creature; the old things passed away; behold, new things have come. Now all these things are from God, who reconciled us to himself through Christ, and gave us the ministry of reconciliation" (2 Corinthians 5:17–18). As Christians we have a biblical mandate to be ambassadors of reconciliation in the name of Christ wherever we encounter brokenness. The purpose of this book has been to focus especially on an area of brokenness that has been grossly neglected by Christians: racial separation and alienation, even within the body of Christ. Thus, throughout these first seven principles we have been lifting up the call for all Christians to reach across the cultural and racial barriers in Christian love, being obedient to the spiritual mandate laid out in 2 Corinthians 5:17–21.

However, the call extends further. Beyond the general call to be ambassadors of reconciliation, some of us will receive God's specific call to make racial reconciliation a primary ministry focus. The call to reconcile can be a specific call to reconcile dysfunctional families as counselors; other nationalities as missionaries; disputes between believers as Christian arbitrators; or alienated races as racial reconcilers.

God's call upon the leaders of Rock Church and Circle Urban Ministries is to be racial reconcilers. Reconciliation is one of our stated goals; that is why we are so intentional about it. And this is the goal of many groups across the country.[1]

We believe this is also a time in history when *God is calling many more believers and churches to embrace racial reconciliation as one of their primary goals.* This needs to happen—churches (both members and leaders) breaking new ground so that others can follow in our footsteps. If we do this, we become pioneer missionaries to those alienated in American society.

The concept of call is so important that we began Part 2, a discussion of the eight principles of racial reconciliation, with a general call to be Christ's "ambassadors of reconciliation" (see chapter 7). Now we are defining Principle 8 itself, call, to include the call to a specialized ministry of racial reconciliation. But just as with the analogy to evangelism, the two aspects of "calling" cannot be divorced from one another. Let's look at how they are intertwined.

All Are Called

The spiritual mandate to be a reconciler should be consistent with our commitment to Christ. Being a reconciler is part and parcel of who we are as a new creation, the fruit of our Christianity. We should be reconcilers in all situations, whether that's broken families or broken friendships or broken relationships in the church. That's who Christ was; He came to heal the broken, and we too must be concerned for the brokenness of the world.

But in the midst of this broader call, we must be open to hear what the Lord is saying to each of us about reconciliation in our own situations. The silence of the American church on the issue of racial alienation and injustice is an incredible inconsistency with our faith. The church has a responsibility to recognize and repent of overt attitudes of prejudice and acts of discrimination, as well as our sins of omission in the area of racial sensitivity.

Therefore, we believe that just as God calls every Christian to be a witness (if not an evangelist), He also calls every believer to seek to develop relationships with people of a different race. Better educational opportunities, open housing laws, and affirmative action programs have meant that most whites in urban and suburban areas meet or could get to know a black or Hispanic or Asian person at work, in the neighborhood, through school activities, or in some other way if they chose to. Most minorities have the same opportunity.

The first relationship may not work out because you aren't otherwise compatible, but don't let that contribute to racial stereotypes. Keep trying; keep reaching across the cultural barriers.

At some point a relationship will click, and the rewards will be great.

Racial reconciliation is not just a need for the inner city. A reconciler who is serious about his or her Christianity will recognize that even an integrated middle-class suburb faces racial alienation within its borders.

It's tempting for whites to think, especially in middle-class situations, that alienation between people is really a class issue between the middle and lower class. To put it another way, as blacks become integrated into middle-class work and neighborhood situations, the race issue just "sort of goes away." In Oak Park and Evanston, two integrated Chicago suburbs, some believe the presence of ethnic minorities means racism is not a key issue. Certainly the disparity is not as obvious (at least to whites) when people earn comparable wages. Yet racism is ever present, no matter the income or level of success. Consider Charles Barkley, pro-basketball all-star who pulls down a seven-figure income each year. Barkley was riding in the first class section of a train when a fellow passenger confronted him with, "You are sitting in the first class section." The other passenger obviously was implying that a black man did not belong there.

Here was one more white person, seeing only a black face, reminding Barkley that it didn't matter if he was famous, earned millions a year, or how high he climbed—he was still just a black man.

We need to be honest and admit that middle-class churches are unreconciled across racial lines, lower-class churches are unreconciled across racial lines, and both are unreconciled across class and cultural lines. These churches are made up of individual believers like you and me.

The observable characteristic of love between Christians, particularly love across racial lines (according to Colossians 3:11–13), is one way we authenticate God's power in our lives. When politics, humanism, government, and the best efforts of secular society are failing miserably, what proves the power of God more than reconciliation between the races?

If all Christians recognized that goal as a call from God, and acted accordingly, it would do dramatic things in our churches across the country—especially if we added to that general mandate the special call God has for some individuals and churches to make racial reconciliation a primary goal of their ministry.

Some Are Called

A call to the pastoral ministry is verified by the gift of preacher/ teacher. A call to be a medical missionary is verified, not only by medical training and skill, but by the gift of service. In the same way, a special call to racial reconciliation is verified by certain spiritual gifts and personal qualities, as well as grace from the Holy Spirit.

To be a racial reconciler (in the sense of a special call), one probably will have gifts similar to those of the missionary who is called to go overseas. Missionaries often must interact with a different race, as well as a different culture, and to do that well they must have the requisite spiritual qualities and gifts that empower them in that setting. In truth, a racial reconciler is a missionary across racial and cultural lines, needing those same gifts and qualities.

Does this person have experience relating cross-culturally? Does this person have sensitivity to people different from himself or herself, and the ability to communicate that sensitivity? Is this person patient and long-suffering, having the stamina to hang in there in spite of misunderstandings and conflict? Those who answer yes to these questions have qualities that suggest skills in being a reconciler.

Those gifted may have other qualities, too. They believe that people of lesser means have something to offer, and they are willing to be vulnerable and honest across racial lines. They stand firm on the essentials of the faith but are willing to compromise on areas of cultural or personal preferences or ways of doing things. Typically they have good conflict resolution skills and are committed to discovering the way of peace and reconciliation.

A person will not be perfect in all these areas, of course, and there will be setbacks in relationships. It's only by the grace of God, knowing that we, Glen and Raleigh, have a unique call to the ministry of reconciliation, that we have been able to endure the struggles and to hang in there, in spite of our weaknesses.

Those who sense a particular call to the ministry of reconciliation should seek the heart of God to determine whether this means "blooming where you are planted" (in your own neighborhood or city), or whether the Lord is specifically calling you to follow Him to a new location. For some, a call to the ministry of

reconciliation will mean relocation, even if that means only moving to the inner city thirty minutes away, because God is calling
them specifically to reach out to the poor. We need more men and
women of faith to answer this call, to breach the tremendous
chasm existing between most of the church and the oppressed in
our own cities.

In February of 1991, missionaries invited us speak in Zaire,
Africa. This was a great privilege, but we were unsure whether our
message of racial reconciliation, forged in the urban crucible,
would apply in the remote jungles of Zaire. We found out that not
only were our principles of reconciliation applicable in Zaire, but
our hearts knit with those missionaries as we openly shared together and struggled with the issues created from the colonial
past. As the missionaries ministered in Zaire, we ministered in
Chicago. We shared the same commitment of being sold out to our
community 100 percent, living among the people, adjusting to a
different culture, being concerned for meeting both the spiritual
needs and the practical needs of the poor and the oppressed. Thus,
all the ingredients that went into making the Zaire missionaries
effective in their setting were the same gifts and commitments we
needed to minister in the Austin community. Zaire, Africa, is a
mission field. Austin, Chicago, is a mission field.

Called to Be Pioneers

Among those God is calling to make racial reconciliation a
primary emphasis of their ministry, we believe, He places certain
people in pioneering efforts to apply those principles of racial reconciliation in service to the poor, the oppressed, and the needy—
the so-called ghettos, where alienation and separation are having
the most devastating effect.

Plowing virgin soil is hard work. Beginning a cross-cultural
ministry is like trying to build on the frontier. You're trying to
build a cabin with raw materials, clearing stumps, hoping the
mule won't drop dead, and discovering holes in your boots, all the
while hoping not to get an arrow in the back. If you're out there
trailblazing, you've got to have a pioneering, stick-to-it spirit—or
you're not going to make it.

But once the ground has been plowed and the cabin is up, it's
going to be easier for folks who follow you. Then more will come,
and they won't all be pioneers, but they'll be "farmers" and "set-

tlers" and "storekeepers" and "road builders." Youth workers, carpenters, and doctors will follow, all with the inner-city call and all wielding the gifts that are necessary to bring about racial reconciliation in our country.

We see this in our own church and ministry. We were among the pioneers, forging a black-white partnership both in our personal relationship and in our ministries. Then others came and helped build Rock Church and Circle Urban Ministries with all its tentacles reaching out into the Austin community. Like many ministries, we have gone through different stages of development; most of the people who were around in the beginning were the pioneer types, adventurers willing to set off into the unknown. But then others came with gifts needed for the long haul. Most of those pioneers have been called on to other things, but we still feel called to be on the forefront, plowing new land where other people have yet to go.

Let's not forget that not all pioneering efforts "succeed." Circle Church was a pioneering effort that ended up with a lot of arrows in the back of the pioneers and the cabin burned down. But that doesn't mean it was wasted effort. The lessons learned at Circle Church have had a great deal of impact on our next pioneering effort.[2]

For one thing, I (Glen) learned that my *commitment to racial reconciliation is not connected to a person, but is connected to a calling.* My commitment preceded my relationship with the black associate pastor at Circle and others with whom I tried to establish a meaningful personal relationship across racial lines. Right now that commitment finds its deepest expression in my relationship with Raleigh Washington. I believe that my understanding has grown and living out that reconciliation is truly happening. But if Raleigh should die tomorrow, that should not affect my call to reconciliation.

The Role of Relationships

In order to be a reconciler, you need to be able to live out that call in your relationships and demonstrate it in your lifestyle. So because I'm called to reconciliation, and racial reconciliation in particular, I have a number of cross-cultural relationships, some of which are deep, while others find their water mark at various levels. Our personalities might not click, so we might not be fast friends, but even in those relationships that may come and go, I should be living out the same principles of reconciliation.

I also learned that you can want something too badly. If you try to force it, you will tend to mess it up. That is what happened when I so desperately felt the need for an equal partnership with a black friend and co-worker. With several people I tried to make it happen, and it blew up in my face. That is why *prayer, accountability to others for the relationship (and/or ministry), and persistence with God's grace and timing are all essential ingredients in racial reconciliation.*

Unlike Glen, I (Raleigh) came into this pioneering effort without a deep call to serve the poor. When Paulette and I first came to Austin, I just wanted to preach. My first preference for planting a church would have been an integrated, middle-class community like Oak Park, not Austin, where Circle Urban Ministries offered to give us space to start a church, with its terrible poverty, gang graffiti everywhere, and drug traffic. I'd had enough of the ghetto growing up; why in the world would I want to go back?

But the more we listened to Glen and Lonni Kehrein—these white folks, after all—talk about their call and commitment to racial reconciliation between black and white, and saw their call and commitment to the poor, the oppressed, and the needy, living in Austin when they could live more comfortably somewhere else, the more God was working on our hearts. "You know," I told Paulette, "if people like us don't return to bring God's hope and resources back into the ghetto, how are we going to facilitate change? I'm a product of the ghetto; all the more reason I need to go back to live out God's reconciling power." If Glen and Lonni could—how could we not?

By the time Glen found the abandoned building complex, God had begun to build deep within Paulette and me an unmistakable call, not only to a cross-cultural ministry but also to the poor, oppressed, and needy in the ghetto.

But neither one of us is a superhero. We can't do this alone—and neither can others who answer the call of God to be pioneers in the area of racial reconciliation. We need each other; we need our brothers and sisters; we need the wider church to hear the call and be part of the partnership. Interdependence is a must!

What About the Kids?

John Perkins's "Three R's" of Christian community develop-ment[3] link "relocation" and "reconciliation." We believe that most of those especially called to be reconcilers will need to relocate into a poor, minority community where brokenness and aliena-tion abound.

But the number one question then becomes: "What about the kids?" When faced with inner-city living, the white family asks, "Does God call me to sacrifice my children on the altar of racial reconciliation?" Meanwhile, the black family, when faced with the challenge to open up and bridge into the white community, asks, "Does God call me to abandon my racial heritage?"

No! we firmly declare. God's call enhances your gift of love for your children as it prepares them to live in an increasingly "colorful" world.

The Washingtons' call included our kids then living at home, Coffee, Reggie, Paul, Matthew, and Rachel. Paulette and I had a summit meeting to tell our children how God had called us to be reconcilers, reaching out into the white community. That meant we needed their help. Our home would (and now does) have white house-guests for meals or even to live for a while. White volunteer groups will come one after the other; white church youth groups will be in and out. And we told our children, "You will be the first or most accessible black person they have met."

The Kehrein kids, Tara, Nathan, and Chelsey, were born into the call and had little choice. Often asked about what living in the black community is like for our kids, I (Glen) put the question to Tara one day. "What's the big deal?" she asked. What should be normal for Christians—cross-cultural living—but is, in fact, a rare and questionable curiosity, for Tara was quite normal. Going on vacation to Yellowstone National Park, Nathan blurted out, "Where are all the black people?" In fact, the Kehreins are quite uncom-fortable in all-white settings—it's feels unnatural!

Art Linkletter taught us that kids bring humor into all aspects of life, and I (Raleigh) learned that during a mission trip to an Evangelical Free church. While in conversation, I heard a child running after another screaming, "Nigger, nigger, nigger." Horri-fied that such a thing was acceptable in a Free church (our denomination), I stepped out of the room to discover that the screamer was my own Petra, age five, taunting a group of little white girls. Watching a talk show a few days earlier, Petra had heard "the N word." She didn't know what it meant, but she had seen it had gotten a big rise out of folks when used!

Not Either/Or but Both/And

Let's return to our analogy of God's call to evangelism. Some churches have a reputation for being "missionary-minded." Those churches usually preach a strong message about the importance of missions at home and around the world. They sponsor numerous missionaries out on the foreign field. Their church budget includes a healthy percentage earmarked for missions.

But what if the individual members thought, "Well, that takes care of my responsibility as far as missions is concerned." And so they go home, put their feet up, and never once share the gospel with their unsaved neighbors next door, neglecting their personal responsibility to evangelize.

Let's turn that situation around. Some churches really emphasize personal evangelism. Evangelism teams go out two-by-two on the weekend in the community surrounding the church; members are encouraged to do "friendship evangelism" with their neighbors and co-workers and to bring them to church. After staff salaries and building expenses, most of the budget is plowed back into local programs.

But what if those same churches shrugged when someone mentioned missions. "Each church is called to minister to its own community. How could we possibly be personally involved clear across town—much less clear across the world?"

No, the church is called to both personal evangelism and mission. Some are called to "bloom where they are planted"; others are called to "go." But both those who stay and those who go are necessary—not "either/or" but "both/and." Those who are out on the front lines, pioneering new paths for the gospel, need the financial, physical, spiritual, and prayer support of the churches "back home." Those who stay home need to see themselves as "missionaries" in their own communities, linked inextricably to what is happening in the inner city, all over the nation, and around the world (Acts 1:8).

■ □ ■ □ ■

Applying the Principle

Each one of us must open his eyes to the brokenness between the races and ethnic groups that make up our own communities and cities, and accept personal responsibility to reach across the racial and cultural barriers to build relationships. Maybe the person waiting for your cross-cultural friendship is a fellow worker on the job, a family in your neighborhood, a parent you met at the PTA, or a fellow pastor from another (ethnically or racially different) church in your town.

Cross-cultural reconciliation is needed on the congregational level as well. Has your church ever thought about establishing a relationship with a "sister congregation" across racial or ethnic lines? Pastoral staff could meet and open their lives to one another; the congregations could visit one another's churches for special events and programs; and the congregations could participate in some joint ministries in their communities.

If your church is located in a racially or ethnically diverse area (which is not necessarily reflected in your congregational membership), consider how to be intentional about racial reconciliation in your own church. For years, Reba Place Church in Evanston, Illinois, sincerely desired to include their black neighbors in the church. But only after the church made racial reconciliation a priority goal for the congregation, after they called a black pastor to join the pastoral staff, after they changed their structure and programs to include more ingredients appealing to the black community—only then did their black neighbors begin to consider that "this church might be for me after all."

And then there are those called to be pioneers, to relocate into areas where people are desperate for the ministry of reconciliation with God and each other but who may have difficulty hearing such a message because of the oppression of their lives. It is a special calling, and God calls the rest of the church to support it. The pioneers of racial reconciliation can't do it alone any more than foreign missionaries can minister overseas without the partnership of believers and churches.

Everyone may not be called to move into the poor community with the poor, but every believer and every church needs to be involved as reconcilers at several levels. It's not either/or but both/ and. To be Christ's ambassadors of reconciliation:

- Each one of us needs to develop at least one personal relationship across racial lines.
- Each church needs to develop a congregational relationship across the ethnic barrier.
- Some of us need to answer the call to make racial reconciliation our primary ministry.
- And all of us need to support the ministries of reconciliation on the front lines, first and foremost with our prayer support, then with our financial support and spiritual support (the interest and concern of the broader Christian community). We can even offer our physical support, like all those wonderful volunteers from other churches, even other states, who have been helping us develop the CUM/Rock Church building complex, room by room!

Christ has called each of us to be His ambassadors of reconciliation. As partners, hand in hand we can reach across the "dividing wall of hostility." Christ has already broken the wall in His death on the cross; now it is up to us to live as reconcilers every day in an everyday way. The opportunity is there, the tools exist— the choice to be a reconciler is yours.

NOTES

1. Four notable organizations working for reconciliation are the John Perkins Foundation for Reconciliation and Development and the foundation's *Urban Family* magazine, both located in Pasadena, California; the Antioch Community in Jackson, Mississippi, directed by Chris Rice and Spencer Perkins; and the Lawndale Community Church of Chicago, led by Wayne Gordon and Carey Casey.

2. Circle Church continues today in Oak Park, Illinois, a suburb neigboring the Austin community, with a somewhat different focus than the open church statment. Rock Church and Circle Urban Ministries enjoy a positive relationship with this vital Chicago church.

3. Perkins cites three R's as vital to proper community development: relocation, redistribution, and reconciliation. For a fuller description, see John Perkins, *With Justice for All* (Glendale, Calif.: Regal, 1982).

PART THREE
AT THE BREACH

■ □ ■ □ ■

After reading the eight principles, you may be thinking strongly of pursuing a cross-cultural relationship, but something is holding you back. Probably it is personal experiences that have brought about attitudes of fear or doubt about the other race, or about your own abilities. Your attitudes are largely a part of your culture as a black or white person. Therefore, in this final section we want to speak directly to you, the black reader, and to you, the white reader. As we see and deal with our own cultural needs, we can walk freely through the breach at the dividing wall, and find the liberty of true friendships that cross racial lines.

The message of Part 3 is the same: Racial reconciliation is a two-way street. But there is another reality at work. Blacks and whites are coming at the problem from different perspectives and backgrounds. Therefore, the agenda for blacks and the agenda for whites differ somewhat, though the goal is the same. In these last two chapters, we write separately to black Christians and white Christians, taking the liberty to give advice from two crusty old veterans. First, some words for our black readers.

■ □ ■ □ ■

CHAPTER 16
FOR BLACK CHRISTIANS ONLY

Talking to fellow African-Americans about relationships with whites gives me (Raleigh) some fear and trembling, because often I'm misunderstood in this area. People tend to hear (and read) what they want to hear, and what they hear (and read) is also filtered by the grid of their own experiences, often taking on a completely different meaning than what is meant. (Glen, by the way, says the same is true for his input.) Nevertheless, because Scripture and the work of Christ—not our experiences—are the foundation of our faith, I would like to speak candidly from my heart to my black brothers and sisters in Christ.

Six Imperatives

Here are six imperatives for us as we seek to reconcile and form friendships that help to break down that wall dividing blacks and whites.

1. Live out the truth of the gospel.

To experience reconciliation, which I believe is a biblical mandate to all Christians regardless of race or ethnic origin, black believers must accept the challenge to live out the truth of the gospel. In several of his letters to the early churches (see Galatians 1–2 in particular), the apostle Paul warns against substituting a different gospel for the truth of the gospel as revealed in Jesus Christ. And it is Christ who "gave us the ministry of reconciliation" and calls us to be His ambassadors (2 Corinthians 5:18, 20).

As new creations in Christ, God empowers us to live in the "new creation" (the kingdom of God) here and now—which is accomplished through the ministry of reconciliation. This ministry includes being reconciled to God, then reconciled to one another across racial and class barriers.

But shouldn't white believers take that initiative? After all, blacks are the ones who have been enslaved and oppressed, and they have suffered many indignities of prejudice and discrimination. Let's remember, the biblical mandate is just as true for the black Christian as for the white Christian. Each of us must take responsibility for breaking down the dividing wall of hostility between ourselves and our white, Hispanic, Asian, and Jewish brothers and sisters in Christ. If we are indeed going to live out the truth of the gospel, we must initiate.

2. Confront racism constructively.

Racism in the Christian arena has many faces, but probably the most prevalent form is institutional racism. Most white believers are not overtly or intentionally racist in the manner of the Ku Klux Klan, the Skinheads, and others who teach race hatred; rather they operate out of ignorance, the status quo, convenience, and fear—fear of the unknown, fear of people different from themselves, fear of the rage that explodes in a race riot, fear of young black men. Their fears and ignorance prompt attitudes and behaviors that are self-preserving, and motivates the racism that we blacks experience today.

Yes, institutional racism exists in Christian institutions. For the Christian black man or woman, it is especially painful when trying to get spiritual training in a Bible school or seminary, most of which are located in white, middle-class communities with white, middle-class professors who teach a white, Euro-centric theology that is often insensitive to the needs of black believers and other ethnic believers as well.

But understanding this reality helps us to know what we are facing and how to deal with the situation. I personally believe we can best challenge institutional racism by becoming a part of these Christian institutions—working from the inside, as it were. That requires sacrifice and adjustment on our part; it's not always comfortable. But I can best influence a church if I become a member and find my way onto one of the governing boards in that church. Likewise, I can best challenge a Bible school or seminary if I win their confidence as a trusted faculty member.

If you are considering attending a Bible college or seminary but worry about the white majority and a predominantly white faculty, I say, "Go." You can influence them to the good, and when you graduate, you will have more than knowledge. You will have influence on both your community and the white Christian world.

Our influence on white institutions will happen only if you and I are willing to take the first step and make the first adjustment. Why would you or I go through the trouble? Because God has given us a mandate of being His ambassadors in the ministry of reconciliation.

3. Recognize that blacks can have racist attitudes, too.

It's difficult for many African-Americans to admit, but blacks as well as whites need to deal with racism, because racism is first of all a condition of the heart. Whenever I don't like somebody or put people in a certain category or stereotype them or expect them to act a certain way primarily because of the color of their skin, that's racism. We as black people get caught up in those attitudes just as much as white people.

As we mentioned in the Preface, a popular sociological definition of racism states that one can only be racist if that person is in a position of power, and uses that power to take advantage of another race of people. I call that racial oppression, which indeed is an evil expression of racism, but is not the sum total of racism. Just as the sin of adultery or murder begins in the heart—even if it is never acted out—racism, too, begins in the heart, even though we may not have the social power to act on it by oppressing those we hate. Yes, often we are victims, but our response cannot be "by any means necessary." As with all sin, the sin of racism must be dealt with by confession and asking forgiveness.

—□■—

4. *Don't get caught up in bitterness.*

I acknowledge that as black people we have faced and continue to face discrimination and oppression in this society. The political and justice systems over the long haul have been unfair to African-Americans. The selection process for jobs, scholarships, and other opportunities have been discriminatory, even in Christian institutions. Unfortunately, it has been the liberal rather than evangelical institutions that have taken initiative to reach out to blacks and other minorities and implement affirmative action programs and scholarships. The evangelical church community has said, "Let's preach and teach the Word of God!"—but has not been as faithful to live out the Word of God in the area of race relations, forgetting that faith without works is dead.

But I strongly encourage my black brothers and sisters in Christ to not get caught up in bitterness because of the wrongs perpetrated against us. Yes, we have a "right" to be bitter; there are real reasons for our anger. But as Christians we lay down our "rights" at the foot of the cross; there is no other way to understand the Sermon on the Mount (Matthew 5–7). Our agenda as Christians is different; love and forgiveness are more powerful weapons than hate and revenge. As Paul said, "Forgetting what lies behind and reaching forward to what lies ahead, I press on toward the goal for the prize of the upward call of God in Christ Jesus" (Philippians 3:13–14).

The ultimate prize is eternal life in peace and harmony with God and man, the end result of our reconciliation with God. But we can't be reconciled to God and at the same time harbor bitterness toward our white brothers and sisters. Martin Luther King, Jr., helped us picture a vision of black and white joining hands in reconciliation, yet to come. If I might paraphrase Dr. King's famous words, at that point we will say:

> *Together at last! Together at last!*
> *Thank God, Almighty, we're together at last!*

5. *Avoid the BBW trap.*

Next, I strongly caution my black brothers and sisters to avoid what I call the BBW trap; that is, black people know how to talk to black people about white people (see chapter 10). When we hear a complaint about a white person from a black brother or sister, we usually assume that it's true because it comes with a lot of familiar baggage. So we commiserate—and immediately we've been caught up in the BBW trap, fanning the flames of bitterness. But I believe that in doing so, we sin. If we continue to practice BBW, we will never be able to follow through and discover how much misunderstanding may be involved, or how best to resolve whatever the tension or issue is. Even though talking with each other about "The Man" is common practice and is often seen as a matter of survival, the BBW trap will inhibit us from being ambassadors of reconciliation and truly living out the truth of the gospel.

As Jesus instructed us, when we have a grievance, we are to go directly to the person to work it out. If we resolve the problem (or the person confesses the sin on his or her part), then "you have won your brother" (Matthew 18:15). If the matter is not resolved, then it is appropriate to draw in others to help mediate. But never once does Scripture mention talking about problems behind a person's back.

6. We need our white brothers and sisters, and they need us.

The face of America reflects an unmistakable reality that African-Americans must come to grips with: we need our white brothers and sisters, and they need us. God has given us as black believers, both individually and corporately, something unique, powerful, and marvelous for which we can give praise and glory to God. But we must acknowledge that God has also given our Hispanic, Asian, and white brothers and sisters something just as unique, wonderful, and marvelous, and I believe it's God intent that we positively infect one another with these great blessings of God.

We also need each other because the problems in the black community are like a forest fire raging out of control. As a black pastor in the middle of the ghetto, I've got one water hose, but my white brothers over there in the suburbs have four water hoses. If I hold my head up stubbornly and say, "Sure, we've got a little fire here, but we don't need your help," then our community will surely be destroyed, because I need five water hoses to put out this fire. But if I am willing to go to my white brothers and sisters saying, "Come and join us, come and help us, we need your prayers and your hoses, because we can't handle this fire alone," they might respond because of the love of God.

We have to be honest about the problems in the black community if we are going to engender support. I believe that black and white should work together side by side in the ghetto for the cause of Christ, and that white believers who are called to the mission field have just as much place in our inner cities as they have in Kenya or China or Japan.

A Word About Afro-centrism

The movement toward Afro-centrism to correct the cultural and historical imbalance of a white-dominated society has many positive motivations and contributions, but I am also concerned about a negative side. (I realize that some of my black brothers and sisters might close this book the minute I make such a statement. But please hear me out.)

First, some acknowledgments. Afro-centrism reminds us of one of our greatest needs as blacks: to demonstrate to ourselves and the world that we are an honorable people, with a rich and valuable heritage; that we hold a meaningful place in biblical history; that in ancient civilizations we were kings and queens; and that we are spiritual and mature. As blacks we have made significant contributions to American society (more than our fair share, because we have done it with less than our fair share of means). For these reasons, we can hold our heads up high to the praise and glory of God. (We already know that we are physically superior, but that's because "White boys can't jump!")

For too long history has been written from a European perspective, meaning that many of the contributions of other ethnic groups, particularly blacks, have been completely left out. Afro-centrism makes a positive contribution both to history and to black self-esteem by unveiling many of these things.

In so doing, however, we need to be careful that our research is balanced and truth-seeking. The same is true in the theological realm. Justice is best served if we do this together with white and Asian and Hispanic Christians who have the same concern about the truth of history and the truth of the Bible. Theology should not be Euro-centric nor Afro-centric, but Bibli-centric. History should not be Euro-centric nor Afro-centric, but histo-centric. That is, our goal should be to discover exactly what happened in history and identify those people who made meaningful contributions regardless of race or nationality—not rewrite history in a way that is imbalanced and extreme in order to satisfy the concerns of different groups. If we are balanced in our approach to history and culture, our efforts will not be divisive but will build up the whole body of Christ and give praise and glory to God.

Developing positive self-esteem in the black community is a meaningful goal. But Afro-centrism can (and in many cases has) brought about a self-centered focus in the drive to achieve that self-esteem. Afro-centrism tries to tell us to say, "White man, we don't need you; we are capable and can do it ourselves. The only thing we require from you is to recognize that fact." Afro-centrism taken to the extreme compels us blacks to put up our defenses against the wrongs whites might do to us, and even to go on the offensive.

But as black Christians we must accept the biblical mandate to "love our enemies" (those who have done injustices to us). Does that exclude European whites? Jews? Asians? Hispanics? No, Christ calls us to love and respect others in the same way that we love and respect ourselves, and to acknowledge that the "eye," the "hand," and the "toe" in the body of Christ all need each other. To get totally caught up in Afro-centrism is to forget that love covers a multitude of sins (1 Peter 4:8).

The challenge is to celebrate the positive aspects of our black heritage and identity, yet live out the truth of the gospel that compels us to be inclusive rather than exclusive.

Our Black Heritage

Some fear that racial reconciliation means a watering down of our identity. That is untrue. Racial reconciliation does not require us to deny our black heritage and who we are. Some black folks in the 'hood have accused me of being an Oreo, of selling out to the white community because Glen Kehrein, my primary partner in ministry, is white. They've said that I am denying my heritage and who I am.

To the contrary. Whenever I speak to white groups, I speak as a black man, out of the wealth of my own culture, heritage, and perspective. I challenge them to leave the comfort of their white world and get to know black folks as real people. I am convinced that whites stand to benefit by living and working shoulder to shoulder with blacks.

As we have said before, true reconciliation means that both parties bring something of value to the relationship. The only difference is, reconciliation celebrates both/and, not either/or.

Facing Our Problems

I believe, however, I must earn the right to be heard. When I admit first the problems in our own culture, then I earn the right to challenge problems in another culture. As black Americans we make a big mistake by denying or avoiding the reality of the problems that are literally destroying us as a people. Admittedly, African-Americans are tired of the barrage of sociological studies and alarming TV reports about "babies having babies," and about the irresponsible young men who make babies but don't marry the mothers. We chafe at reports about black on black crime and the statistics that 25 percent of our black men in their twenties are either in jail, on parole, or on probation.

Many blacks get impatient when these topics come up and shove them aside, fearing that the many positive things blacks are doing are being downplayed or overlooked—another "racist conspiracy" to paint blacks in a negative light.

But we can't close our eyes, pretending the problems don't exist. Alvin Poussaint, a black psychologist at Harvard University, has said that unless these trends are reversed, black America will self-destruct by the year 2000.

The Bible talks about different parts of the body having different functions, and that the Spirit gives different gifts with the same purpose—to build up the whole body of Christ. In the same way, different ones of us in the black community are called to focus on different things for different reasons. Some of us can be encouragers, lifting up our black heritage and accomplishments and building the self-esteem of our young people. Others need to be willing to be spokesmen in the spirit of the Old Testament prophets, boldly addressing the issues of sin ripping the heart out of the black community. What will your role be in helping your brothers and sisters?

Hearing about sin is discomfiting for all of us (especially if the shoe pinches). But we must confront both at the same time— the strengths and the weaknesses in the black community today. We must measure what these contemporary prophets are saying, not by whether it feels good or worrying about what "other people" are going to think, but by whether it's the truth.

I have been frequently criticized for hanging out our dirty laundry in front of white folks because I deal with the issues and problems facing the black community when I speak in a white church. But I'm not telling them anything they don't know (the majority of these statistics are compiled by white researchers, and white folks read the papers). But when I address these problems as a black man to a white audience, I can fill in the cold statistics with real people, give a better definition of the cause, and show how Rock Church and Circle are providing a biblical solution.

The Problem Is Sin, Not Skin

I tell people that the problem is not skin; the problem is sin. The same problems of sexual immorality, violence, and family breakdown are just as present in the white community, though they may be "white-washed." The devastation may be more visible in the black community, where it is compounded by racism and poverty. For instance, pregnant black teenagers tend to keep their babies and go on welfare; pregnant white teenagers often feel more pressure to get an abortion or give up their babies to adoption. It's the same sin—sexual immorality—but you see the manifestation of that sin walking around as fatherless babies in the black community. The basic problem of sin is the same.

My challenge to my black brothers and sisters is to speak the truth in what we see so that we can bring the power of the gospel to deal with it. Only as we acknowledge our need for spiritual renewal—spiritual solutions to spiritual problems—can we bring God's redeeming power to resolve the problems facing us as a people.

CHAPTER 17
FOR WHITE CHRISTIANS ONLY

As Christians who are also white, we realize Jesus calls on us to be different from the world in our values and lifestyle, even while not separating ourselves from the people of the world. This is a powerful combination: living "in" the world, but not "of" the world. Jesus described the effect as "salt and light," preserving society from rot and bringing illumination (truth) to a confused, darkened world.

Through the ages some white believers have faithfully followed the footsteps of Christ in breaking down the barriers of race and class. Tragically, however, the evangelical church as a whole has not been salt and light when confronted with racial alienation. Instead, we have often separated ourselves from the poor and oppressed; we have conformed to the world in our attitudes about race rather than becoming a transforming agent. In many cases we have set our racial values by middle-class American standards and then baptized them as "Christian." We neither have a unique Christian perspective nor have we behaved in distinctly Christian ways, different from the world, in order to bring down the barriers that separate black and white believers.

I write this chapter to my white brothers and sisters to point out our unique background, to remind us of our blind spots, and to give specific pointers for entering the breach and making reconciliation part of our lives and ministries. We must acknowledge our corporate failure in this area, but we can step forward confidently if we do so in humble dependence on God and the power of His Spirit.

Here are six imperatives for us as we seek to reconcile and form friendships across racial lines. Following these will help to break down that wall dividing blacks and whites.

1. Don't deny the reality of racism.

The first step we must take is to acknowledge the reality of racism and its effect on us today. For many, the civil rights movement and television programs such as "Roots" have brought home the truth that the racism and segregation of the past were evil and wrong. Still, our guilt about slavery and accusations about past injustice make us easily defensive. You may have said or thought about past racial injustices, "That doesn't have anything to do with us now. Today there is equal opportunity for everyone."

Confronted with staggering statistics of gangs, drugs, poverty, and babies being born out of wedlock in the black community, we have gotten very good at analyzing the problem but denying any responsibility. But I challenge white Christians to be honest about the reality of racism in the present and its ongoing effects from the past on our black brothers and sisters. To discover the truth in this area, we must leave our comfort zones and become intentional about pursuing the reality that blacks live with every day. We cannot depend on what we've heard and "know" from our own social circles and family background, because they are probably too limited. We must encounter and talk with blacks. Talking with whites alone will only ensure our falling into the WWB trap (see chapter 10).

White Christians have a unique responsibility to address the tremendous pain surrounding racism, because racism at its core is sin, and Satan has used racism as a primary tool to divide not only our nation but the church as well. Yes, on Sunday morning black and white Christians demonstrate that they are an alienated people.

As the Kerner Commission predicted after the riots in 1968, our country has become two nations—the haves and the have-nots. Essentially, middle- and upper-class whites are the haves, while most blacks and the underclass have been largely cut off from the American Dream. As Christians, we need to take responsibility for allowing ourselves to be carried along that mainstream.

2. Don't look for simple answers to complex problems.

When whites do become concerned about our responsibility, a common question is, "What should we do?" First, we must avoid looking for simple answers to complex problems. Television has programmed us to think in terms of half-hour plots and thirty-second commercials (problem: dirt; solution: Brand X cleaner). White society wants an easy answer that will solve the problem of race quickly, but it's not going to happen that way.

Because other racial groups rarely enter our daily experience, most of us don't understand just how alienated and separated our society is. A remnant of Christians has spoken up for the poor and dispossessed and against injustice, but most evangelical Christians and leaders have labeled these concerns as a "liberal agenda" and remain silent. The black community sees that silence as agreement with the status quo, which has cut out the black community. Our complicity in what is seen by blacks as an unjust system has created a tremendous sense of alienation and distrust.

When whites come into a black community wanting to right the wrongs of the past, our attitude is usually, "I'm a good guy, you can trust me." Then we confront anger and hostility, and we are bewildered. As white people, we don't often personally experience the anger bred by oppression because most interaction with blacks is on our turf—at work or a sporting event—where whites are in a majority; in those settings, hostility is well hidden. But when whites come into the turf of those who feel oppressed, angry, and alienated, those feelings will not be hidden.

Though whites may desire involvement in the inner city, when black people begin to question our motives or confront us with what they see as racism, our response is often, "I didn't come here to subject myself to this." Because we have the option to pull out whenever we want to, it's tempting to do so.

There are no simple answers, but there is a simple word: *time.* To build a bridge over a gulf created by hundreds of years of pain and injustice, we must recognize there are some dues to be paid. When so much damage exists, we must realize that *we can only build trust with time and commitment.* If we're sincere about reaching toward the goal of racial reconciliation, we must be willing to pay the price. Part of that price is to realize that it will take time and comprehensive strategies.

At times I wonder if it is too much to expect to see a lot of progress in my lifetime. That is why our children are important. If I raise my children as reconcilers without the baggage my generation must struggle through, I believe they will effect greater results.

My challenge to white Christians is to choose to identify with the pain of the poor and the oppressed. As Christ experienced pain and sorrow when He identified with us as human beings, we must be intentional about crossing the barriers. Get tough; the investment must be for the long haul.

3. *Become a learner by first admitting you don't know very much about black people.*

African-Americans usually live in a world controlled by white society. Even if they live in a predominantly black community, at many points they must deal with the white world. The reverse is not true for us. Whites have not had to learn about the culture of African-Americans, so when we come into the black community to serve or get involved, we must understand from the beginning that we have a lot to learn.

The white people in our ministry who have become good cross-cultural folks have worked hard at submitting to black leadership, becoming part of the program, and recognizing that they know very little about the culture. This willingness to learn helps temper the fact that white people often act in a manner interpreted as "superior" by blacks. Indeed, the heart of our racial problem may be that we white people often see ourselves as superior in accomplishment, intelligence, and power. We like to make the decisions and are comfortable when we are in control.

We often determine how things ought to operate by the standards of our culture, and we devalue the culture of the minority. This issue of superiority and inferiority is often unexpressed, very subtle, and lying beneath the surface. But it is devastating to relationships. The solution is to be a learner, asking black people for advice and respecting their opinions.

4. *Get beyond guilt to action.*

Guilt plays an appropriate role in helping whites to recognize and repent of sin. If we don't understand the guilt of our sin, we will never ask for forgiveness in a way that allows us to get beyond it. And if we recognize our sins but deny our responsibility, saying, "Someone else caused this," we ignore our own complicity.

You may recognize your guilt and yet feel paralyzed by it. False guilt says, "What whites have done to black people in America is terrible . . . but I'm only one person; there's not much I can do." So you don't act at all. That's false guilt, because it doesn't lead anywhere or have any productive purpose.

Though we cannot change the past, neither can we deny how its injustice has created tremendous problems in the present. Our guilt occurs when we participate in a lifestyle that perpetuates injustice without question or concern. As white Christians, we must look at our privileged place in America as an opportunity to contribute to a true reconciliation.

Many white Christians, watching the ongoing civil rights movement, have become more aware of the tremendous alienation between blacks and whites. We are unsure about what to do with our concern. But we can move beyond guilt to action. We can do many things to bridge that gap. First, we can move beyond guilt to repentance. Repentance leads to changes not only in attitudes but in choices, and that's action.

For instance, too many white Christians give little thought that their neighborhoods would not welcome anybody of color living there. A truly Christian response would mean either (1) not moving there in the first place, or (2) determining to bring a Christian perspective, challenging others on their attitudes while developing relationships that would help break down those barriers (for instance, inviting black friends and co-workers home for dinner). By crossing those barriers as Christian witnesses, we move beyond guilt to action.

5. *How much you accomplish depends on how much you invest.*

Jesus said, "From everyone who has been given much shall much be required; and to whom they entrusted much, of him they will ask all the more" (Luke 12:48). Realizing we have been given so much should prompt Christians to significant action. Unfortunately, we typically don't really want to change our lifestyle too much.

The principle of commitment (chapter 8) implies you will need to invest time. Cross-cultural ministry will cost more than two hours on a Saturday afternoon helping with a food drive or a church cleanup in the inner city. As in business, the return on your investment relates directly to the time you invest. To have a major impact on racial reconciliation, you (and your church) must invest time with people.

In the aftermath of the Rodney King verdict and the ensuing riots, many Christian denominations and groups drafted resolutions about racial reconciliation. While making resolutions might be a good start, such responses won't bring about a whole lot of change unless the churches put those words into action. We must move beyond just investing a little and then wondering why we see few lasting changes.

6. White churches must become part of the solution.

A few years ago, Bill Moyers did a television special called "Crisis in America: The Vanishing Black Family." After graphically laying out the tremendous problems of the black underclass, he assembled a panel of experts to suggest "solutions." Incredibly, no one represented the church. (Rev. Jesse Jackson may have come closest, but he speaks predominantly as a political figure and certainly not as an evangelical.) The evangelical church is perceived as a nonplayer in the arena of race relations. In this arena we have become salt that has lost its flavor, without much value except to be trampled underfoot.

Racial alienation is a cancer eating away the core of our society. When the disease eventually appears in a community like Los Angeles, it is easy to focus on the manifestations of anger—the rioting and looting. While condemning the obvious corporate sin of the rebellious mobs we easily miss the other side of the coin: how deep must feelings of alienation be to destroy stores even in one's own community? Ask yourself, What corporate action can we as believers take to answer the great anger and hostility of racial minorities?

We must recognize as white church members and leaders that if we are not part of the solution we are part of the problem. Denying responsibility means that we refuse to work toward a solution and refuse to admit our role in the conflict. The alienation and separation continue to broaden, moving us closer to an inevitable clash.

But accepting responsibility does not require flagellation—becoming the racial "whipping boy." Instead, we must do something—anything—to demonstrate that we are reconcilers. Imagine what would happen in our society if racial reconciliation became an evangelical agenda as important as abortion? Where government mandates have failed, Christian choices could succeed. Such is the power of love.

Taking Risks

If you choose to be part of the solution and get involved, you can expect misunderstanding and conflict. But if we desire to be reconcilers, we have to take risks. We must use our sphere of influence to open doors of opportunity for others who don't naturally have that access.

For instance, the radio program "Urban Alternative," featuring black pastor Tony Evans, is now syndicated on more than 150 radio stations nationwide. Through the program Evans's ministry is building bridges between the black community and the white community. But in the beginning, most conservative white radio stations wouldn't consider airing the program. Most Christian stations are owned by white, conservative evangelicals, and they would not accept the show without an endorsement by someone willing to take a risk and put his reputation on the line.

The first person to take that risk was George Sweeting, then president of Moody Bible Institute. With Sweeting's endorsement, and the support of the Moody Broadcasting Network, Tony Evans received a national platform for his message. Later, Sweeting's successor, Joseph Stowell, and James Dobson, host of the popular Christian radio broadcast "Focus on the Family," promoted the program to station managers and their white audiences. Taking the risk expanded that ministry in a way that might otherwise have taken years to realize. Sweeting, Stowell, and Dobson took risks and thus became part of a plan to get an excellent black messenger on the airwaves.

When we take risks and cross the barriers into areas where society is not comfortable, it doesn't always work out; it sometimes blows up. That's why it's called a risk.

—□—■—

Risk often means spending money on cross-cultural pioneering efforts. Because the white community controls much of the financial resources and many avenues of opportunity, I believe we whites must be willing to take the initiative to open those doors.

A good formula to help Christians understand when it's right to take that risk is to ask: "Is it right in the economy of God? Will it bring value to the kingdom of God?" Even if the "risk" of endorsing Tony Evans had met with failure (for instance, listeners might have called radio stations to complain; donors might have withdrawn support), the answer to those questions even before the results were seen was yes. Dr. Evans preaches the gospel from the urban perspective. There was a valid basis for knowing it was right to take the risk.

An Opportunity to Grow

When whites, new to cross-cultural ministry, start to experience conflict with blacks, they usually are critical of the other person while justifying their own reactions (that's Whites Know in action). Sometimes a white person tells me, "I just don't know if it's worth it. I'm not sure I want to stick with this."

"I understand what you're going through, but hang in there; there are some deep things God wants to teach you," I usually reply. "This is actually a good time in your life, a great opportunity to see God at work. He is putting you through the fire and burning off some garbage in your life."

And it's true. The realities of cross-cultural ministry can bring on painful struggles, but those struggles are really opportunities to grow. Rather than using those tough times as an excuse to cut and run, we must learn to see suffering as a godly opportunity to give and to grow.

Some TV viewers may have been surprised when Billy Graham told ABC newswoman Diane Sawyer that "racial division and strife" represent a major evil in the world. But Graham did not hesitate in his reply, and we should not hesitate in our response. Racial reconciliation in our nation should become a major priority in our lives. When it does, Christians will demonstrate to an unbelieving world that Christ does, indeed, break down walls to bring people together—black, yellow, brown, and white.

More About CUM and Rock Church

The eight principles of reconciliation in this book derive from our personal lives and the proving ground of two cross-cultural, inner city ministries. Circle Urban Ministries (CUM) and Rock of Our Salvation Church are partners in a wholistic ministry that unite faith and works.

Rock Church, affiliated with the Evangelical Free Church of America, is a Bible centered church living out the truth of the gospel. Begun in 1983 in the predominantly black Austin community on Chicago's West Side, Rock Church is committed to cross-cultural ministry; 70 percent of its attenders are black and 30 percent are white.

The church has a strong emphasis on evangelism and discipleship, typified by Harvest Week of concentrated outreach, which yields hundreds of souls coming to Christ.

CUM began in 1973 when a small band of people moved into a racially changing community, intent on providing social services and Christian counsel for the poor in the Austin community. Today almost one hundred staff members operate a multifaceted community development program with a distinctively Christian emphasis.

Services include legal aid, medical care, transitional homeless shelters, food and clothing, and education. Evangelism and a chaplaincy address the spiritual needs of the clients. CUM's community development activities include rehabilitation and management of almost four hundred housing units, help in beginning community businesses, and youth development programs.

All these programs support CUM's mission statement: "to bring good news to the poor of our community by applying the power of the *whole gospel* of Jesus Christ, resulting in *transformation* of individual lives and the surrounding community."

CUM and Rock Church remain on the front lines, reclaiming the inner city of Chicago, because of the prayers and support of many friends. If you would like more information, please contact us at:

Circle Urban Ministries or Rock Church
118 N. Central
Chicago IL 60644